SACRED SPACE

SACRED SPACE

The Prayer Book 2025

from the website www.sacredspace.ie

Prayer from the Irish Jesuits

LOYOLA PRESS.
A JESUIT MINISTRY

LOYOLAPRESS.
A JESUIT MINISTRY

www.loyolapress.com

This edition of *Sacred Space Prayer Book* is published by arrangement with Messenger Publications, 37 Lower Leeson Street, Dublin D02 W938, Ireland.

Loyola Press in Chicago thanks the Irish Jesuits and Messenger Press for preparing this book for publication.

Cover art credit: Yifei Fang/Moment/Getty Images

ISBN: 978-0-8294-5788-9

Published in Chicago, IL
Printed in the United States of America.
24 25 26 27 28 29 30 31 32 33 LakeBook 10 9 8 7 6 5 4 3 2 1

Contents

Sacred Space Prayer

Bless all who worship you, almighty God,
from the rising of the sun to its setting:
from your goodness enrich us,
by your love inspire us,
by your Spirit guide us,
by your power protect us,
in your mercy receive us,
now and always.

Preface

In 1999 an Irish Jesuit named Alan McGuckian had the simple—but at the time radical—idea of bringing daily prayer to the Internet. No one imagined that his experimental project would grow into a global community with volunteers translating the prayer experience into seventeen different languages.

Millions of people, from numerous Christian traditions, visit www. sacredspace.ie each year, and what they find is an invitation to step away from their busy routines for a few minutes a day to concentrate on what is really important in their lives. Sacred Space offers its visitors the opportunity to grow in prayerful awareness of their friendship with God.

Besides the daily prayer experience, Sacred Space also offers Living Space, with commentaries on the Scripture readings for each day's Catholic Mass. The Chapel of Intentions allows people to add their own prayers, while Pray with the Pope joins the community to the international Apostleship of Prayer. In addition, Sacred Space provides Lenten and Advent retreats, often in partnership with Pray as You Go, and audio prayer service from the British Jesuits.

The contents of this printed edition, first produced in 2004, are taken directly from our Internet site. Despite the increased use of Sacred Space on mobile devices, many people want a book they can hold and carry; in addition, this book has proven especially helpful for prayer groups.

In 2014 the Irish Jesuits entered into an apostolic agreement with the Chicago-Detroit Jesuits, and Sacred Space now operates in partnership with Loyola Press.

I am delighted to bring you the *Sacred Space* book, and I pray that your prayer life will flourish with its help.

Yours in Christ
Paul Campbell SJ

Introduction to
Sacred Space 2025

We sometimes like going through or into a space that's different from normal. An uncle of mine had a very special space. It was his armchair. When he sat in that armchair, nobody was to disturb him. Because that's where he read the paper. From front to back and back to front again. It was his sort of 'sacred' space. You may find different spaces where you can relax, where you take time out from the stresses of life.

Sacred Space 2025, with its content of daily prayer, invites us to find and enjoy the sacred space that gives us time to pray and to learn a bit more about God, about ourselves, about others and about life.

We can go off into the sacred space of a lovely mountain or look down at a river and give thanks for the continuous beauty of creation. Or we might find that space in a church or garden. We can share the space with another or others, with spouses, friends and family, and in faith communities. My parents had a space we used to go to, and whenever we were on the road towards that place, my father would say to my mother something like, 'This is our space.' We didn't know what that meant at the time, but later realised it was where they 'walked out' in their younger, pre-marriage days. It was special to them.

We have our sacred space for God, where, again and again, we pray and hear God's word. The message given by Jesus Christ is easily enough summed up in three truths that lie behind all he said and did:

God loves you.

We are all brothers and sisters.

Good will overcome evil.

Sacred Space, with its daily Scripture and its inspiration points, will give a clue each day to the deeper meaning of the gospel.

Our sacred space is a place for 'relaxing into the mystery of being loved by God', to quote the late Fr Michael Paul Gallagher SJ.

Each of us, depending on our age, upbringing, mood and the events of our lives, has our own way of praying. Aids to daily prayer are not the prayer itself, but are pointers to what to do when praying. *Sacred Space* gives ways of being in that space of the love of God which is sometimes in the atmosphere of silence. We relax into the mystery of being loved by God.

. . . relax—we let go of our cares, and find ways for that to happen.

. . . into the mystery—the best things in life, like love, faith and humour, cannot easily be understood.

. . . of being loved—we recall in our space the loves of our life, past and present.

. . . by God—the God of creation is the God of nearness to each of us. God is no further from us than our very self!

And so to pray:

1. Enter prayer . . . stay in that silence for as long as you wish. You may never get to the content!
2. Ask for the grace God may give you today in prayer and throughout the day.
3. When you wish, go to your content.
4. Read the Scripture. If you are alone you may like to read it aloud.
5. Pause and let what is connecting with you sink in.
6. Speak to God in your own words if this helps.
7. End with a prayer, perhaps to Our Lady, or the Glory Be.

Perhaps an image would help? Imagine going into a dark room and having to fumble on the wall for the switch. It could take you a while to find it. And then you turn it on and the darkness goes. So, in some way we find where God switches on that light for us. He switches it on, and the light of our sacred space is the light of God in prayer, in a creation walk, in love and friendship. We can then switch on the light for others, asking ourselves, how can my prayer benefit others?

The year 2025 is a Holy Year, with an emphasis on prayer.

Pope Francis asked that 2024 be marked as a Year of Prayer, to recover the desire to be in the presence of the Lord, to listen to him and adore him and to put the need for a profound relationship with the Lord back at the centre of people's lives, through the many forms of prayer to be found in the rich Catholic tradition of prayer.

Pope Francis is expected to initiate the Jubilee Year 2025 just before Christmas by opening the Holy Door of St Peter's Basilica in a rite dating back to the year 1500. 2025 will be his second jubilee. The first was the extraordinary Jubilee of Mercy, which he opened in Bangui, the capital of the war-torn Central African Republic, on 29 November 2015.

Vatican organisers of the Jubilee Year 2025 expect the event to attract around 30 million pilgrims to the Eternal City, and Rome is already preparing in anticipation of their arrival.

Our twenty-sixth *Sacred Space Prayerbook* is one of the contributions of Messenger Publications to this Holy Year.

Donal Neary SJ

Something to think and pray about each day this week:

Just as we are never conscious of air, because God's presence is always around us, we never notice it. The journey of faith is a gift of a loving God who takes the first step and waits patiently, silently, almost shyly for the human response. Life is a vocation, a call to seek this shy God.

As we prepare to celebrate the moment the Word became flesh our faith needs deepening. Ours is a faith that sincerely accepts the darkness surrounding the search for more light. Consequently, Advent is a time of loving adoration, a true act of supernatural hope and of loving surrender to this shy God.

Life is about relationships, not about things. The greatest joy comes from good relationships—the greatest sorrow and suffering come not from loss of job or property but from broken and betrayed relationships. All relationships of love are rooted in the love this shy God has for all of us.

Vincent Sherlock,
Let Advent Be Advent

The Presence of God
'Be still, and know that I am God.' Lord, your words lead us to the calmness and greatness of your presence.

Freedom
I am free. When I look at these words in writing, they seem to create in me a feeling of awe. Yes, a wonderful feeling of freedom. Thank you, God.

Consciousness
At this moment, Lord, I turn my thoughts to you. I will leave aside my chores and preoccupations. I will take rest and refreshment in your presence, Lord.

The Word
The word of God comes down to us through the Scriptures. May the Holy Spirit enlighten my mind and my heart to respond to the Gospel teachings. *(Please turn to the Scripture on the following pages. Inspiration points are there, should you need them. When you are ready, return here to continue.)*

Conversation
Begin to talk with Jesus about the Scripture you have just read. What part of it strikes a chord in you? Perhaps the words of a friend—or some story you have heard recently—will slowly rise to the surface of your consciousness. If so, does the story throw light on what the Scripture passage may be trying to say to you?

Conclusion
Glory be to the Father, and to the Son, and to the Holy Spirit,
As it was in the beginning, is now and ever shall be,
World without end. Amen.

Sunday 1 December
First Sunday of Advent
Luke 21:25–28, 34–36

'There will be signs in the sun, the moon, and the stars, and on the earth distress among nations confused by the roaring of the sea and the waves. People will faint from fear and foreboding of what is coming upon the world, for the powers of the heavens will be shaken. Then they will see "the Son of Man coming in a cloud" with power and great glory. Now when these things begin to take place, stand up and raise your heads, because your redemption is drawing near. . . .

'Be on guard so that your hearts are not weighed down with dissipation and drunkenness and the worries of this life, and that day does not catch you unexpectedly, like a trap. For it will come upon all who live on the face of the whole earth. Be alert at all times, praying that you may have the strength to escape all these things that will take place, and to stand before the Son of Man.'

- In Advent we are to prepare to celebrate the coming of our saviour Jesus Christ into our world as one of us. St Luke advises us to live so that we can stand with confidence before our God when he comes a second time to judge the world. May this time of Advent be for us a time of renewal and deeper faith.

- Our God is always inviting us to come to him and to place him at the centre of our lives. Do I always put him first in my life? God can never take second place.

Monday 2 December
Matthew 8:5–11

When he entered Capernaum, a centurion came to him, appealing to him and saying, 'Lord, my servant is lying at home paralysed, in terrible distress.' And he said to him, 'I will come and cure him.' The centurion answered, 'Lord, I am not worthy to have you come under my roof; but only speak the word, and my servant will be healed. For I also am a man under authority, with soldiers under me; and I say to one, "Go", and he goes, and to another, "Come", and he comes, and to my slave, "Do this", and the slave does it.' When Jesus heard him, he was amazed and said to those who followed him, 'Truly I tell you, in no one in Israel have I found such faith. I tell you, many will come from east and west and will eat with Abraham and Isaac and Jacob in the kingdom of heaven.'

- In this foreigner who comes to Jesus we have one of the best examples of faith we can find in the Gospels. We recall it in every Mass as we are preparing to receive our Lord in communion.

- It brought great joy to Jesus whenever he encountered faith in those he met as with this centurion. To doubting Thomas he said, 'You believe because you can see me. Blessed are those who have not seen and yet believe.' Lord, help me to grow in my faith by using whatever little faith I have. In our prayer now we can give him this great joy by believing him and trusting in him.

Tuesday 3 December
Luke 10:21–24

At that same hour Jesus rejoiced in the Holy Spirit and said, 'I thank you, Father, Lord of heaven and earth, because you have hidden these things from the wise and the intelligent and have revealed them to infants; yes, Father, for such was your gracious will. All things have been handed over to me by my Father; and no one knows who the Son is except the Father, or who the Father is except the Son and anyone to whom the Son chooses to reveal him.'

Then turning to the disciples, Jesus said to them privately, 'Blessed are the eyes that see what you see! For I tell you that many prophets and kings desired to see what you see, but did not see it, and to hear what you hear, but did not hear it.'

- Jesus is always the best model to teach us how we should pray. He simply speaks from his heart to his beloved Father using his own words in whatever situation he finds himself in. Let us learn from the Master and speak from our hearts to him who is here with us.

- Unlike those 'many prophets and kings' we have the benefit of Christ's example and his words. Let us take the advice of St Teresa of Ávila and look at him with eyes of faith and recall that the Holy Spirit is dwelling within us.

Wednesday 4 December
Matthew 15:29–37

After Jesus had left that place, he passed along the Sea of Galilee, and he went up the mountain, where he sat down. Great crowds came to him, bringing with them the lame, the maimed, the blind, the mute, and many others. They put them at his feet, and he cured them, so that the crowd was amazed when they saw the mute speaking, the maimed whole, the lame walking, and the blind seeing. And they praised the God of Israel.

Then Jesus called his disciples to him and said, 'I have compassion for the crowd, because they have been with me now for three days and have nothing to eat; and I do not want to send them away hungry, for they might faint on the way.' The disciples said to him, 'Where are we to get enough bread in the desert to feed so great a crowd?' Jesus asked them, 'How many loaves have you?' They said, 'Seven, and a few small fish.' Then ordering the crowd to sit down on the ground, he took the seven loaves and the fish; and after giving thanks he broke them and gave them to the disciples, and the disciples gave them to the crowds. And all of them ate and were filled; and they took up the broken pieces left over, seven baskets full.

- Jesus always had compassion for the crowds that came to hear him. He feeds them first through his preaching on the level of their spirits, and then he looks after their bodily needs. Jesus said, 'The words that I have spoken to you are spirit and life.' Let us take his words into our hearts and respond to them with whatever words come to mind.

- Jesus is still our Shepherd today and in prayer we can be in his company. We can now take the words of Psalm 23, 'The Lord is my Shepherd', and allow them to speak to us, responding with whatever comes to mind.

Thursday 5 December
Matthew 7:21, 24–27

Then Jesus said to his disciples, 'Not everyone who says to me, "Lord, Lord", will enter the kingdom of heaven, but only one who does the will of my Father in heaven. . . .

'Everyone then who hears these words of mine and acts on them will be like a wise man who built his house on rock. The rain fell, the floods came, and the winds blew and beat on that house, but it did not fall, because it had been founded on rock. And everyone who hears these words of mine and does not act on them will be like a foolish man who built his house on sand. The rain fell, and the floods came, and the winds blew and beat against that house, and it fell—and great was its fall!'

- When Jesus was told his family were outside and wanted to speak to him, he replied by saying his family are those who do the will of his Father. So not one who simply says, 'Lord, Lord.' Love is proved by deeds, not words. Jesus said, 'When you are praying, do not heap up empty phrases as the Gentiles do; for they think that they will be heard because of their many words.' You may wish to speak simply with the Lord in your own words about whatever is going on in your life.

- If we build our lives and our faith on the rock that is Christ no storms can overcome us. May we be filled with confidence when Jesus tells us, 'But take courage; I have conquered the world!' By his life, death and resurrection he has won for us every grace we will ever need.

Friday 6 December
Matthew 9:27–31

As Jesus went on from there, two blind men followed him, crying loudly, 'Have mercy on us, Son of David!' When he entered the house, the blind men came to him; and Jesus said to them, 'Do you believe that I am able to do this?' They said to him, 'Yes, Lord.' Then he touched their eyes and said, 'According to your faith let it be done to you.' And their eyes were opened. Then Jesus sternly ordered them, 'See that no one knows of this.' But they went away and spread the news about him throughout that district.

- As the two blind men continue to plead with Jesus he appears to ignore them. Yet he still grants them their request. Every prayer we make is heard by God, but for our good he often delays his response to our petitions. By persevering in prayer our faith grows stronger. We pray for this grace.

- Jesus, you told us to ask for all our needs. May we trust in your unchanging love for us. You always know what is best for us.

Saturday 7 December
Matthew 9:35—10:1, 5–8

Then Jesus went about all the cities and villages, teaching in their synagogues, and proclaiming the good news of the kingdom, and curing every disease and every sickness. When he saw the crowds, he had compassion for them, because they were harassed and helpless, like sheep without a shepherd. Then he said to his disciples, 'The harvest is plentiful, but the labourers are few; therefore ask the Lord of the harvest to send out labourers into his harvest.'

Then Jesus summoned his twelve disciples and gave them authority over unclean spirits, to cast them out, and to cure every disease and every sickness. . . .

These twelve Jesus sent out with the following instructions: 'Go nowhere among the Gentiles, and enter no town of the Samaritans, but go rather to the lost sheep of the house of Israel. As you go, proclaim the good news, "The kingdom of heaven has come near." Cure the sick, raise the dead, cleanse the lepers, cast out demons. You received without payment; give without payment.'

- In his compassion and love, Jesus continues to sustain and love all people, and he wants them to come to know him. 'I came that they may have life and have it abundantly.' Jesus knew that in his humanity he could not reach every place and that after his death and his return to his Father he would need his apostles and his disciples, namely us, to bring the Good News to his people.

- Pope Francis reminds us that each of us has a mission. We are to witness to our God by how we live. Lord, we pray that you help us to live our faith in accordance with your will.

Something to think and pray about each day this week:

During this time of the year, I notice myself withdrawing from the busy pace of the world to seek quiet time for reflection. Nature is integral to my daily spiritual life. In the sacred space of the natural world, I feel a profound sense of what it means to be part of the web of life—to belong to a bigger cosmic consciousness.

For me, my intimate connection to God in nature is the Holy Spirit in action. I have long held a strong connection to all living things on the planet. My desire to live in a more sustainable, conscious way is how I respond to the call of *Laudato Si'* to have an ecological conversion.

A nature-based approach to spirituality could hold the solution to our feelings of alienation and disconnection from the Church, our global community and even our role in the current global climate change crisis. As we make it our intention to restore this connection in order to overcome the current socio-ecological crises that threaten our survival as a species on the planet, we also deepen our own faith. As Thomas Berry wisely observed, 'The destiny of humans cannot be separated from the destiny of earth.'

Andrea Hayes,
The Sacred Heart Messenger,
December 2021

The Presence of God

'Come to me, all you that are weary and are carrying heavy burdens, and I will give you rest.' Here I am, Lord. I come to seek your presence. I long for your healing power.

Freedom

'In these days, God taught me as a schoolteacher teaches a pupil.' —St Ignatius

I remind myself that there are things God has to teach me yet, and I ask for the grace to hear those things and let them change me.

Consciousness

Help me, Lord, to be more conscious of your presence. Teach me to recognise your presence in others. Fill my heart with gratitude for the times your love has been shown to me through the care of others.

The Word

God speaks to each of us individually. I listen attentively to hear what he is saying to me. Read the text a few times, then listen. *(Please turn to the Scripture on the following pages. Inspiration points are there, should you need them. When you are ready, return here to continue.)*

Conversation

Conversation requires talking and listening. As I talk to Jesus, may I also learn to be still and listen. I picture the gentleness in his eyes and the smile full of love as he gazes on me. I can be totally honest with Jesus as I tell him of my worries and my cares. I will open my heart to him as I tell him of my fears and my doubts. I will ask him to help me place myself fully in his care and abandon myself to him, knowing that he always wants what is best for me.

Conclusion

I thank God for these moments we have spent together and for any insights I have been given concerning the text.

Sunday 8 December
Second Sunday of Advent
Luke 3:1–6

In the fifteenth year of the reign of Emperor Tiberius, when Pontius Pilate was governor of Judea, and Herod was ruler of Galilee, and his brother Philip ruler of the region of Ituraea and Trachonitis, and Lysanias ruler of Abilene, during the high-priesthood of Annas and Caiaphas, the word of God came to John son of Zechariah in the wilderness. He went into all the region around the Jordan, proclaiming a baptism of repentance for the forgiveness of sins, as it is written in the book of the words of the prophet Isaiah,

'The voice of one crying out in the wilderness:
"Prepare the way of the Lord,
    make his paths straight.
Every valley shall be filled,
    and every mountain and hill shall be made low,
and the crooked shall be made straight,
    and the rough ways made smooth;
and all flesh shall see the salvation of God."'

• St Luke, writing for the Gentile world, announces the beginning of the public ministry of John the Baptist, the last of the prophets before Christ. He is to prepare the way for the Messiah through hearts that are purified by their repentance for their sins. Only hearts that have turned away from sinful ways can receive the message of the Good News.

• John the Baptist attracts a large following by his preaching and by his witnessing to a simple and austere life. Are we willing to make changes in our lifestyle to be more open to the message of Christ?

Monday 9 December
The Immaculate Conception of the BVM
Luke 1:26–38

In the sixth month the angel Gabriel was sent by God to a town in Galilee called Nazareth, to a virgin engaged to a man whose name was Joseph, of the house of David. The virgin's name was Mary. And he came to her and said, 'Greetings, favoured one! The Lord is with you.' But she was much perplexed by his words and pondered what sort of greeting this might be. The angel said to her, 'Do not be afraid, Mary, for you have found favour with God. And now, you will conceive in your womb and bear a son, and you will name him Jesus. He will be great, and will be called the Son of the Most High, and the Lord God will give to him the throne of his ancestor David. He will reign over the house of Jacob for ever, and of his kingdom there will be no end.' Mary said to the angel, 'How can this be, since I am a virgin?' The angel said to her, 'The Holy Spirit will come upon you, and the power of the Most High will overshadow you; therefore the child to be born will be holy; he will be called Son of God. And now, your relative Elizabeth in her old age has also conceived a son; and this is the sixth month for her who was said to be barren. For nothing will be impossible with God.' Then Mary said, 'Here am I, the servant of the Lord; let it be with me according to your word.' Then the angel departed from her.

- Mary was chosen by God for her great role as Christ's Mother, but she is left free in how she will respond to the angel's message. She becomes, by her faith, her trust and her charity, the model for all Christians. She is truly the servant of God in all the ways she cares for and loves her Son.

- Next to Jesus, Mary is the holiest person who has ever lived on this earth. We give thanks to God for the honour bestowed through her upon the whole human race, and ask for the grace to follow her example.

Tuesday 10 December
Matthew 18:12–14

Jesus said to them, 'What do you think? If a shepherd has a hundred sheep, and one of them has gone astray, does he not leave the ninety-nine on the mountains and go in search of the one that went astray? And if he finds it, truly I tell you, he rejoices over it more than over the ninety-nine that never went astray. So it is not the will of your Father in heaven that one of these little ones should be lost.'

- The theme of God as the Shepherd of his people Israel and the people of God as his flock is very strong in both the Old and New Testaments.

Psalm 23 is entirely devoted to it. In John's Gospel it is a major theme and there Jesus says he will lay down his life for his sheep.

- It is clear that our God is a God of mercy. As we look back over our lives let us give him thanks for his many mercies shown to us.

Wednesday 11 December
Matthew 11:28–30

Jesus said, 'Come to me, all you that are weary and are carrying heavy burdens, and I will give you rest. Take my yoke upon you, and learn from me; for I am gentle and humble in heart, and you will find rest for your souls. For my yoke is easy, and my burden is light.'

- What is God like? The apostle Philip once asked Jesus to show them the Father. Jesus replied by saying, 'Have I been with you all this time, Phillip, and you still do not know me? Whoever has seen me has seen the Father.' Jesus came to reveal the Father to us.

- In our prayer we share our joys, our sorrows and our hopes with Jesus, this friend who is gentle and humble of heart. 'But I have calmed and quieted my soul, like a weaned child with its mother; my soul is like the weaned child that is with me.' (Psalm 131).

Thursday 12 December
Matthew 11:11–15

Jesus said to them, 'Truly I tell you, among those born of women no one has arisen greater than John the Baptist; yet the least in the kingdom of heaven is greater than he. From the days of John the Baptist until now the kingdom of heaven has suffered violence, and the violent take it by force. For all the prophets and the law prophesied until John came; and if you are willing to accept it, he is Elijah who is to come. Let anyone with ears listen!'

- John the Baptist's preaching came at the end of the Old Testament and as the New Testament was about to begin with the life, death and resurrection of Jesus. We have the greater privilege of living in the era of the New Testament and with the witness of the example of a multitude of saints and martyrs in over two thousand years of Christianity. However, we still have to struggle to attain the kingdom of heaven.

• We have the gift of the Holy Spirit given to us and to our Church. How well do we use these gifts that we have received?

Friday 13 December
Matthew 11:16–19

Jesus said to them, 'But to what will I compare this generation? It is like children sitting in the market-places and calling to one another,

"We played the flute for you, and you did not dance;
    we wailed, and you did not mourn."

For John came neither eating nor drinking, and they say, "He has a demon"; the Son of Man came eating and drinking, and they say, "Look, a glutton and a drunkard, a friend of tax-collectors and sinners!" Yet wisdom is vindicated by her deeds.'

• The people in Judea and Galilee were given an extraordinary opportunity, as their God walked among them and worked great wonders. For centuries people had longed to see what they saw, to hear what they heard. But in the hardness of their hearts their leaders shut the eyes of their minds to it. There are none so blind as those who do not want to see.

• How open am I to the message of the Good News? Do I take the means to grow in my understanding of it and to know the Lord more and more?

Saturday 14 December
Matthew 17:10–13

And the disciples asked him, 'Why, then, do the scribes say that Elijah must come first?' He replied, 'Elijah is indeed coming and will restore all things; but I tell you that Elijah has already come, and they did not recognise him, but they did to him whatever they pleased. So also the Son of Man is about to suffer at their hands.' Then the disciples understood that he was speaking to them about John the Baptist.

- John the Baptist was seen by many as a great prophet or as Elijah returned in some way. In his ministry he brought a reminder of the old prophecies as he prepared the way for the eventual fulfilment of those prophecies.
- Jesus knew that they would treat him as they had treated the prophets of old. Talk to him now about what it was like to carry within him the burden of this knowledge as he went about his mission in the face of opposition.

Third Week of Advent
15–21 December 2024

Something to think and pray about each day this week:

Christmas is often described as a 'magical' season: festive gatherings, songs and movies, the excitement on little faces on Christmas morning, the traditions we carry with us from childhood—all of these evoke strong emotions. But there's something that transcends all of this, and that is the familiar story of the shepherds.

Some 2,000-plus years later, our own daily routines are put on pause by the arrival of Christmas and this 'good news of great joy' (Luke 2:10). Like the shepherds, we are invited to step out of our everyday life with its challenges and worries, and 'go now to Bethlehem' to meet the child Jesus in the manger in all his newness and human vulnerability. We live in a world that can feel increasingly uncertain, dark and frightening. We cannot escape the daily news of war, famine, mass shootings, hateful attacks on minorities, worrying news about our climate and our planet. It is important to be engaged, but the barrage of bad news can leave us feeling anxious about the future and about the security of ourselves and our loved ones. This Christmas Day, we have an opportunity, like the shepherds, to step out of our routine and visit the Christmas crib. This scene still has the power to move and amaze us. We bring our worries and anxieties, and perhaps we can leave them behind a while as, like Mary, we reflect deeply and treasure this mystery of God with us. The world will still be there to return to, as it was for the shepherds, with a new perspective and renewed hope.

Tríona Doherty and Jane Mellett,
*The Deep End: A Journey with the Sunday Gospels
in the Year of Mark*

The Presence of God

'I am standing at the door, knocking,' says the Lord. What a wonderful privilege that the Lord of all creation desires to come to me. I welcome his presence.

Freedom

Leave me here freely all alone. / In cell where never sunlight shone. / Should no one ever speak to me. / This golden silence makes me free!

—Part of a poem written by a prisoner
at Dachau concentration camp

Consciousness

How am I really feeling? Lighthearted? Heavyhearted? I may be very much at peace, happy to be here. Equally, I may be frustrated, worried or angry. I acknowledge how I really am. It is the real me whom the Lord loves.

The Word

I take my time to read the word of God slowly, a few times, allowing myself to dwell on anything that strikes me. *(Please turn to the Scripture on the following pages. Inspiration points are there, should you need them. When you are ready, return here to continue.)*

Conversation

Do I notice myself reacting as I pray with the word of God? Do I feel challenged, comforted, angry? Imagining Jesus sitting or standing by me, I speak out my feelings, as one trusted friend to another.

Conclusion

Glory be to the Father, and to the Son, and to the Holy Spirit,
As it was in the beginning, is now and ever shall be,
World without end. Amen.

Sunday 15 December
Third Sunday of Advent
Luke 3:10–18

And the crowds asked him, 'What then should we do?' In reply he said to them, 'Whoever has two coats must share with anyone who has none; and whoever has food must do likewise.' Even tax-collectors came to be baptized, and they asked him, 'Teacher, what should we do?' He said to them, 'Collect no more than the amount prescribed for you.' Soldiers also asked him, 'And we, what should we do?' He said to them, 'Do not extort money from anyone by threats or false accusation, and be satisfied with your wages.'

As the people were filled with expectation, and all were questioning in their hearts concerning John, whether he might be the Messiah, John answered all of them by saying, 'I baptize you with water; but one who is more powerful than I is coming; I am not worthy to untie the thong of his sandals. He will baptize you with the Holy Spirit and fire. His winnowing-fork is in his hand, to clear his threshing-floor and to gather the wheat into his granary; but the chaff he will burn with unquenchable fire.'

So, with many other exhortations, he proclaimed the good news to the people.

- As they listened to John the Baptist's call for repentance his hearers rightly asked what change they needed to make in their lives. In his reply the law of charity came first, as he urged them to share with the poor and to deal honestly with all. Lord, may we show our love by our care for and treatment of others.

- John the Baptist in his humility acknowledges that he is not worthy even to untie our Lord's sandals. We are all called to grow in humility and to acknowledge our own littleness and our complete dependence on our God. We ask God to reveal this more and more to us.

Monday 16 December
Matthew 21:23–27

When he entered the temple, the chief priests and the elders of the people came to him as he was teaching, and said, 'By what authority are you doing these things, and who gave you this authority?' Jesus said to them, 'I will also ask you one question; if you tell me the answer, then I will also tell you by what authority I do these things. Did the baptism of John come from heaven, or was it of human origin?' And they argued with one another, 'If we say, "From heaven", he will say to us, "Why then did you not believe him?" But if we say, "Of human origin", we are afraid of the crowd; for all regard John as a prophet.' So they answered Jesus, 'We do not know.' And he said to them, 'Neither will I tell you by what authority I am doing these things.'

- The attacks of the chief priests and elders on Jesus were inspired by jealousy and because they felt their own authority was being undermined. In his replies to them Jesus shows his quickness of mind. He always speaks the truth with courage and conviction.

- As we live our Christian lives in an increasingly secular age, we are being asked to witness to the truth that we hold. May we have the confidence to continue doing this in simplicity and sincerity. St Peter tells us we should always have an answer for those who ask us about our faith.

Tuesday 17 December
Matthew 1:1–17

An account of the genealogy of Jesus the Messiah, the son of David, the son of Abraham.

Abraham was the father of Isaac, and Isaac the father of Jacob, and Jacob the father of Judah and his brothers, and Judah the father of Perez and Zerah by Tamar, and Perez the father of Hezron, and Hezron the father of Aram, and Aram the father of Aminadab, and Aminadab the father of Nahshon, and Nahshon the father of Salmon, and Salmon the father of Boaz by Rahab, and Boaz the father of Obed by Ruth, and Obed the father of Jesse, and Jesse the father of King David.

And David was the father of Solomon by the wife of Uriah, and Solomon the father of Rehoboam, and Rehoboam the father of Abijah, and Abijah the father of Asaph, and Asaph the father of Jehoshaphat, and Jehoshaphat the father of Joram, and Joram the father of Uzziah, and Uzziah the father of Jotham, and Jotham the father of Ahaz, and Ahaz the father of Hezekiah, and Hezekiah the father of Manasseh, and Manasseh the father of Amos, and Amos the father of Josiah, and Josiah the father of Jechoniah and his brothers, at the time of the deportation to Babylon.

And after the deportation to Babylon: Jechoniah was the father of Salathiel, and Salathiel the father of Zerubbabel, and Zerubbabel the father of Abiud, and Abiud the father of Eliakim, and Eliakim the father of Azor, and Azor the father of Zadok, and Zadok the father of Achim, and Achim the father of Eliud, and Eliud the father of Eleazar, and Eleazar the father of Matthan, and Matthan the father of Jacob, and Jacob the father of Joseph the husband of Mary, of whom Jesus was born, who is called the Messiah.

So all the generations from Abraham to David are fourteen generations; and from David to the deportation to Babylon, fourteen generations; and from the deportation to Babylon to the Messiah, fourteen generations.

- Matthew, writing for a mainly Jewish audience, gives us this list of the past generations, beginning with Abraham, the father of Israel, to make clear that the coming into the world of Jesus Christ as the Messiah was the fulfilment of a long line of God's prophecies to his people. He introduces this with a reference to Jesus the son of David, because this is the genealogy of Jesus Christ, the royal anointed one.

- We have inherited not only our genes but also our faith from a long line of our ancestors. Do we thank God enough for these people who have passed on so much to us?

Wednesday 18 December
Matthew 1:18–24

Now the birth of Jesus the Messiah took place in this way. When his mother Mary had been engaged to Joseph, but before they lived together, she was found to be with child from the Holy Spirit. Her husband Joseph, being a righteous man and unwilling to expose her to public disgrace, planned to dismiss her quietly. But just when he had resolved to do this, an angel of the Lord appeared to him in a dream and said, 'Joseph, son of David, do not be afraid to take Mary as your wife, for the child conceived in her is from the Holy Spirit. She will bear a son, and you are to name him Jesus, for he will save his people from their sins.' All this took place to fulfil what had been spoken by the Lord through the prophet:

'Look, the virgin shall conceive and bear a son,
     and they shall name him Emmanuel',

which means, 'God is with us.' When Joseph awoke from sleep, he did as the angel of the Lord commanded him; he took her as his wife.

- This must have been a very difficult time for both Mary and Joseph. It is clear that Joseph puzzled over what he should do and finally resolved on a particular course of action, before the angel intervened. We too are often left by God to puzzle over what we should do in difficult circumstances. Through prayer and careful discernment in the light of the Gospels we need to trust that God will show us the way.

- Joseph, like Mary, is specially chosen by God. He is, we read, 'a righteous man', and in his goodness he wants to spare Mary any embarrassment and shame among her neighbours. In his obedience to the message of the angel and in the carrying out of what is being asked of him, he becomes a model for all Christians who seek to do God's will. We ask for the grace to know and do God's will, and we pray especially for all married couples.

Thursday 19 December
Luke 1:5–25

In the days of King Herod of Judea, there was a priest named Zechariah, who belonged to the priestly order of Abijah. His wife was a descendant of Aaron, and her name was Elizabeth. Both of them were righteous before God, living blamelessly according to all the commandments and regulations of the Lord. But they had no children, because Elizabeth was barren, and both were getting on in years.

Once when he was serving as priest before God and his section was on duty, he was chosen by lot, according to the custom of the priesthood, to enter the sanctuary of the Lord and offer incense. Now at the time of the incense-offering, the whole assembly of the people was praying outside. Then there appeared to him an angel of the Lord, standing at the right side of the altar of incense. When Zechariah saw him, he was terrified; and fear overwhelmed him. But the angel said to him, 'Do not be afraid, Zechariah, for your prayer has been heard. Your wife Elizabeth will bear you a son, and you will name him John. You will have joy and gladness, and many will rejoice at his birth, for he will be great in the sight of the

Lord. He must never drink wine or strong drink; even before his birth he will be filled with the Holy Spirit. He will turn many of the people of Israel to the Lord their God. With the spirit and power of Elijah he will go before him, to turn the hearts of parents to their children, and the disobedient to the wisdom of the righteous, to make ready a people prepared for the Lord.' Zechariah said to the angel, 'How will I know that this is so? For I am an old man, and my wife is getting on in years.' The angel replied, 'I am Gabriel. I stand in the presence of God, and I have been sent to speak to you and to bring you this good news. But now, because you did not believe my words, which will be fulfilled in their time, you will become mute, unable to speak, until the day these things occur.'

Meanwhile, the people were waiting for Zechariah, and wondered at his delay in the sanctuary. When he did come out, he could not speak to them, and they realised that he had seen a vision in the sanctuary. He kept motioning to them and remained unable to speak. When his time of service was ended, he went to his home.

After those days his wife Elizabeth conceived, and for five months she remained in seclusion. She said, 'This is what the Lord has done for me when he looked favourably on me and took away the disgrace I have endured among my people.'

• In the story of Zechariah there is a contrast between how Mary believed in the message of the archangel Gabriel and how Zechariah did not. Zechariah is terrified, while Mary is perplexed and ponders the message. Because of his lack of faith he cannot speak about the message. Are there times when our lack of faith keeps us from speaking out the truth and witnessing to our faith when we should?

Friday 20 December
Luke 1:26–38

In the sixth month the angel Gabriel was sent by God to a town in Galilee called Nazareth, to a virgin engaged to a man whose name was Joseph, of the house of David. The virgin's name was Mary. And he came to her and said, 'Greetings, favoured one! The Lord is with you.' But she was much perplexed by his words and pondered what sort of greeting this might be. The angel said to her, 'Do not be afraid, Mary, for you have found favour with God. And now, you will conceive in your womb and bear a son, and you will name him Jesus. He will be great, and will be called the Son of the Most High, and the Lord God will give to him the throne of his ancestor David. He will reign over the house of Jacob for ever, and of his kingdom there will be no end.' Mary said to the angel, 'How can this be, since I am a virgin?' The angel said to her, 'The Holy Spirit will come upon you, and the power of the Most High will overshadow you; therefore the child to be born will be holy; he will be called Son of God. And now, your relative Elizabeth in her old age has also conceived a son; and this is the sixth month for her who was said to be barren. For nothing will be impossible with God.' Then Mary said, 'Here am I, the servant of the Lord; let it be with me according to your word.' Then the angel departed from her.

- Nothing is impossible with God. Through the power of the Holy Spirit Mary will conceive in her womb a child who will be the Son of God. This mystery is no less awesome than a tiny wafer, through the power of the Holy Spirit, becoming truly the sacred body and blood, soul and divinity of Jesus Christ the Son of God.

- Mary was always a woman of prayer. Her whole life was to be that of the perfect servant of God, living out her 'yes' to God. We too are being asked to interweave our prayer life with how we live our Christian lives so that they become one.

Saturday 21 December
Luke 1:39–45

In those days Mary set out and went with haste to a Judean town in the hill country, where she entered the house of Zechariah and greeted Elizabeth. When Elizabeth heard Mary's greeting, the child leapt in her womb. And Elizabeth was filled with the Holy Spirit and exclaimed with a loud cry, 'Blessed are you among women, and blessed is the fruit of your womb. And why has this happened to me, that the mother of my Lord comes to me? For as soon as I heard the sound of your greeting, the child in my womb leapt for joy. And blessed is she who believed that there would be a fulfilment of what was spoken to her by the Lord.'

- Elizabeth's praise of Mary and her child still find a voice whenever we pray the Hail Mary. There is a great difference between saying prayers and praying prayers. All real prayer is spoken to a person. Whenever we say 'Hail Mary', Mary is immediately attentive to us.

- Enlightened by the Holy Spirit, Elizabeth recognises in Mary the Mother of her God. The Holy Spirit is always active in whatever God wills. It is the same Spirit who has spoken through the prophets. We should often pray to the Holy Spirit for light and guidance in our lives and to serve God in peace and joy.

Something to think and pray about each day this week:

Many people find winter difficult; with cold weather and very little sunlight, it can be a tough time. But it is during these weeks that Christians celebrate something amazing: God entering into humanity, putting on skin and living among us as a full human person, in a way that we still find hard to put into words. Jesus—a Palestinian Jew, who was born into a homeless family in an animal shelter in a remote part of the Roman Empire—was marginalised from the very beginning. Yet he transformed history and continues to transform our lives today.

Into all the harrowing struggles of our world, then and now, God is born. Christ is born again each year in our hearts, if we can make room for him there, and in our world, if we look with awareness in ordinary places. As we light the white candle on the Advent wreath on Christmas morning, let us remember what it represents: the peace, unity and hope for which the world desperately longs. We are invited to rejoice with the angels and the shepherds, joining together in praise, singing, 'Glory to God in the highest heaven and on earth peace, good will among people'.

Tríona Doherty and Jane Mellett,
*The Deep End: A Journey with the Sunday Gospels
in the Year of Mark*

The Presence of God
'Be still, and know that I am God!' Lord, may your spirit guide me to seek your loving presence more and more for it is there I find rest and refreshment from this busy world.

Freedom
By God's grace I was born to live in freedom. Free to enjoy the pleasures he created for me. Dear Lord, grant that I may live as you intended, with complete confidence in your loving care.

Consciousness
How am I today? Where am I with God? With others? Do I have something to be grateful for? Then I give thanks. Is there something I am sorry for? Then I ask forgiveness.

The Word
God speaks to each of us individually. I need to listen, to hear what he is saying to me. Read the text a few times, then listen. *(Please turn to the Scripture on the following pages. Inspiration points are there, should you need them. When you are ready, return here to continue.)*

Conversation
How has God's word moved me? Has it left me cold? Has it consoled me or moved me to act in a new way? I imagine Jesus standing or sitting beside me. I turn and share my feelings with him.

Conclusion
I thank God for these moments we have spent together and for any insights I have been given concerning the text.

Sunday 22 December
Fourth Sunday of Advent
Luke 1:39–45

In those days Mary set out and went with haste to a Judean town in the hill country, where she entered the house of Zechariah and greeted Elizabeth. When Elizabeth heard Mary's greeting, the child leapt in her womb. And Elizabeth was filled with the Holy Spirit and exclaimed with a loud cry, 'Blessed are you among women, and blessed is the fruit of your womb. And why has this happened to me, that the mother of my Lord comes to me? For as soon as I heard the sound of your greeting, the child in my womb leapt for joy. And blessed is she who believed that there would be a fulfilment of what was spoken to her by the Lord.'

- Mary in her kindness hastens to go to her elderly cousin, knowing that she will need help in her pregnancy. Elizabeth recognises the great privilege being given to her. Today we have the privilege of being able to speak to our God and to Mary.

- Elizabeth praises Mary for her great faith in believing the message of the angel. As Jesus grew up in Mary's home from childhood to manhood it must have been extraordinarily difficult for her to realise that this is God. In our prayer let us ponder with Mary over this mystery of our God who became one of us and who is with us now through his Spirit within us.

Monday 23 December
Luke 1:57–66

Now the time came for Elizabeth to give birth, and she bore a son. Her neighbours and relatives heard that the Lord had shown his great mercy to her, and they rejoiced with her.

On the eighth day they came to circumcise the child, and they were going to name him Zechariah after his father. But his mother said, 'No; he is to be called John.' They said to her, 'None of your relatives has this name.' Then they began motioning to his father to find out what name he wanted to give him. He asked for a writing-tablet and wrote, 'His name is John.' And all of them were amazed. Immediately his mouth was opened and his tongue freed, and he began to speak, praising God. Fear came over all their neighbours, and all these things were talked about throughout the entire hill country of Judea. All who heard them pondered them and said, 'What then will this child become?' For, indeed, the hand of the Lord was with him.

- The name 'John' is of Hebrew origin and means 'God is gracious'. Both Elizabeth and Zechariah recognised that God had indeed been gracious to them. Our God is continuously gracious to each of us, loving us with an everlasting love.

- In Isaiah we read, 'I have called you by your name, you are mine' (Isaiah 43:1). In the garden of the resurrection, Mary of Magdala recognised Jesus when he called her by her name. Allow him now in your prayer to call you by your name and respond to his immense love for you in whatever way you wish.

Tuesday 24 December
Luke 1:67–69

Then his father Zechariah was filled with the Holy Spirit and spoke this prophecy:
    'Blessed be the Lord God of Israel,
        for he has looked favourably on his people and redeemed them.
    He has raised up a mighty saviour for us
        in the house of his servant David.'

- Zechariah had served his God faithfully in his ministry in the temple. At this initiation rite for his son John, Zechariah's voice is restored to him, and his mind is enlightened by the Holy Spirit. Each of us is also called to a life of fidelity to our God and we have been given the gift of the Holy Spirit to lead us. How open are we to that same Spirit and do we frequently ask his help in our prayer?

Wednesday 25 December
The Nativity of the Lord
John 1:1–18

In the beginning was the Word, and the Word was with God, and the Word was God. He was in the beginning with God. All things came into being through him, and without him not one thing came into being. What has come into being in him was life, and the life was the light of all people. The light shines in the darkness, and the darkness did not overcome it.

There was a man sent from God, whose name was John. He came as a witness to testify to the light, so that all might believe through him. He himself was not the light, but he came to testify to the light. The true light, which enlightens everyone, was coming into the world.

He was in the world, and the world came into being through him; yet the world did not know him. He came to what was his own, and his own people did not accept him. But to all who received him, who believed in his name, he gave power to become children of God, who were born, not of blood or of the will of the flesh or of the will of man, but of God.

And the Word became flesh and lived among us, and we have seen his glory, the glory as of a father's only son, full of grace and truth. (John testified to him and cried out, 'This was he of whom I said, "He who comes after me ranks ahead of me because he was before me."') From his fullness we have all received, grace upon grace. The law indeed was given through Moses; grace and truth came through Jesus Christ. No one has ever seen God. It is God the only Son, who is close to the Father's heart, who has made him known.

- Today we begin John's Gospel with its prologue, which used to be read at the end of Mass. Written towards the end of the first century, this Gospel is the fruit of much theological reflection. The divinity of Jesus will be emphasised throughout and already we read that all creation comes through Jesus. He is the light come into a darkened world.

- In the Incarnation our God has become one of us and like us in all things but sin. In our prayer now we can relate to him as we would to a really close friend and brother. He loves us and longs for our friendship with him to grow.

Thursday 26 December
St Stephen, Martyr
Matthew 10:17–22

Jesus said to them, 'Beware of them, for they will hand you over to councils and flog you in their synagogues; and you will be dragged before governors and kings because of me, as a testimony to them and the Gentiles. When they hand you over, do not worry about how you are to speak or what you are to say; for what you are to say will be given to you at that time; for it is not you who speak, but the Spirit of your Father speaking through you. Brother will betray brother to death, and a father his child, and children will rise against parents and have them put to death; and you will be hated by all because of my name. But the one who endures to the end will be saved.'

- Jesus foretells the coming persecutions for his followers but he promises salvation to those who persevere. In one of his letters St Paul tells us that the Lord said to him, 'My grace is sufficient for you.' Lord, you have told us that you will never forsake us or fail us. Help us to have the courage to place our complete trust in you, knowing that your Holy Spirit is within us.

Friday 27 December
St John, Apostle and Evangelist
John 20:2–8

So she ran and went to Simon Peter and the other disciple, the one whom Jesus loved, and said to them, 'They have taken the Lord out of the tomb, and we do not know where they have laid him.' Then Peter and the other disciple set out and went towards the tomb. The two were running together, but the other disciple outran Peter and reached the tomb first. He bent down to look in and saw the linen wrappings lying there, but he did not go in. Then Simon Peter came, following him, and went into the tomb. He saw the linen wrappings lying there, and the cloth that had been on Jesus' head, not lying with the linen wrappings but rolled up in a place by itself. Then the other disciple, who reached the tomb first, also went in, and he saw and believed.

- Jesus gave the first news of his resurrection to the women who had faithfully followed him, even to the foot of the cross. When they go and tell the apostles the news they are not believed. But something of Jesus' own words to them before his death seems to have come back to them, and Peter and John run to the tomb to see for themselves.

- It has been said that human beings can take in very little of reality. Are there times when we have wavered in our faith in the love and faithfulness of our God towards us? Our prayer so often can be the prayer of the father whose son the disciples of Jesus were unable to cure: 'I believe; help my unbelief!'

Saturday 28 December
The Holy Innocents
Matthew 2:13–18

Now after they had left, an angel of the Lord appeared to Joseph in a dream and said, 'Get up, take the child and his mother, and flee to Egypt, and remain there until I tell you; for Herod is about to search for the child, to destroy him.' Then Joseph got up, took the child and his mother by night, and went to Egypt, and remained there until the death of Herod. This was to fulfil what had been spoken by the Lord through the prophet, 'Out of Egypt I have called my son.'

When Herod saw that he had been tricked by the wise men, he was infuriated, and he sent and killed all the children in and around Bethlehem who were two years old or under, according to the time that he had learned from the wise men. Then was fulfilled what had been spoken through the prophet Jeremiah:

'A voice was heard in Ramah,
     wailing and loud lamentation,
Rachel weeping for her children;
     she refused to be consoled, because they are no more.'

- The holy innocents lose their lives because of the hatred of Herod for the child Jesus, and so they become martyrs. The long line of martyrs for the sake of Christ continues down to our present day.

- St Joseph, led by the Holy Spirit, protects the child and his mother who have been entrusted to him. We pray to St Joseph, asking him to help us to care for and protect all those for whom we have responsibility.

29 December 2024–4 January 2025

Something to think and pray about each day this week:

Silvano Fausti SJ wrote a version of the Christmas story that is popular in Italian elementary schools: Caleb was the poorest of the shepherds near Bethlehem on that holy night. He had just two sheep. When the angel appeared to the shepherds and told them to go to town to find their Saviour in a manger inside a cave, they quickly gathered up some gifts, whatever was at hand. One brought a chicken, another some freshly baked bread and another a basket of fruit. Caleb followed them but, being so poor, he had no gift to bring.

When the shepherds reached the cave they proceeded inside, each bearing their gift, and kneeled before Jesus. Soon other people arrived, each bringing a gift to honour the sacred child. Caleb remained some way off, too embarrassed to approach the scene empty-handed.

Mary and Joseph felt overwhelmed by their visitors. They found it difficult to manage the crowd and all those useful presents, especially as Mary was also holding Jesus. Noticing Caleb standing some way off, with his empty hands and sad expression, she asked him to come closer. Then she placed the baby in his arms. Caleb's hands were no longer empty. They were, in fact, holding the greatest gift of all.

Even if we have little or nothing to offer the Lord this Christmas, that poverty, in itself, may be enough of a gift to welcome the Son of God.

Gerard Condon,
The Sacred Heart Messenger,
December 2023

The Presence of God
As I sit here, the beating of my heart, the ebb and flow of my breathing, the movements of my mind are all signs of God's ongoing creation of me. I pause for a moment and become aware of this presence of God within me.

Freedom
Everything has the potential to draw from me a fuller love and life. Yet my desires are often fixed, caught, on illusions of fulfilment. I ask that God, through my freedom, may orchestrate my desires in a vibrant loving melody rich in harmony.

Consciousness
I ask, how am I within myself today? Am I particularly tired, stressed or off-form? If any of these characteristics apply, can I try to let go of the concerns that disturb me?

The Word
I read the word of God slowly, a few times over, and I listen to what God is saying to me. *(Please turn to the Scripture on the following pages. Inspiration points are there, should you need them. When you are ready, return here to continue.)*

Conversation
I begin to talk with Jesus about the Scripture I have just read. What part of it strikes a chord in me? Perhaps the words of a friend or a story I have heard recently will slowly rise to the surface of my consciousness. If so, does the story throw light on what the Scripture passage may be trying to say to me?

Conclusion
Glory be to the Father, and to the Son, and to the Holy Spirit,
As it was in the beginning, is now and ever shall be,
World without end. Amen.

Sunday 29 December
The Holy Family
Luke 2:41–52

Now every year his parents went to Jerusalem for the festival of the Passover. And when he was twelve years old, they went up as usual for the festival. When the festival was ended and they started to return, the boy Jesus stayed behind in Jerusalem, but his parents did not know it. Assuming that he was in the group of travellers, they went a day's journey. Then they started to look for him among their relatives and friends. When they did not find him, they returned to Jerusalem to search for him. After three days they found him in the temple, sitting among the teachers, listening to them and asking them questions. And all who heard him were amazed at his understanding and his answers. When his parents saw him they were astonished; and his mother said to him, 'Child, why have you treated us like this? Look, your father and I have been searching for you in great anxiety.' He said to them, 'Why were you searching for me? Did you not know that I must be in my Father's house?' But they did not understand what he said to them. Then he went down with them and came to Nazareth, and was obedient to them. His mother treasured all these things in her heart.

And Jesus increased in wisdom and in years, and in divine and human favour.

- Jesus mixed so well with relatives and acquaintances that his parents could set out for home trusting he was with their friends. We thank the Father for sending his only Son into our world as a full human being, making it easier for us to relate to him.

- Most of Jesus' life on earth was spent in a small unimportant town doing the very ordinary work of carpentry. We go to God through our humanity. There is a great lesson to be learned here. We can link our own often humdrum lives to his and, like Mary, ponder in prayer the mystery of God with us.

Monday 30 December
Luke 2:36–40

There was also a prophet, Anna the daughter of Phanuel, of the tribe of Asher. She was of a great age, having lived with her husband for seven years after her marriage, then as a widow to the age of eighty-four. She never left the temple but worshipped there with fasting and prayer night and day. At that moment she came, and began to praise God and to speak about the child to all who were looking for the redemption of Jerusalem.

When they had finished everything required by the law of the Lord, they returned to Galilee, to their own town of Nazareth. The child grew and became strong, filled with wisdom; and the favour of God was upon him.

- Anna had lived a very long widowhood and her life was one of fidelity in her worship of God in the temple through prayer and sacrifice. For such a life she is rewarded even on earth by recognising, through the power of the Holy Spirit, the promised Messiah. God will never be outdone in his generosity. May the lives of the saints who have gone before us be an inspiration to us.

- As followers of Jesus Christ may we always strive to put God first in our lives and give time each day to praying with gratitude and offering him our sacrifices.

Tuesday 31 December
John 1:1–18

In the beginning was the Word, and the Word was with God, and the Word was God. He was in the beginning with God. All things came into being through him, and without him not one thing came into being. What has come into being in him was life, and the life was the light of all people. The light shines in the darkness, and the darkness did not overcome it.

There was a man sent from God, whose name was John. He came as a witness to testify to the light, so that all might believe through him. He himself was not the light, but he came to testify to the light. The true light, which enlightens everyone, was coming into the world.

He was in the world, and the world came into being through him; yet the world did not know him. He came to what was his own, and his own people did not accept him. But to all who received him, who believed in his name, he gave power to become children of God, who were born, not of blood or of the will of the flesh or of the will of man, but of God.

And the Word became flesh and lived among us, and we have seen his glory, the glory as of a father's only son, full of grace and truth. (John testified to him and cried out, 'This was he of whom I said, "He who comes after me ranks ahead of me because he was before me."') From his fullness we have all received, grace upon grace. The law indeed was given through Moses; grace and truth came through Jesus Christ. No one has ever seen God. It is God the only Son, who is close to the Father's heart, who has made him known.

• Light is a favourite theme in John's Gospel, with emphasis on the enlightenment of our minds that opens them to the revelation of God. Jesus is the light come into the world to enlighten all who will accept him. He comes to reveal what God his Father is really like. In Matthew 11:27 we read, 'No one knows the Father except the Son and anyone to whom the Son chooses to reveal him.'

• By reading the Gospels frequently we come to know more about the kind of person Jesus is. But it is only through meeting him in heartfelt prayer that we come to know him personally. Lord, may our praying to you each day become a joyful encounter with you.

Wednesday 1 January
Mary, Mother of God
Luke 2:16–21

So they went with haste and found Mary and Joseph, and the child lying in the manger. When they saw this, they made known what had been told them about this child; and all who heard it were amazed at what the shepherds told them. But Mary treasured all these words and pondered them in her heart. The shepherds returned, glorifying and praising God for all they had heard and seen, as it had been told them.

After eight days had passed, it was time to circumcise the child; and he was called Jesus, the name given by the angel before he was conceived in the womb.

- Very few of Mary's words are given in the New Testament. She achieved so much by her silent presence along with her son at many of the key moments in his life, his birth, his first miracle at Cana, and his death on the cross. She is for us a model of silent contemplation as she ponders with great faith and devotion the mystery that unfolded before her in the life of her Son.

- The name Jesus is a Greek translation from the commonly used biblical Hebrew Yeshua or Joshua, meaning 'one who saves'. St Peter, speaking to the Jewish authorities after the resurrection, said, 'There is no other name under heaven . . . by which we must be saved.' Let us unite our prayer with the prayer of Jesus to the Father in the Spirit.

Thursday 2 January
John 1:19–28

This is the testimony given by John when the Jews sent priests and Levites from Jerusalem to ask him, 'Who are you?' He confessed and did not deny it, but confessed, 'I am not the Messiah.' And they asked him, 'What then? Are you Elijah?' He said, 'I am not.' 'Are you the prophet?' He answered, 'No.' Then they said to him, 'Who are you? Let us have an answer for those who sent us. What do you say about yourself?' He said,

'I am the voice of one crying out in the wilderness,
    "Make straight the way of the Lord",
    as the prophet Isaiah said.'

Now they had been sent from the Pharisees. They asked him, 'Why then are you baptizing if you are neither the Messiah, nor Elijah, nor the prophet?' John answered them, 'I baptize with water. Among you stands one whom you do not know, the one who is coming after me; I am not worthy to untie the thong of his sandal.' This took place in Bethany across the Jordan where John was baptizing.

- John the Baptist always spoke the truth fearlessly to all who would listen as he called people to repent and turn from sin so that they could be open to the coming of the Messiah. He chastises King Herod for unlawfully marrying his brother's wife and is killed because of this. We are all called to a life of fidelity to the truth.

- John's ministry took place near Bethany, which was a place our Lord later loved to visit, as his friends Martha and Mary and their brother Lazarus lived there. Jesus has asked us to make our home in him, just as he makes his home in us (John 14:23). We pray for the grace to welcome him into our hearts.

Friday 3 January
John 1:29–34

The next day he saw Jesus coming towards him and declared, 'Here is the Lamb of God who takes away the sin of the world! This is he of whom I said, "After me comes a man who ranks ahead of me because he was before me." I myself did not know him; but I came baptizing with water for this reason, that he might be revealed to Israel.' And John testified, 'I saw the Spirit descending from heaven like a dove, and it remained on him. I myself did not know him, but the one who sent me to baptize with water said to me, "He on whom you see the Spirit descend and remain is the one who baptizes with the Holy Spirit." And I myself have seen and have testified that this is the Son of God.'

- John the Baptist was someone who was very attuned to the Holy Spirit. He was blessed by God, who had given him his mission, and the Holy Spirit revealed to him in a special way that Jesus was truly the Son of God.

- In John's Gospel (14:21), Jesus has promised that he would reveal himself to us. We pray for the grace to be open to his fulfilment of this promise through our fidelity to daily prayer from the heart.

Saturday 4 January
John 1:35–42

The next day John again was standing with two of his disciples, and as he watched Jesus walk by, he exclaimed, 'Look, here is the Lamb of God!' The two disciples heard him say this, and they followed Jesus. When Jesus turned and saw them following, he said to them, 'What are you looking for?' They said to him, 'Rabbi' (which translated means Teacher), 'where are you staying?' He said to them, 'Come and see.' They came and saw where he was staying, and they remained with him that day. It was about four o'clock in the afternoon. One of the two who heard John speak and followed him was Andrew, Simon Peter's brother. He first found his brother Simon and said to him, 'We have found the Messiah' (which is translated Anointed). He brought Simon to Jesus, who looked at him and said, 'You are Simon son of John. You are to be called Cephas' (which is translated Peter).

- These two disciples of John had taken to heart his preaching about the One who was to come. Now that he has pointed Jesus out to them they will not miss this chance to meet him. Their response to his invitation to 'Come and see' will change their lives totally. We, too, are invited to 'Come and see.'

- One of the first questions Jesus asks of all his disciples is, 'What are you looking for?' In his Spiritual Exercises St Ignatius stresses the importance of the desire for God. 'When you search for me, you will find me; if you seek me with all your heart. . . .'

Something to think and pray about each day this week:

We often pray, 'Heart of Jesus, make our hearts like yours.' We pray to be as large-hearted as Jesus in compassion and care for all creation.

The god of Herod in the story of the Magi is tiny, created in Herod's image and likeness. His god is as small as his influence, which did not last, and as small as the precious stone in his crown. He has made God as tiny as the outreach of his heart, which looked to others only for what he could get, not what he could give. His zest for power is so strong that he kills even tiny children who might threaten him. A bit of him wanted to see and hear Jesus later in life, but only to condemn him.

The God of the Magi was a big god! Big enough to bring the wise men on the long road to Bethlehem. They followed the star of love, goodness, faith, courage, endurance and justice, guided by a star whose light, the light of God, never fails. Their God was big enough to be recognised in a small baby. They searched and found what they were searching for, even though they may not have been sure what they would find.

The star that guides us is the star of the loves and questions, joys and sorrows of our life's journey. It lives in the hearts of all we meet. Like St Francis of Assisi, we see in a crowd of people not a mob, but the love and image of God multiplied in all. His God was wide, and, like Jesus, his care for God's world went to every person God created, every blade of grass and everything that has life.

Donal Neary SJ,
The Sacred Heart Messenger,
January 2023

The Presence of God
Dear Jesus, I come to you today longing for your presence. I desire to love you as you love me. May nothing ever separate me from you.

Freedom
Lord, grant me the grace to be free from the excesses of this life. Let me not get caught up with the desire for wealth. Keep my heart and mind free to love and serve you.

Consciousness
Where do I sense hope, encouragement and growth in my life? By looking back over the past few months, I may be able to see which activities and occasions have produced rich fruit. If I do notice such areas, I will determine to give those areas both time and space in the future.

The Word
God speaks to each of us individually. I listen attentively to hear what he is saying to me. Read the text a few times, then listen. *(Please turn to the Scripture on the following pages. Inspiration points are there, should you need them. When you are ready, return here to continue.)*

Conversation
What is stirring in me as I pray? Am I consoled, troubled, left cold? I imagine Jesus standing or sitting at my side, and I share my feelings with him.

Conclusion
Glory be to the Father, and to the Son, and to the Holy Spirit,
As it was in the beginning, is now and ever shall be,
World without end. Amen.

Sunday 5 January
Second Sunday of Christmas
The Epiphany of the Lord (USA)
John 1:1–18

In the beginning was the Word, and the Word was with God, and the Word was God. He was in the beginning with God. All things came into being through him, and without him not one thing came into being. What has come into being in him was life, and the life was the light of all people. The light shines in the darkness, and the darkness did not overcome it.

There was a man sent from God, whose name was John. He came as a witness to testify to the light, so that all might believe through him. He himself was not the light, but he came to testify to the light. The true light, which enlightens everyone, was coming into the world.

He was in the world, and the world came into being through him; yet the world did not know him. He came to what was his own, and his own people did not accept him. But to all who received him, who believed in his name, he gave power to become children of God, who were born, not of blood or of the will of the flesh or of the will of man, but of God.

And the Word became flesh and lived among us, and we have seen his glory, the glory as of a father's only son, full of grace and truth. (John testified to him and cried out, 'This was he of whom I said, "He who comes after me ranks ahead of me because he was before me."') From his fullness we have all received, grace upon grace. The law indeed was given through Moses; grace and truth came through Jesus Christ. No one has ever seen God. It is God the only Son, who is close to the Father's heart, who has made him known.

- Because we could not go to God, God came to us and dwelt among us. As Fr Canice Egan SJ put it, 'In the silence of the night Love Itself stole down unseen to embrace the hearts of all.' That the Creator of the universe would deign to take on the nature of his creature and become one of us is so astonishing that we cannot take it in. We ask God to reveal himself to us as he promised he would.

Monday 6 January
The Epiphany of the Lord (Ireland)
Matthew 2:1–12

In the time of King Herod, after Jesus was born in Bethlehem of Judea, wise men from the East came to Jerusalem, asking, 'Where is the child who has been born king of the Jews? For we observed his star at its rising, and have come to pay him homage.' When King Herod heard this, he was frightened, and all Jerusalem with him; and calling together all the chief priests and scribes of the people, he inquired of them where the Messiah was to be born. They told him, 'In Bethlehem of Judea; for so it has been written by the prophet:

"And you, Bethlehem, in the land of Judah,
    are by no means least among the rulers of Judah;
  for from you shall come a ruler
      who is to shepherd my people Israel."'

Then Herod secretly called for the wise men and learned from them the exact time when the star had appeared. Then he sent them to Bethlehem, saying, 'Go and search diligently for the child; and when you have found him, bring me word so that I may also go and pay him homage.' When they had heard the king, they set out; and there, ahead of them, went the star that they had seen at its rising, until it stopped over the place where the child was. When they saw that the star had stopped, they were overwhelmed with joy. On entering the house, they saw the child with Mary his mother; and they knelt down and paid him homage. Then, opening their treasure-chests, they offered him gifts of gold, frankincense, and myrrh. And having been warned in a dream not to return to Herod, they left for their own country by another road.

• The wise men came on a long journey to find the One who was born king of the Jews. Herod urges them to search diligently for him. Where indeed is God to be found? How earnestly do we seek to find him? The decision to put God and his will in the first place in our life must override all our other decisions, as he can never take second place.

- The wise men were not put off by the humble circumstances in which they found the child-king. It is with the eyes of faith that we must look for God beyond any appearances. 'I believe; help my unbelief!'

Tuesday 7 January
Matthew 4:12–17, 23–25

Now when Jesus heard that John had been arrested, he withdrew to Galilee. He left Nazareth and made his home in Capernaum by the lake, in the territory of Zebulun and Naphtali, so that what had been spoken through the prophet Isaiah might be fulfilled:
'Land of Zebulun, land of Naphtali,
   on the road by the sea, across the Jordan, Galilee of the Gentiles—
the people who sat in darkness
   have seen a great light,
and for those who sat in the region and shadow of death
   light has dawned.'
From that time Jesus began to proclaim, 'Repent, for the kingdom of heaven has come near.'

Jesus went throughout Galilee, teaching in their synagogues and proclaiming the good news of the kingdom and curing every disease and every sickness among the people. So his fame spread throughout all Syria, and they brought to him all the sick, those who were afflicted with various diseases and pains, demoniacs, epileptics, and paralytics, and he cured them. And great crowds followed him from Galilee, the Decapolis, Jerusalem, Judea, and from beyond the Jordan.

- After he had moved from Nazareth to Capernaum, we see Jesus in the full exercise of his public ministry, teaching about the kingdom of God, preaching repentance and healing all manner of sickness. By reading we come to know about him, but only by meeting him in prayer do we come to know him.

- He is truly the Light come into a world that had such great need of him. As his fame spread throughout Palestine, huge crowds sought him out in their hunger and need. It was said among the people, 'The whole world has gone after him.' We ask for the grace to deepen our desire to know and love him.

Wednesday 8 January
Mark 6:34–44

As he went ashore, he saw a great crowd; and he had compassion for them, because they were like sheep without a shepherd; and he began to teach them many things. When it grew late, his disciples came to him and said, 'This is a deserted place, and the hour is now very late; send them away so that they may go into the surrounding country and villages and buy something for themselves to eat.' But he answered them, 'You give them something to eat.' They said to him, 'Are we to go and buy two hundred denarii worth of bread, and give it to them to eat?' And he said to them, 'How many loaves have you? Go and see.' When they had found out, they said, 'Five, and two fish.' Then he ordered them to get all the people to sit down in groups on the green grass. So they sat down in groups of hundreds and of fifties. Taking the five loaves and the two fish, he looked up to heaven, and blessed and broke the loaves, and gave them to his disciples to set before the people; and he divided the two fish among them all. And all ate and were filled; and they took up twelve baskets full of broken pieces and of the fish. Those who had eaten the loaves numbered five thousand men.

• Even when it grew late these hungry 'sheep' did not grumble and complain about Jesus preaching to them in this 'deserted place'. They were being fed in their spirits by his words and his message. When the soul is being fed the needs of the body are lessened and we can attend more to the hunger in our souls.

• Our God is a God who provides for all our needs. Let us thank him for everything, but especially for the bread of life that we receive in the Eucharist.

Thursday 9 January
Mark 6:45–52

Immediately he made his disciples get into the boat and go on ahead to the other side, to Bethsaida, while he dismissed the crowd. After saying farewell to them, he went up on the mountain to pray.

When evening came, the boat was out on the lake, and he was alone on the land. When he saw that they were straining at the oars against an adverse wind, he came towards them early in the morning, walking on the lake. He intended to pass them by. But when they saw him walking on the lake, they thought it was a ghost and cried out; for they all saw him and were terrified. But immediately he spoke to them and said, 'Take heart, it is I; do not be afraid.' Then he got into the boat with them and the wind ceased. And they were utterly astounded, for they did not understand about the loaves, but their hearts were hardened.

- It was already late when the crowd were fed and Jesus, worn out by a long day of teaching, felt the need to go and be with his Father in prayer. We know he loved to go aside into a quiet place and, as it were, recharge his batteries. As Matthew puts it in his version of this account, 'He went up the mountain by himself to pray.'

- Prayer is always an invitation to sit with the Master and spend time in his company. Through our imagination we can be with him as he goes to a quiet place to be with his Father. Let us now join this same Jesus who went up the mountain to pray.

Friday 10 January
Luke 4:14–22

Then Jesus, filled with the power of the Spirit, returned to Galilee, and a report about him spread through all the surrounding country. He began to teach in their synagogues and was praised by everyone.

When he came to Nazareth, where he had been brought up, he went to the synagogue on the sabbath day, as was his custom. He stood up to read, and the scroll of the prophet Isaiah was given to him. He unrolled the scroll and found the place where it was written:
'The Spirit of the Lord is upon me,
    because he has anointed me
        to bring good news to the poor.
He has sent me to proclaim release to the captives
    and recovery of sight to the blind,
        to let the oppressed go free,
to proclaim the year of the Lord's favour.'
And he rolled up the scroll, gave it back to the attendant, and sat down. The eyes of all in the synagogue were fixed on him. Then he began to say to them, 'Today this scripture has been fulfilled in your hearing.' All

spoke well of him and were amazed at the gracious words that came from his mouth. They said, 'Is not this Joseph's son?'

- It was the custom in Jesus' time for local preachers to be invited to address the people in the synagogue. With great curiosity his former villagers came to listen to him. His gracious words amazed them, but we know from the other versions about this return to Nazareth that jealousy and lack of faith were at work. Do we ever resent the gifts that are given to others, or do we instead give praise and thanks for them?

- As we listen to the words of Jesus in the Gospels do we receive them with faith and gratitude? The same Jesus who spoke in that synagogue in Nazareth is with us now in prayer.

Saturday 11 January
Luke 5:12–16

Once, when he was in one of the cities, there was a man covered with leprosy. When he saw Jesus, he bowed with his face to the ground and begged him, 'Lord, if you choose, you can make me clean.' Then Jesus stretched out his hand, touched him, and said, 'I do choose. Be made clean.' Immediately the leprosy left him. And he ordered him to tell no one. 'Go', he said, 'and show yourself to the priest, and, as Moses commanded, make an offering for your cleansing, for a testimony to them.' But now more than ever the word about Jesus spread abroad; many crowds would gather to hear him and to be cured of their diseases. But he would withdraw to deserted places and pray.

- Jesus never refused anyone who came to him with faith asking to be healed. Lepers were not supposed even to approach other people for fear of infecting them. Yet Jesus reaches out and touches and heals the leper. This leper knows he can freely come to Jesus. We know that we too can always come to him to be healed.

- Jesus Christ, yesterday, today, the same for ever, always wants whatever is best for us and gives us healing.

First Week in Ordinary Time
12–18 January 2025

Something to think and pray about each day this week:

In a strange city I had been told to attach myself to a native of the city to cross the road—with him I'd be safe. Otherwise I was scared stiff in a city crowded with traffic. My fear was overcome with the help of another person, someone who could help me cross.

Many of our fears dissolve if we share them; they don't exactly go away immediately but they're different. We can help each other because we're all afraid at times, just as people had their fear (and still do) of Covid. In bereavement we're frightened of being lonely, being left alone. It's the same in our older years. All of us have fears like these, and we can bring them into our relationship with God. Job in the Old Testament was like that. He even feared he was losing his God, but by being honest with God, he could live with his fear. Jesus was afraid in the Garden of Gethsemane, but very soon afterward, with trust in his Father, he went to his death unafraid.

May God bless us with the joy of walking with him, accompanying us at times of fear, helping us to live our lives with trust and confidence. A hymn based on Scripture says 'Be not afraid. I go before you always. Come, follow me.' Our prayer can be: 'Lord, help me believe that nothing can happen that you and I together cannot face and overcome.'

Donal Neary SJ,
The Sacred Heart Messenger,
July 2023

The Presence of God

At any time of the day or night we can call on Jesus. He is always waiting, listening for our call. What a wonderful blessing. No phone needed, no e-mails, just a whisper.

Freedom

If God were trying to tell me something, would I know? If God were reassuring me or challenging me, would I notice? I ask for the grace to be free of my own preoccupations and open to what God may be saying to me.

Consciousness

Help me, Lord, become more conscious of your presence. Teach me to recognise your presence in others. Fill my heart with gratitude for the times your love has been shown to me through the care of others.

The Word

In this expectant state of mind, please turn to the text for the day with confidence. Believe that the Holy Spirit is present and may reveal whatever the passage has to say to you. Read reflectively, listening with a third ear to what may be going on in your heart. *(Please turn to the Scripture on the following pages. Inspiration points are there, should you need them. When you are ready, return here to continue.)*

Conversation

Conversation requires talking and listening. As I talk to Jesus, may I also learn to pause and listen. I picture the gentleness in his eyes and the love in his smile. I can be totally honest with Jesus as I tell him my worries and cares. I will open my heart to Jesus as I tell him my fears and doubts. I will ask him to help me place myself fully in his care, knowing that he always desires good for me.

Conclusion

I thank God for these moments we have spent together and for any insights I have been given concerning the text.

Sunday 12 January
The Baptism of the Lord
Luke 3:15–16, 21–22

As the people were filled with expectation, and all were questioning in their hearts concerning John, whether he might be the Messiah, John answered all of them by saying, 'I baptize you with water; but one who is more powerful than I is coming; I am not worthy to untie the thong of his sandals. He will baptize you with the Holy Spirit and fire.' . . .

Now when all the people were baptized, and when Jesus also had been baptized and was praying, the heaven was opened, and the Holy Spirit descended upon him in bodily form like a dove. And a voice came from heaven, 'You are my Son, the Beloved; with you I am well pleased.'

- John preached repentance and the washing away of sins through baptism in water. As God, Jesus did not need to be baptized, but in his human nature as representing all of humanity he is baptized and receives the Holy Spirit coming down like a dove upon him. He can be seen as the first of the new creation God is forming. 'If anyone is in Christ, there is a new creation' (2 Corinthians 5:17).

- Let us pray for the renewal of the graces of our baptism, and to live the new life that Christ has won for us by his life, death and resurrection.

Monday 13 January
Mark 1:14–20

Now after John was arrested, Jesus came to Galilee, proclaiming the good news of God, and saying, 'The time is fulfilled, and the kingdom of God has come near; repent, and believe in the good news.'

As Jesus passed along the Sea of Galilee, he saw Simon and his brother Andrew casting a net into the lake—for they were fishermen. And Jesus said to them, 'Follow me and I will make you fish for people.' And immediately they left their nets and followed him. As he went a little farther, he saw James son of Zebedee and his brother John, who were in their boat mending the nets. Immediately he called them; and they left their father Zebedee in the boat with the hired men, and followed him.

- Jesus always knew that for his mission to succeed he would need a special group of followers who would become his devoted companions and who would be formed through hearing his teachings and by his presence among them. The four that he calls in this Gospel had already met him and heard him preach. Andrew had spent a day with him and later introduced him to his brother Peter, saying, 'We have found the Messiah.'

- They were simple fishermen but they were to become apostles to the world. Nothing is impossible to God. In John's Gospel we read, 'You did not choose me but I chose you. And I appointed you to go and bear fruit.' We pray that our lives may make a difference for others.

Tuesday 14 January
Mark 1:21–28

They went to Capernaum; and when the sabbath came, he entered the synagogue and taught. They were astounded at his teaching, for he taught them as one having authority, and not as the scribes. Just then there was in their synagogue a man with an unclean spirit, and he cried out, 'What have you to do with us, Jesus of Nazareth? Have you come to destroy us? I know who you are, the Holy One of God.' But Jesus rebuked him, saying, 'Be silent, and come out of him!' And the unclean spirit, throwing him into convulsions and crying with a loud voice, came out of him. They were all amazed, and they kept on asking one another, 'What is this? A new teaching—with authority! He commands even the unclean spirits, and they obey him.' At once his fame began to spread throughout the surrounding region of Galilee.

- In the Gospels about Jesus' preaching we see again and again that his hearers were so often struck by how different he was from their own preachers, the Pharisees and elders. He spoke with authority and with a new message that touched their hearts. They were to say, 'Never has anyone spoken like this!'

- Jesus is always the headline for us in how to live our lives. Let us pray as St Ignatius advises in his Spiritual Exercises, to know the Lord better so that we may love him more deeply and follow him more closely in our lives.

Wednesday 15 January
Mark 1:29–39

As soon as they left the synagogue, they entered the house of Simon and Andrew, with James and John. Now Simon's mother-in-law was in bed with a fever, and they told him about her at once. He came and took her by the hand and lifted her up. Then the fever left her, and she began to serve them.

That evening, at sunset, they brought to him all who were sick or possessed with demons. And the whole city was gathered around the door. And he cured many who were sick with various diseases, and cast out many demons; and he would not permit the demons to speak, because they knew him.

In the morning, while it was still very dark, he got up and went out to a deserted place, and there he prayed. And Simon and his companions hunted for him. When they found him, they said to him, 'Everyone is searching for you.' He answered, 'Let us go on to the neighbouring towns, so that I may proclaim the message there also; for that is what I came out to do.' And he went throughout Galilee, proclaiming the message in their synagogues and casting out demons.

- Word of Jesus' power to heal has spread and the people crowd around the door of the house he has entered, bringing to him those who are sick. Each one is precious to him and he heals them all.

- We all need to have a strong conviction that taking time each day to pray is essential if we are to grow in our Christian faith. Lord, we pray that you help us discover the joy that awaits in a life of fidelity to prayer.

Thursday 16 January
Mark 1:40–45

A leper came to him begging him, and kneeling he said to him, 'If you choose, you can make me clean.' Moved with pity, Jesus stretched out his hand and touched him, and said to him, 'I do choose. Be made clean!' Immediately the leprosy left him, and he was made clean. After sternly warning him he sent him away at once, saying to him, 'See that you say nothing to anyone; but go, show yourself to the priest, and offer for your cleansing what Moses commanded, as a testimony to them.' But he went out and began to proclaim it freely, and to spread the word, so that Jesus could no longer go into a town openly, but stayed out in the country; and people came to him from every quarter.

- Jesus was always deeply moved when he encountered human suffering. On meeting the leper, he reaches out, touches the untouchable and heals him.

- Lord Jesus, you looked on everyone with deep compassion. Just being in your presence brought a healing of body and mind. Help us in our day to be your eyes and hands that reach out to help others.

Friday 17 January
Mark 2:1–12

When he returned to Capernaum after some days, it was reported that he was at home. So many gathered around that there was no longer room for them, not even in front of the door; and he was speaking the word to them. Then some people came, bringing to him a paralysed man, carried by four of them. And when they could not bring him to Jesus because of the crowd, they removed the roof above him; and after having dug through it, they let down the mat on which the paralytic lay. When Jesus saw their faith, he said to the paralytic, 'Son, your sins are forgiven.' Now some of the scribes were sitting there, questioning in their hearts, 'Why does this fellow speak in this way? It is blasphemy! Who can forgive sins but God alone?' At once Jesus perceived in his spirit that they were discussing these questions among themselves; and he said to them, 'Why do you raise such questions in your hearts? Which is easier, to say to the paralytic, "Your sins are forgiven", or to say, "Stand up and take your mat and walk"? But so that you may know that the Son of Man has authority on earth to forgive sins'—he said to the paralytic—'I say to you, stand up, take your mat and go to your home.' And he stood up, and immediately took the mat and went out before all of them; so that they were all amazed and glorified God, saying, 'We have never seen anything like this!'

- The good friends of the paralytic showed how determined they were to bring him into contact with Jesus. Each of us can be instruments of God to bring others to Jesus in spite of the many apparent obstacles.

- In our Christian lives the action of Jesus in first forgiving the paralytic his sins and then healing his body reminds us of what our priorities should be. Lord, you are a God of mercy. You know where we are most in need of healing.

Saturday 18 January
Mark 2:13–17

Jesus went out again beside the lake; the whole crowd gathered around him, and he taught them. As he was walking along, he saw Levi son of Alphaeus sitting at the tax booth, and he said to him, 'Follow me.' And he got up and followed him.

And as he sat at dinner in Levi's house, many tax-collectors and sinners were also sitting with Jesus and his disciples—for there were many who followed him. When the scribes of the Pharisees saw that he was eating with sinners and tax-collectors, they said to his disciples, 'Why does he eat with tax-collectors and sinners?' When Jesus heard this, he said to them, 'Those who are well have no need of a physician, but those who are sick; I have come to call not the righteous but sinners.'

- Was this Levi's farewell meal for his friends before he took to the road and followed Jesus? In the call to follow Jesus we have to leave many things behind. What are the things we still cling to that hinder our total commitment to being followers of Jesus?

- The Pharisees wanted to have nothing to do with those they deemed sinners. In contrast, Jesus always sought out the company of sinners and worked tirelessly to bring them back to God. All of us remain sinners and in constant need of God's merciful forgiveness and healing. We ask the Lord to show us this more fully.

19–25 January 2025

Something to think and pray about each day this week:

Worry is the cause of many of the world's problems, and it can be a warning sign that God is not first in my life at this point in time.

A day of worrying can be more exhausting than a day of hard work. Nothing wastes more energy than worrying. It's a total waste of time and it's useless. Worry can damage your health. It can raise your blood pressure, cause depression, increase your stress levels and give you sleepless nights. It can be a slow killer.

There is no pill you can take to stop you from worrying; no seminar, book or CD will stop you from worrying. The answer is to put God in control of your life. Trust him. Leave tomorrow to God. Don't cross bridges until you reach them. Don't open your umbrella until it starts raining.

Hand over everything to God: yourself, your problems, plans and health, everything. Surrender and abandon yourself to him. Your future is in God's hands and in God's hands you are in safe hands. Trust him and all will be well. Easier said than done. It may take time. But it works.

Terence Harrington OFMCap,
The Sacred Heart Messenger,
December 2023

The Presence of God

As I sit here, the beating of my heart, the ebb and flow of my breathing, the movements of my mind are all signs of God's ongoing creation of me. I pause for a moment and become aware of this presence of God within me.

Freedom

It is so easy to get caught up with the trappings of wealth in this life. Grant, O Lord, that I may be free from greed and selfishness. Remind me that the best things in life are free: love, laughter, caring and sharing.

Consciousness

Knowing that God loves me unconditionally, I can afford to be honest about how I am. How has the day been, and how do I feel now? I share my feelings openly with the Lord.

The Word

Lord Jesus, you became human to communicate with me. You walked and worked on this earth. You endured the heat and struggled with the cold. All your time on this earth was spent in caring for humanity. You healed the sick, you raised the dead. Most important of all, you saved me from death. *(Please turn to the Scripture on the following pages. Inspiration points are there, should you need them. When you are ready, return here to continue.)*

Conversation

Sometimes I wonder what I might say if I were to meet you in person, Lord. I think I might say, 'Thank you', because you are always there for me.

Conclusion

I thank God for these moments we have spent together and for any insights I have been given concerning the text.

Sunday 19 January
Second Sunday in Ordinary Time
John 2:1–11

On the third day there was a wedding in Cana of Galilee, and the mother of Jesus was there. Jesus and his disciples had also been invited to the wedding. When the wine gave out, the mother of Jesus said to him, 'They have no wine.' And Jesus said to her, 'Woman, what concern is that to you and to me? My hour has not yet come.' His mother said to the servants, 'Do whatever he tells you.' Now standing there were six stone water-jars for the Jewish rites of purification, each holding twenty or thirty gallons. Jesus said to them, 'Fill the jars with water.' And they filled them up to the brim. He said to them, 'Now draw some out, and take it to the chief steward.' So they took it. When the steward tasted the water that had become wine, and did not know where it came from (though the servants who had drawn the water knew), the steward called the bridegroom and said to him, 'Everyone serves the good wine first, and then the inferior wine after the guests have become drunk. But you have kept the good wine until now.' Jesus did this, the first of his signs, in Cana of Galilee, and revealed his glory; and his disciples believed in him.

- In our Christian lives there are times for joyful celebration and being in the company of friends. The presence of Jesus and his mother was truly a blessing for this young couple as they began married life. May we invite the Lord into all the events of our lives.

- Mary the mother of Jesus has been given to us as our mother too, and she takes her role seriously, as we know from her apparitions to us over the centuries. Here we see her compassion for this young couple and her complete trust in her Son. She will be no different with us; she will always bring us closer to her Son. Let us speak to her now or prayerfully repeat the words of the Memorare.

Monday 20 January
Mark 2:18–22

Now John's disciples and the Pharisees were fasting; and people came and said to him, 'Why do John's disciples and the disciples of the Pharisees fast, but your disciples do not fast?' Jesus said to them, 'The wedding-guests cannot fast while the bridegroom is with them, can they? As long as they have the bridegroom with them, they cannot fast. The days will come when the bridegroom is taken away from them, and then they will fast on that day.

'No one sews a piece of unshrunk cloth on an old cloak; otherwise, the patch pulls away from it, the new from the old, and a worse tear is made. And no one puts new wine into old wineskins; otherwise, the wine will burst the skins, and the wine is lost, and so are the skins; but one puts new wine into fresh wineskins.'

- For everything under heaven there is a time, a time to fast and a time to refrain from fasting. The path of our Christian journey is never a continuously smooth one, but has its ups and downs. We pray for the grace to persevere in the bad times and the good times, always trusting in the infinite love of our God.

- New wineskins are needed for new wine and the wine of the kingdom of God is indeed new. St John Henry Newman wrote, 'To live is to change, and to be perfect is to have changed often.' Let us ask that we might be able to discern the will of God in these changing times, and to worship him in ways that are authentic.

Tuesday 21 January
Mark 2:23–28

One sabbath he was going through the cornfields; and as they made their way his disciples began to pluck heads of grain. The Pharisees said to him, 'Look, why are they doing what is not lawful on the sabbath?' And he said to them, 'Have you never read what David did when he and his companions were hungry and in need of food? He entered the house of God, when Abiathar was high priest, and ate the bread of the Presence, which it is not lawful for any but the priests to eat, and he gave some to his companions.' Then he said to them, 'The sabbath was made for humankind, and not humankind for the sabbath; so the Son of Man is lord even of the sabbath.'

- Jesus in his humanity knows what it is like to be hungry and thirsty, and he approves of David's actions. Our religion should never become a religion of do's and don'ts but one where we become more and more trusting in our God's loving providence.

- The Jewish manmade rules about keeping the sabbath were a frequent source of dispute between Jesus and the Jewish religious leaders. Jesus always sought the good of people, so the keeping of the sabbath is for our benefit. God is not in need of our worship for his happiness, but we have need of God. We acknowledge this by giving time to prayer.

Wednesday 22 January
Mark 3:1–6

Again he entered the synagogue, and a man was there who had a withered hand. They watched him to see whether he would cure him on the sabbath, so that they might accuse him. And he said to the man who had the withered hand, 'Come forward.' Then he said to them, 'Is it lawful to do good or to do harm on the sabbath, to save life or to kill?' But they were silent. He looked around at them with anger; he was grieved at their hardness of heart and said to the man, 'Stretch out your hand.' He stretched it out, and his hand was restored. The Pharisees went out and immediately conspired with the Herodians against him, how to destroy him.

- In all the healing scenes in the Gospels the Pharisees never seem to show any compassion for the afflicted person. To them the sick were sinners who deserved their ailments. But Jesus will not allow their narrow attitudes to prevent him from doing good. Do we sometimes allow the critical attitudes of others to stop us from helping and loving those in need?

- We ask for the courage to do the right thing, and to follow our conscience regardless of what others may think of us.

Thursday 23 January
Mark 3:7–12

Jesus departed with his disciples to the lake, and a great multitude from Galilee followed him; hearing all that he was doing, they came to him in great numbers from Judea, Jerusalem, Idumea, beyond the Jordan, and the region around Tyre and Sidon. He told his disciples to have a boat ready for him because of the crowd, so that they would not crush him; for he had cured many, so that all who had diseases pressed upon him to touch him. Whenever the unclean spirits saw him, they fell down before him and shouted, 'You are the Son of God!' But he sternly ordered them not to make him known.

- Those who serve in public life know well how demanding the public can be. Jesus does not spare himself as the crowd presses upon him. A prayer associated with St Ignatius is, 'To give and not to count the cost, to fight and not to heed the wounds, to toil and not to seek for rest, to labour and to look for no reward save that of knowing that I do the will of God.'
- The people have seen the healing power of Jesus, and they seek to come in contact with him. We too in our need can contact this same Jesus through our faith-filled prayer with him.

Friday 24 January
Mark 3:13–19

He went up the mountain and called to him those whom he wanted, and they came to him. And he appointed twelve, whom he also named apostles, to be with him, and to be sent out to proclaim the message, and to have authority to cast out demons. So he appointed the twelve: Simon (to whom he gave the name Peter); James son of Zebedee and John the brother of James (to whom he gave the name Boanerges, that is, Sons of Thunder); and Andrew, and Philip, and Bartholomew, and Matthew, and Thomas, and James son of Alphaeus, and Thaddaeus, and Simon the Cananaean, and Judas Iscariot, who betrayed him.

- In St Luke's account of Jesus choosing his apostles we read that Jesus spent the whole of the previous night in prayer. In our big decisions we too need to pray earnestly, especially to the Holy Spirit, for light and guidance.
- It is consoling for us that from a human point of view Jesus did not get it totally right—he chose Judas Iscariot—but then we are always left free in our following of Jesus. May we use this freedom well in our decisions.

Saturday 25 January
The Conversion of St Paul, Apostle
Mark 16:15–18

And he said to them, 'Go into all the world and proclaim the good news to the whole creation. The one who believes and is baptized will be saved; but the one who does not believe will be condemned. And these signs will accompany those who believe: by using my name they will cast out demons; they will speak in new tongues; they will pick up snakes in their hands, and if they drink any deadly thing, it will not hurt them; they will lay their hands on the sick, and they will recover.'

- As Pope Francis reminds us, we all have a mission to witness to the truth of our faith. May our lives, in their own quiet way, proclaim the message of the Good News.

- The Spirit of Jesus has been given to the church, and Jesus has promised to be with us always. His healing power has passed on into the sacraments. In every sacrament we encounter him. Let us pray for a deeper trust in his saving power.

Something to think and pray about each day this week:

Sometimes people don't pray because they feel they're not worthy of it. They think it's not for them. Mention the word 'contemplation' and they run a mile. They think it's for monks and people who have all sorts of qualifications. Prayer and contemplation are nothing more than simply 'sitting with God'.

The world we live in can be very distracting. Everything gets broken down or torn apart, important concepts are shredded into little bits and pieces. Prayer, and particularly contemplation, allows you to enter into the heart of God, knowing that this world beats as one, that there's a harmony on the world. You are more than broken bits and pieces and individual parts. To be at peace you have to see the whole, get the picture of the whole, get the sense of the whole, and it is prayer and contemplation that help you achieve this.

I find that when I pray in the morning I go out into my day with a greater sense of purpose. I'm not just fiddling with little bits and pieces and trying to fit them together chaotically.

Alan Hilliard,
Dipping into Life: 40 Reflections for a Fragile Earth

The Presence of God

'Come to me, all you that are weary and are carrying heavy burdens, and I will give you rest.' Here I am, Lord. I come to seek your presence. I long for your healing power.

Freedom

God is not foreign to my freedom. The Spirit breathes life into my most intimate desires, gently nudging me towards all that is good. I ask for the grace to let myself be enfolded by the Spirit.

Consciousness

I remind myself that I am in the presence of the Lord. I will take refuge in his loving heart. He is my strength in times of weakness. He is my comforter in times of sorrow.

The Word

I take my time to read the word of God slowly, a few times, allowing myself to dwell on anything that strikes me. *(Please turn to the Scripture on the following pages. Inspiration points are there, should you need them. When you are ready, return here to continue.)*

Conversation

Jesus, you always welcomed little children when you walked on this earth. Teach me to have a childlike trust in you. Teach me to live in the knowledge that you will never abandon me.

Conclusion

Glory be to the Father, and to the Son, and to the Holy Spirit,
As it was in the beginning, is now and ever shall be,
World without end. Amen.

Sunday 26 January
Third Sunday in Ordinary Time
Luke 1:1–4; 4:14–21

Since many have undertaken to set down an orderly account of the events that have been fulfilled among us, just as they were handed on to us by those who from the beginning were eyewitnesses and servants of the word, I too decided, after investigating everything carefully from the very first, to write an orderly account for you, most excellent Theophilus, so that you may know the truth concerning the things about which you have been instructed. . . .

Then Jesus, filled with the power of the Spirit, returned to Galilee, and a report about him spread through all the surrounding country. He began to teach in their synagogues and was praised by everyone.

When he came to Nazareth, where he had been brought up, he went to the synagogue on the sabbath day, as was his custom. He stood up to read, and the scroll of the prophet Isaiah was given to him. He unrolled the scroll and found the place where it was written:

'The Spirit of the Lord is upon me,
because he has anointed me
to bring good news to the poor.
He has sent me to proclaim release to the captives
and recovery of sight to the blind,
to let the oppressed go free,
to proclaim the year of the Lord's favour.'

And he rolled up the scroll, gave it back to the attendant, and sat down. The eyes of all in the synagogue were fixed on him. Then he began to say to them, 'Today this scripture has been fulfilled in your hearing.'

- Our God speaks to us today through his inspired words in the Bible and especially in the Gospels. 'O that today you would listen to his voice! Do not harden your hearts, as at Meribah' (Psalm 95). May we always be open to whatever he wishes to teach us through his word.

- Jesus returns to his native village to bring the gift of the Good News to all those he had grown up with. With great longing Jesus wants to give to each of us the Good News of our salvation. He has promised us that he will reveal himself to us, but he needs us to give him that opportunity through our heartfelt encounters with him in prayer.

Monday 27 January
Mark 3:2–30

They watched him to see whether he would cure him on the sabbath, so that they might accuse him. And he said to the man who had the withered hand, 'Come forward.' Then he said to them, 'Is it lawful to do good or to do harm on the sabbath, to save life or to kill?' But they were silent. He looked around at them with anger; he was grieved at their hardness of heart and said to the man, 'Stretch out your hand.' He stretched it out, and his hand was restored. The Pharisees went out and immediately conspired with the Herodians against him, how to destroy him.

Jesus departed with his disciples to the lake, and a great multitude from Galilee followed him; hearing all that he was doing, they came to him in great numbers from Judea, Jerusalem, Idumea, beyond the Jordan, and the region around Tyre and Sidon. He told his disciples to have a boat ready for him because of the crowd, so that they would not crush him; for he had cured many, so that all who had diseases pressed upon him to touch him. Whenever the unclean spirits saw him, they fell down before him and shouted, 'You are the Son of God!' But he sternly ordered them not to make him known.

He went up the mountain and called to him those whom he wanted, and they came to him. And he appointed twelve, whom he also named apostles, to be with him, and to be sent out to proclaim the message, and to have authority to cast out demons. So he appointed the twelve: Simon (to whom he gave the name Peter); James son of Zebedee and John the brother of James (to whom he gave the name Boanerges, that is, Sons of Thunder); and Andrew, and Philip, and Bartholomew, and Matthew, and Thomas, and James son of Alphaeus, and Thaddaeus, and Simon the Cananaean, and Judas Iscariot, who betrayed him.

Then he went home; and the crowd came together again, so that they could not even eat. When his family heard it, they went out to restrain him, for people were saying, 'He has gone out of his mind.' And the scribes who came down from Jerusalem said, 'He has Beelzebul, and by the ruler of the demons he casts out demons.' And he called them to him, and spoke to them in parables, 'How can Satan cast out Satan? If a kingdom is divided against itself, that kingdom cannot stand. And if a house is divided against itself, that house will not be able to stand. And if Satan has risen up against himself and is divided, he cannot stand, but his end has come. But no one can enter a strong man's house and plunder his property without first tying up the strong man; then indeed the house can be plundered.

'Truly I tell you, people will be forgiven for their sins and whatever blasphemies they utter; but whoever blasphemes against the Holy Spirit can never have forgiveness, but is guilty of an eternal sin'—for they had said, 'He has an unclean spirit.'

- We always have a choice to do good or to do harm. Jesus has told us that it is out of the human heart that good or bad comes. Let us pray for goodness of heart.

- From the Gospels we see that Jesus had very mixed success in his efforts to spread his Father's kingdom. Although great crowds of people sought to listen to him, some, like the Pharisees, closed their hearts to his message, and it grieved him. Do I respond to his message with generosity and try to put his teachings into practice?

Tuesday 28 January
Mark 3:31–35

Then his mother and his brothers came; and standing outside, they sent to him and called him. A crowd was sitting around him; and they said to him, 'Your mother and your brothers and sisters are outside, asking for you.' And he replied, 'Who are my mother and my brothers?' And looking at those who sat around him, he said, 'Here are my mother and my brothers! Whoever does the will of God is my brother and sister and mother.'

- Through his coming amongst us as one of us and by his life, death and resurrection, Jesus has become our brother and made all who seek to follow him his new family. In having the one Spirit of Jesus within us we are united together and become brothers and sisters of each other. Let us join with Jesus in his prayer for unity among all Christians.

Wednesday 29 January
Mark 4:1–20

Again he began to teach beside the lake. Such a very large crowd gathered around him that he got into a boat on the lake and sat there, while the whole crowd was beside the lake on the land. He began to teach them many things in parables, and in his teaching he said to them: 'Listen! A sower went out to sow. And as he sowed, some seed fell on the path, and the birds came and ate it up. Other seed fell on rocky ground, where it did not have much soil, and it sprang up quickly, since it had no depth of soil. And when the sun rose, it was scorched; and since it had no root, it withered away. Other seed fell among thorns, and the thorns grew up and choked it, and it yielded no grain. Other seed fell into good soil and brought forth grain, growing up and increasing and yielding thirty and sixty and a hundredfold.' And he said, 'Let anyone with ears to hear listen!'

- As we listen to the words of this Gospel it will be helpful to reflect on our own lives and to recall how the seed of the word of God found a different reception in us at different times. Let us acknowledge that in varying degrees we have been the rocky and dry ground and the thorny ground, as well as the good soil. We ask for the grace to be open to God's working in our lives.

- At our baptism we received the gift of the Holy Spirit, opening us to receive the seed of the word of God. Our subsequent Christian formation led to the silent maturing of the seeds of our Christian lives. But many things can block the growth of this life within us. Let us reflect in prayer where the precious seeds may have become withered or parched through our neglect, and also where they have become fruitful.

Thursday 30 January
Mark 4:21–25

He said to them, 'Is a lamp brought in to be put under the bushel basket, or under the bed, and not on the lampstand? For there is nothing hidden, except to be disclosed; nor is anything secret, except to come to light. Let anyone with ears to hear listen!' And he said to them, 'Pay attention to what you hear; the measure you give will be the measure you get, and still more will be given you. For to those who have, more will be given; and from those who have nothing, even what they have will be taken away.'

- Jesus urges us to listen to his words with real openness. It has been said that the language of God is silence and love. Are we content to sit in his presence and listen to his loving us here and now? When we can't find what words to say, just have our Lord say to us, 'I don't need your words. I just want your presence and your love.'

- St Paul reminds us that 'you shine like stars in the world'. St Thérèse of Lisieux wrote about 'the prayer that ignites a fire of love'. May we bear witness by our lives to the light and love of Jesus Christ.

Friday 31 January
Mark 4:26–34

He also said, 'The kingdom of God is as if someone would scatter seed on the ground, and would sleep and rise night and day, and the seed would sprout and grow, he does not know how. The earth produces of itself, first the stalk, then the head, then the full grain in the head. But when the grain is ripe, at once he goes in with his sickle, because the harvest has come.'

He also said, 'With what can we compare the kingdom of God, or what parable will we use for it? It is like a mustard seed, which, when sown upon the ground, is the smallest of all the seeds on earth; yet when it is sown it grows up and becomes the greatest of all shrubs, and puts forth large branches, so that the birds of the air can make nests in its shade.'

With many such parables he spoke the word to them, as they were able to hear it; he did not speak to them except in parables, but he explained everything in private to his disciples.

- A farmer sows tiny seeds in the ground and leaves them to grow silently at their own pace. In John 5 Jesus has told us that both he and his Father are at work in us. Often it is only when we look back at our lives that we see the fruit of his silent working in us. We give him thanks and entrust ourselves more and more to his loving care.

Saturday 1 February
Mark 4:35–41

On that day, when evening had come, he said to them, 'Let us go across to the other side.' And leaving the crowd behind, they took him with them in the boat, just as he was. Other boats were with him. A great gale arose, and the waves beat into the boat, so that the boat was already being swamped. But he was in the stern, asleep on the cushion; and they woke him up and said to him, 'Teacher, do you not care that we are perishing?' He woke up and rebuked the wind, and said to the sea, 'Peace! Be still!' Then the wind ceased, and there was a dead calm. He said to them, 'Why are you afraid? Have you still no faith?' And they were filled with great awe and said to one another, 'Who then is this, that even the wind and the sea obey him?'

- St Mark alone mentions the little detail of Jesus asleep on the cushion. Physically exhausted, even the motion of the boat did not awaken him. This is a scene we can often bring to prayer, as so often our God seems to be asleep or absent when we go to meet him in prayer. But Jesus clearly expects our faith to overcome this illusion.

- Yes, indeed, 'Who then *is* this, that even the wind and the sea obey him?' In our long journey of coming to know the Lord this will be a constant question and a constant mystery for us to ponder and to talk to the Lord about in prayer. At its heart is the Incarnation and the immense love of our God for us.

Something to think and pray about each day this week:

February has many themes, starting with St Brigid and ending with the possibility of a leap year. In the middle of it all is the feast of St Valentine. There were many Valentines in the early church. The first Valentine, who may be the original St Valentine, died around AD 270 for reputedly celebrating the marriage of the early Christians, a practice forbidden by law.

When love is celebrated we sometimes wonder what is being celebrated. Is it a passing, fleeting moment of emotional ecstasy? Or is it the pain of loss? Or are we marking something that is eternal, joyful and beyond words?

A starting point might be to name the source of love—we may think that we are the source of our love. Or we can ask does love come from somewhere else? If love comes from somewhere other than the self, then it doesn't depend on us. The love from elsewhere can be my strength and sustenance in the act of loving and being loved. It can also tell us how to repair that love. Our Christian faith gives us the story of Jesus of Nazareth as he teaches us how to weave forgiveness, sacrifice, support, care, memory and healing into our story of love.

'Beloved, let us love one another, for love is from God, and whoever loves has been born of God and knows God' (1 John 4:7). Believing this, we know that loving doesn't depend on us, but on the source of it all:

Alan Hilliard,
The Sacred Heart Messenger,
February 2021

The Presence of God
What is present to me is what has a hold on my becoming. I reflect on the presence of God always there in love, amidst the many things that have a hold on me. I pause and pray that I may let God affect my becoming in this precise moment.

Freedom
By God's grace I was born to live in freedom. Free to enjoy the pleasures he created for me. Dear Lord, grant that I may live as you intended, with complete confidence in your loving care.

Consciousness
I exist in a web of relationships: links to nature, people, God. I trace out these links, giving thanks for the life that flows through them. Some links are twisted or broken; I may feel regret, anger, disappointment. I pray for the gift of acceptance and forgiveness.

The Word
God speaks to each of us individually. I listen attentively to hear what he is saying to me. Read the text a few times, then listen. *(Please turn to the Scripture on the following pages. Inspiration points are there, should you need them. When you are ready, return here to continue.)*

Conversation
I begin to talk with Jesus about the Scripture I have just read. What part of it strikes a chord in me? Perhaps the words of a friend—or some story I have heard recently—will rise to the surface in my consciousness. If so, does the story throw light on what the Scripture passage may be saying to me?

Conclusion
Glory be to the Father, and to the Son, and to the Holy Spirit,
As it was in the beginning, is now and ever shall be,
World without end. Amen.

Sunday 2 February
The Presentation of the Lord
Luke 2:22–40

When the time came for their purification according to the law of Moses, they brought him up to Jerusalem to present him to the Lord (as it is written in the law of the Lord, 'Every firstborn male shall be designated as holy to the Lord'), and they offered a sacrifice according to what is stated in the law of the Lord, 'a pair of turtle-doves or two young pigeons.'

Now there was a man in Jerusalem whose name was Simeon; this man was righteous and devout, looking forward to the consolation of Israel, and the Holy Spirit rested on him. It had been revealed to him by the Holy Spirit that he would not see death before he had seen the Lord's Messiah. Guided by the Spirit, Simeon came into the temple; and when the parents brought in the child Jesus, to do for him what was customary under the law, Simeon took him in his arms and praised God, saying,

'Master, now you are dismissing your servant in peace,
according to your word;
for my eyes have seen your salvation,
which you have prepared in the presence of all peoples,
a light for revelation to the Gentiles
and for glory to your people Israel.'

And the child's father and mother were amazed at what was being said about him. Then Simeon blessed them and said to his mother Mary, 'This child is destined for the falling and the rising of many in Israel, and to be a sign that will be opposed so that the inner thoughts of many will be revealed—and a sword will pierce your own soul too.'

There was also a prophet, Anna the daughter of Phanuel, of the tribe of Asher. She was of a great age, having lived with her husband for seven years after her marriage, then as a widow to the age of eighty-four. She never left the temple but worshipped there with fasting and prayer night and day. At that moment she came, and began to praise God and to speak about the child to all who were looking for the redemption of Jerusalem.

When they had finished everything required by the law of the Lord, they returned to Galilee, to their own town of Nazareth. The child grew and became strong, filled with wisdom; and the favour of God was upon him.

- Simeon, enlightened by the Holy Spirit, recognises Jesus as the Messiah. He prophesies that he will be opposed. No human life is without its difficulties. To be true followers of Jesus we must take up our cross daily.

- Mary's own sword of sorrow will take her to the foot of the cross to be present at her Son's execution. Her yes to God at the Annunciation included all that would happen in her life. We pray to accept all the events of our own lives and to see and accept them from the hands of God.

Monday 3 February
Mark 5:1–20

They came to the other side of the lake, to the country of the Gerasenes. And when he had stepped out of the boat, immediately a man out of the tombs with an unclean spirit met him. He lived among the tombs; and no one could restrain him any more, even with a chain; for he had often been restrained with shackles and chains, but the chains he wrenched apart, and the shackles he broke in pieces; and no one had the strength to subdue him. Night and day among the tombs and on the mountains he was always howling and bruising himself with stones. When he saw Jesus from a distance, he ran and bowed down before him; and he shouted at the top of his voice, 'What have you to do with me, Jesus, Son of the Most High God? I adjure you by God, do not torment me.' For he had said to him, 'Come out of the man, you unclean spirit!' Then Jesus asked him, 'What is your name?' He replied, 'My name is Legion; for we are many.' He begged him earnestly not to send them out of the country. Now there on the hillside a great herd of swine was feeding; and the unclean spirits begged him, 'Send us into the swine; let us enter them.' So he gave them permission. And the unclean spirits came out and entered the swine; and the herd, numbering about two thousand, rushed down the steep bank into the lake, and were drowned in the lake.

The swineherds ran off and told it in the city and in the country. Then people came to see what it was that had happened. They came to Jesus and saw the demoniac sitting there, clothed and in his right mind, the very man who had had the legion; and they were afraid. Those who had seen what had happened to the demoniac and to the swine reported it. Then they began to beg Jesus to leave their neighbourhood. As he was getting into the boat, the man who had been possessed by demons begged him that he might be with him. But Jesus refused, and said to him, 'Go home to your friends, and tell them how much the Lord has done for you, and what mercy he has shown you.' And he went away and began to proclaim in the Decapolis how much Jesus had done for him; and everyone was amazed.

- There is a great contrast between the demoniac howling among the tombs and gashing himself with stones, and the demoniac clothed and sitting quietly by the side of Jesus. The presence of Jesus brings healing into even the most agonising situation in which we may find ourselves. With this picture of the demoniac sitting with Jesus before us let us speak now to the Lord.

- The people of the area asked Jesus to leave. Some people may see the cost of discipleship as too high and decide to go and live a different way. As G. K. Chesterton wrote, 'Christianity has not failed. It has been found to be difficult and not tried.' Are we willing to pay the price?

Tuesday 4 February
Mark 5:21–43

When Jesus had crossed again in the boat to the other side, a great crowd gathered round him; and he was by the lake. Then one of the leaders of the synagogue named Jairus came and, when he saw him, fell at his feet and begged him repeatedly, 'My little daughter is at the point of death. Come and lay your hands on her, so that she may be made well, and live.' So he went with him.

And a large crowd followed him and pressed in on him. Now there was a woman who had been suffering from haemorrhages for twelve years. She had endured much under many physicians, and had spent all that she had; and she was no better, but rather grew worse. She had heard about Jesus, and came up behind him in the crowd and touched his cloak, for she said, 'If I but touch his clothes, I will be made well.' Immediately her haemorrhage stopped; and she felt in her body that she was healed of her disease. Immediately aware that power had gone forth from him, Jesus turned about in the crowd and said, 'Who touched my clothes?' And his disciples said to him, 'You see the crowd pressing in on you; how can you say, "Who touched me?"' He looked all round to see who had done it. But the woman, knowing what had happened to her, came in fear and trembling, fell down before him, and told him the whole truth. He said to her, 'Daughter, your faith has made you well; go in peace, and be healed of your disease.'

While he was still speaking, some people came from the leader's house to say, 'Your daughter is dead. Why trouble the teacher any further?' But overhearing what they said, Jesus said to the leader of the synagogue, 'Do not fear, only believe.' He allowed no one to follow him except Peter, James, and John, the brother of James. When they came to the house of the leader of the synagogue, he saw a commotion, people weeping and wailing loudly. When he had entered, he said to them, 'Why do you make a commotion and weep? The child is not dead but sleeping.' And they laughed at him. Then he put them all outside, and took the child's father and mother and those who were with him, and went in where the child was. He took her by the hand and said to her, 'Talitha cum', which means, 'Little girl, get up!' And immediately the girl got up and began to walk about (she was twelve years of age). At this they were overcome with amazement. He strictly ordered them that no one should know this, and told them to give her something to eat.

- Unlike the centurion who said, 'only speak the word, and my servant will be healed', Jairus wants Jesus to come and lay his hands on his dying daughter and Jesus goes with him. Our God in his compassion accepts that we can only pray with whatever faith we have at each moment. Let us ask God to increase our faith as we pray, 'I believe; help my unbelief!'

- Shakespeare wrote, 'Our little life is rounded with a sleep.' For those who die in Christ a reawakening into a new life awaits. Here we see the gentleness of Jesus as he gives their little daughter back to her distraught parents and reminds them to give her something to eat. Jesus said, 'Come to me . . . for I am gentle and humble in heart, and you will find rest for your souls.'

Wednesday 5 February
Mark 6:1–6

He left that place and came to his home town, and his disciples followed him. On the sabbath he began to teach in the synagogue, and many who heard him were astounded. They said, 'Where did this man get all this? What is this wisdom that has been given to him? What deeds of power are being done by his hands! Is not this the carpenter, the son of Mary and brother of James and Joses and Judas and Simon, and are not his sisters here with us?' And they took offence at him. Then Jesus said to them, 'Prophets are not without honour, except in their home town, and among their own kin, and in their own house.' And he could do no deed of power there, except that he laid his hands on a few sick people and cured them. And he was amazed at their unbelief.

Then he went about among the villages teaching.

- Most likely this was the last time Jesus set foot in his home village after they took offence at him out of jealousy or hardness of heart. He had brought the treasure of the Good News to them and no doubt he had hoped for a welcome from them and that he would cure the sick. In my own blindness do I thwart God's plans to give himself to me?

- The surprise of his former fellow villagers at this 'new' Jesus speaks volumes about how ordinary his growing up in Nazareth as the son of the carpenter had been. For most of us our lives will be ordinary, but in God's eyes each one is precious and unique. We thank him for the wonder of our being.

Thursday 6 February
Mark 6:7–13

He called the twelve and began to send them out two by two, and gave them authority over the unclean spirits. He ordered them to take nothing for their journey except a staff; no bread, no bag, no money in their belts; but to wear sandals and not to put on two tunics. He said to them, 'Wherever you enter a house, stay there until you leave the place. If any place will not welcome you and they refuse to hear you, as you leave, shake off the dust that is on your feet as a testimony against them.' So they went out and proclaimed that all should repent. They cast out many demons, and anointed with oil many who were sick and cured them.

- The apostles and disciples of Jesus were on a training course and did not realise it. Jesus knew that he would be in need of them if his Father's kingdom was to spread. Today God asks each of us to be his hands, his feet, his voice, to bring the message of the gospel to others by the witness of our Christian lives. May we not disappoint him.

- Jesus has promised to be with us always and works through us for the good of others. Our acts of kindness and even a smile can bring comfort and healing to those in need.

Friday 7 February
Mark 6:14–29

King Herod heard of it, for Jesus' name had become known. Some were saying, 'John the baptizer has been raised from the dead; and for this reason these powers are at work in him.' But others said, 'It is Elijah.' And others said, 'It is a prophet, like one of the prophets of old.' But when Herod heard of it, he said, 'John, whom I beheaded, has been raised.'

For Herod himself had sent men who arrested John, bound him, and put him in prison on account of Herodias, his brother Philip's wife, because Herod had married her. For John had been telling Herod, 'It is not lawful for you to have your brother's wife.' And Herodias had a grudge against him, and wanted to kill him. But she could not, for Herod feared John, knowing that he was a righteous and holy man, and he protected him. When he heard him, he was greatly perplexed; and yet he liked to listen to him. But an opportunity came when Herod on his birthday gave a banquet for his courtiers and officers and for the leaders of Galilee. When his daughter Herodias came in and danced, she pleased Herod and his guests; and the king said to the girl, 'Ask me for whatever you wish, and I will give it.' And he solemnly swore to her, 'Whatever you ask me, I will give you, even half of my kingdom.' She went out and said to her mother, 'What should I ask for?' She replied, 'The head of John the baptizer.' Immediately she rushed back to the king and requested, 'I want you to give me at once the head of John the Baptist on a platter.' The king was deeply grieved; yet out of regard for his oaths and for the guests, he did not want to refuse her. Immediately the king sent a soldier of the guard with orders to bring John's head. He went and beheaded him in the prison, brought his head on a platter, and gave it to the girl. Then the girl gave it to her mother. When his disciples heard about it, they came and took his body, and laid it in a tomb.

- Herod in his heart knew that John the Baptist was 'a righteous and holy man', and he liked to listen to him. Nevertheless, he remained perplexed by John and refused to accept his teaching and to repent of his own sinful life. Habits of sin in our lives will always be a barrier to our prayer and will block God's working in us. We ask for the grace of repentance.

- Herod puts the good opinions of his guests before the correct following of his conscience. How often am I swayed by the false praise and opinion of others to do what I know is wrong and unjust in my treatment of vulnerable people?

Saturday 8 February
Mark 6:30–34

The apostles gathered around Jesus, and told him all that they had done and taught. He said to them, 'Come away to a deserted place all by yourselves and rest a while.' For many were coming and going, and they had no leisure even to eat. And they went away in the boat to a deserted place by themselves. Now many saw them going and recognised them, and they hurried there on foot from all the towns and arrived ahead of them. As he went ashore, he saw a great crowd; and he had compassion for them, because they were like sheep without a shepherd; and he began to teach them many things.

- After their missionary endeavours the disciples are in need of a break. Jesus knows this and invites them to spend some time alone with him. We all need time and space in our busy lives, both to rest and to reflect on what is important. Let us hear the Master's invitation to spend some time with him in prayer or on a weekend retreat. 'Come away to a deserted place . . . '.

- The people were so enthralled by the teaching of Jesus that they were prepared to go to great lengths to hear more from him. This same Jesus in his compassion wants to teach us today by his word in the Scriptures and by his presence.

Something to think and pray about each day this week:

I'm sure Noah would never get his ark completed today. The flood would well and truly have passed over him before he started building. There are so many rules and regulations governing the simplest of tasks. There are mountains of paperwork that have to be completed, forms to be filled in, permissions to be got and standards to be reached.

He'd have to complete an environmental impact statement, let the planning authority know he was creating a temporary structure, undergo a health and safety audit, let the tax office know where he got the money from just in case he was laundering, and he'd have to ensure that all the animal rights organisations were happy with the accommodation he was hoping to provide to the animals.

The world has become a very complicated place. Some of us may dream of an idyllic, simple life where things can be done with ease and basic camaraderie, but that dream is getting further and further from view. It's as if the world has been made to destroy initiative and keep the status quo in place. On reflection this is not new. I'm sure Noah had equivalent problems in his day. Sure, Jesus was a leader too, and it was the status quo who had him crucified.

Alan Hilliard,
Dipping into Life: 40 Reflections for a Fragile Earth

The Presence of God
'Be still, and know that I am God!' Lord, your words lead us to the calmness and greatness of your presence.

Freedom
'In these days, God taught me as a schoolteacher teaches a pupil' (St Ignatius). I remind myself that there are things God has to teach me yet, and I ask for the grace to hear them and let them change me.

Consciousness
How am I really feeling? Lighthearted? Heavyhearted? I may be very much at peace, happy to be here. Equally, I may be frustrated, worried, or angry. I acknowledge how I really am. It is the real me whom the Lord loves.

The Word
God speaks to each of us individually. I listen attentively to hear what he is saying to me. Read the text a few times, then listen. *(Please turn to the Scripture on the following pages. Inspiration points are there, should you need them. When you are ready, return here to continue.)*

Conversation
Do I notice myself reacting as I pray with the word of God? Do I feel challenged, comforted, angry? Imagining Jesus sitting or standing by me, I speak out my feelings, as one trusted friend to another.

Conclusion
I thank God for these moments we have spent together and for any insights I have been given concerning the text.

Sunday 9 February
Fifth Sunday in Ordinary Time
Luke 5:1–11

Once while Jesus was standing beside the lake of Gennesaret, and the crowd was pressing in on him to hear the word of God, he saw two boats there at the shore of the lake; the fishermen had gone out of them and were washing their nets. He got into one of the boats, the one belonging to Simon, and asked him to put out a little way from the shore. Then he sat down and taught the crowds from the boat. When he had finished speaking, he said to Simon, 'Put out into the deep water and let down your nets for a catch.' Simon answered, 'Master, we have worked all night long but have caught nothing. Yet if you say so, I will let down the nets.' When they had done this, they caught so many fish that their nets were beginning to break. So they signalled to their partners in the other boat to come and help them. And they came and filled both boats, so that they began to sink. But when Simon Peter saw it, he fell down at Jesus' knees, saying, 'Go away from me, Lord, for I am a sinful man!' For he and all who were with him were amazed at the catch of fish that they had taken; and so also were James and John, sons of Zebedee, who were partners with Simon. Then Jesus said to Simon, 'Do not be afraid; from now on you will be catching people.' When they had brought their boats to shore, they left everything and followed him.

• Peter and his companions had fished all night but had caught nothing. Tired and discouraged they could have asked, 'What's the point?' But because Jesus had asked them to throw out the nets again, they obeyed him and had huge success. If at first we don't succeed, try and try again. Being a Christian is about trying to be a Christian. For us praying is always about trying to pray. We must never give it up.

• Jesus has told us in the story of the vine and the branches, 'Apart from me you can do nothing.' Together with him we can achieve whatever is asked of us in life. Let us pray for a deeper trust in him.

Monday 10 February
Mark 6:53–56

When they had crossed over, they came to land at Gennesaret and moored the boat. When they got out of the boat, people at once recognized him, and rushed about that whole region and began to bring the sick on mats to wherever they heard he was. And wherever he went, into villages or cities or farms, they laid the sick in the market-places, and begged him that they might touch even the fringe of his cloak; and all who touched it were healed.

- St Mark often provides little details in his Gospel that are not found in the other Gospels. Here, by just touching the fringe of Jesus' cloak, the people receive healing. By our faith we too can touch his cloak in prayer and be graced and healed. Every prayer from our hearts is heard by God and we are blessed and changed. God is always at work in us, but in his own way and in his own time. By looking back at the graced times in our lives we can become more aware of his help.

Tuesday 11 February
Mark 7:1–13

Now when the Pharisees and some of the scribes who had come from Jerusalem gathered around him, they noticed that some of his disciples were eating with defiled hands, that is, without washing them. (For the Pharisees, and all the Jews, do not eat unless they thoroughly wash their hands, thus observing the tradition of the elders; and they do not eat anything from the market unless they wash it; and there are also many other traditions that they observe, the washing of cups, pots, and bronze kettles.) So the Pharisees and the scribes asked him, 'Why do your disciples not live according to the tradition of the elders, but eat with defiled hands?' He said to them, 'Isaiah prophesied rightly about you hypocrites, as it is written,

"This people honours me with their lips,
    but their hearts are far from me;
in vain do they worship me,
    teaching human precepts as doctrines."
You abandon the commandment of God and hold to human
    tradition.'

Then he said to them, 'You have a fine way of rejecting the commandment of God in order to keep your tradition! For Moses said, "Honour your father and your mother"; and, "Whoever speaks evil of father or mother must surely die." But you say that if anyone tells father or mother,

"Whatever support you might have had from me is Corban" (that is, an offering to God)—then you no longer permit doing anything for a father or mother, thus making void the word of God through your tradition that you have handed on. And you do many things like this.'

- Sadly the hearts of many of the Pharisees and scribes were far from God. They had put their trust for their salvation in their own man-made laws and customs. In their hypocrisy they judged others by how well these customs were observed. Do I keep the tenets of my religion just to be well regarded by others?

- God does not want to be honoured just by our lips but by our love for him expressed from our hearts. In my praying do I simply repeat the same words over and over, without meaning them in my heart and without speaking them to a Person?

Wednesday 12 February
Mark 7:14–23

Then he called the crowd again and said to them, 'Listen to me, all of you, and understand: there is nothing outside a person that by going in can defile, but the things that come out are what defile.'

When he had left the crowd and entered the house, his disciples asked him about the parable. He said to them, 'Then do you also fail to understand? Do you not see that whatever goes into a person from outside cannot defile, since it enters, not the heart but the stomach, and goes out into the sewer?' (Thus he declared all foods clean.) And he said, 'It is what comes out of a person that defiles. For it is from within, from the human heart, that evil intentions come: fornication, theft, murder, adultery, avarice, wickedness, deceit, licentiousness, envy, slander, pride, folly. All these evil things come from within, and they defile a person.'

- Here Jesus declares not only that all foods are clean but also that our human bodies are good and holy. The source of our doing evil comes from the selfishness that is in the spirit (heart) of all of us. We ask God to purify our hearts and to help us truly to understand the source of why we do bad things.

- St Thérèse of Lisieux wrote, 'I said no to self and it made all the difference.' It became a pivotal moment for her on her road to sanctity.

Thursday 13 February
Mark 7:24–30

From there he set out and went away to the region of Tyre. He entered a house and did not want anyone to know he was there. Yet he could not escape notice, but a woman whose little daughter had an unclean spirit immediately heard about him, and she came and bowed down at his feet. Now the woman was a Gentile, of Syrophoenician origin. She begged him to cast the demon out of her daughter. He said to her, 'Let the children be fed first, for it is not fair to take the children's food and throw it to the dogs.' But she answered him, 'Sir, even the dogs under the table eat the children's crumbs.' Then he said to her, 'For saying that, you may go—the demon has left your daughter.' So she went home, found the child lying on the bed, and the demon gone.

- Jesus knew that he had been sent first of all to the lost sheep of the house of Israel, but in his love and compassion he embraced all people, seeing them as the beloved of his Father. Here he seems to snub and even insult this Gentile woman, but in fact he is testing her faith as he does so often with us. Her persistence and trust in him are rewarded. We ask for the grace never to give up prayer and to grow in our faith and trust in the compassion and love our God has for each of us.

Friday 14 February
Mark 7:31–37

Then he returned from the region of Tyre, and went by way of Sidon towards the Sea of Galilee, in the region of the Decapolis. They brought to him a deaf man who had an impediment in his speech; and they begged him to lay his hand on him. He took him aside in private, away from the crowd, and put his fingers into his ears, and he spat and touched his tongue. Then looking up to heaven, he sighed and said to him, 'Ephphatha', that is, 'Be opened.' And immediately his ears were opened, his tongue was released, and he spoke plainly. Then Jesus ordered them to tell no one; but the more he ordered them, the more zealously they proclaimed it. They were astounded beyond measure, saying, 'He has done everything well; he even makes the deaf to hear and the mute to speak.'

- We know that Jesus could have healed all who came to him with just a word, but on a few occasions, as here, he delays and goes through a kind of ritual. It may be to deepen the faith of the sick person. When we ask for something we need to leave it entirely in his hands and trust that he will help us.

- This miracle of Jesus is again one of the signs of the Messiah foretold by the prophets. It is one thing to hear the word of God but we need also to listen on a deeper level that engages our hearts if we are to learn how to imitate the Master who has done all things well.

Saturday 15 February
Mark 8:1–10

In those days when there was again a great crowd without anything to eat, he called his disciples and said to them, 'I have compassion for the crowd, because they have been with me now for three days and have nothing to eat. If I send them away hungry to their homes, they will faint on the way—and some of them have come from a great distance.' His disciples replied, 'How can one feed these people with bread here in the desert?' He asked them, 'How many loaves do you have?' They said, 'Seven.' Then he ordered the crowd to sit down on the ground; and he took the seven loaves, and after giving thanks he broke them and gave them to his disciples to distribute; and they distributed them to the crowd. They had also a few small fish; and after blessing them, he ordered that these too should be distributed. They ate and were filled; and they took up the broken pieces left over, seven baskets full. Now there were about four thousand people. And he sent them away. And immediately he got into the boat with his disciples and went to the district of Dalmanutha.

- The human Jesus is so caring and understanding that he knows that this vast crowd must be hungry by now and will struggle to make their way home. Too often we pamper and attend so much to the needs and wants of our bodies that we neglect the needs of our souls. The body will always want more and more. Let us do more to redress the balance between the needs of both body and spirit.

- There is nothing we have that has not been given to us by God. He provides the food that sustains our bodies, and with his own body and blood he feeds our souls in the Eucharist. It is through the Eucharist that we give him the greatest thanks because it is the offering and prayer of his own Son.

Something to think and pray about each day this week:

Reflection on the journey of life invites us to appreciate our gifts as well as our areas of struggle, so that we can grow in openness to the Lord and to his way. During their time in the wilderness, the Chosen People were changed in their relationship with God, with Moses and with each other. Sometimes these changes were positive but, on other occasions, that was not so. The Commandments taught them about a God of love who called them into a true relationship with God and with each other. They reminded them that God was close to them, concerned about them and committed to them. Their image of God underwent change, as did their relationship with God. The covenant made them into a people bonded with the Lord in a special way. The law of love was to guide their relationships. While that did guide them at times, on other occasions they went their own way, even making and worshipping false gods. Selfish interests took precedence at times, and the bigger vision was lost. Similarly, we are made in the image of God with the potential to grow. As people of the New Covenant we are given a special dignity, and invited to a closer relationship with God. Our image of God and of the self can undergo change. Growing in self-knowledge, we can expand the freedom we have to respond to the Lord in living the commandment of love. We can also go our own way, however, by finding and worshipping false gods. The choices we make have implications for our relationship with the Lord and with each other. By reflecting on our experience and learning from it, the way is opened to change and more faithful living in the truth the Lord reveals to us.

Michael Drennan SJ,
See God Act: The Ministry of Spiritual Direction

The Presence of God
I remind myself that, as I sit here now, God is gazing on me with love and holding me in being. I pause for a moment and think of this.

Freedom
'There are very few people who realise what God would make of them if they abandoned themselves into his hands, and let themselves be formed by his grace' (St Ignatius). I ask for the grace to trust myself totally to God's love.

Consciousness
Where do I sense hope, encouragement, and growth in my life? By looking back over the past few months, I may be able to see which activities and occasions have produced rich fruit. If I do notice such areas, I will determine to give those areas both time and space in the future.

The Word
Lord Jesus, you became human to communicate with me. You walked and worked on this earth. You endured the heat and struggled with the cold. All your time on this earth was spent in caring for humanity. You healed the sick, you raised the dead. Most important of all, you saved me from death. *(Please turn to the Scripture on the following pages. Inspiration points are there, should you need them. When you are ready, return here to continue.)*

Conversation
What is stirring in me as I pray? Am I consoled, troubled, left cold? I imagine Jesus standing or sitting at my side, and I share my feelings with him.

Conclusion
Glory be to the Father, and to the Son, and to the Holy Spirit,
As it was in the beginning, is now and ever shall be,
World without end. Amen.

Sunday 16 February
Sixth Sunday in Ordinary Time
Luke 6:17, 20–26

He came down with them and stood on a level place, with a great crowd of his disciples and a great multitude of people from all Judea, Jerusalem, and the coast of Tyre and Sidon. . . .

Then he looked up at his disciples and said:
'Blessed are you who are poor,
> for yours is the kingdom of God.
'Blessed are you who are hungry now,
> for you will be filled.
'Blessed are you who weep now,
> for you will laugh.
'Blessed are you when people hate you, and when they exclude you,
> revile you, and defame you on account of the Son of Man.
> Rejoice on that day and leap for joy, for surely your reward
> is great in heaven; for that is what their ancestors did to the
> prophets.
'But woe to you who are rich,
> for you have received your consolation.
'Woe to you who are full now,
> for you will be hungry.
'Woe to you who are laughing now,
> for you will mourn and weep.
'Woe to you when all speak well of you, for that is what their ancestors did to the false prophets.'

- It is those who recognise their inner poverty and their complete dependence on God who possess the kingdom of God. The values and ways of the world will always be different from those of the kingdom, so there will be opposition from a secular society. Let us pray for all who are persecuted for their faith and ask for the grace of perseverance in our fidelity to Christ.

Monday 17 February
Mark 8:11–13

The Pharisees came and began to argue with him, asking him for a sign from heaven, to test him. And he sighed deeply in his spirit and said, 'Why does this generation ask for a sign? Truly I tell you, no sign will be given to this generation.' And he left them, and getting into the boat again, he went across to the other side.

- Jesus came to call sinners to repentance and he never ceased to love the Pharisees and the scribes who tried to thwart him again and again in his mission. But their hardness of heart sorely tried his patience, as we read in this Gospel. God never gives up on us. We read in Revelation 3:20, 'Listen! I am standing at the door, knocking; if you hear my voice and open the door, I will come in to you and eat with you, and you with me'

Tuesday 18 February
Mark 8:14–21

Now the disciples had forgotten to bring any bread; and they had only one loaf with them in the boat. And he cautioned them, saying, 'Watch out—beware of the yeast of the Pharisees and the yeast of Herod.' They said to one another, 'It is because we have no bread.' And becoming aware of it, Jesus said to them, 'Why are you talking about having no bread? Do you still not perceive or understand? Are your hearts hardened? Do you have eyes, and fail to see? Do you have ears, and fail to hear? And do you not remember? When I broke the five loaves for the five thousand, how many baskets full of broken pieces did you collect?' They said to him, 'Twelve.' 'And the seven for the four thousand, how many baskets full of broken pieces did you collect?' And they said to him, 'Seven.' Then he said to them, 'Do you not yet understand?'

- Jesus' reaction to his disciples here is so very human in his frustration. Many years ago I attended a stage performance by Alec McCowen where he recited the Gospel of Mark. When he came to this part he expressed very well with his voice the frustration of Jesus. How often God has to be patient with us in our own blindness and lack of faith. Let us talk to him about this now and ask for the grace to be patient with our own slowness to understand and our lack of trust.

Wednesday 19 February
Mark 8:22–26

They came to Bethsaida. Some people brought a blind man to him and begged him to touch him. He took the blind man by the hand and led him out of the village; and when he had put saliva on his eyes and laid his hands on him, he asked him, 'Can you see anything?' And the man looked up and said, 'I can see people, but they look like trees, walking.' Then Jesus laid his hands on his eyes again; and he looked intently and his sight was restored, and he saw everything clearly. Then he sent him away to his home, saying, 'Do not even go into the village.'

- In this miracle there is an extraordinary intimacy between Jesus the incarnate Son of God and the blind man as he puts his own human spittle on his eyes, almost like a balm, and restores his sight. 'For I am gentle and humble of heart.' We go to God through living our humanity.

- 'Do not even go into the village.' After a conversion, which is seeing in a new way, we must not go back to our old ways of living.

Thursday 20 February
Mark 8:27–33

Jesus went on with his disciples to the villages of Caesarea Philippi; and on the way he asked his disciples, 'Who do people say that I am?' And they answered him, 'John the Baptist; and others, Elijah; and still others, one of the prophets.' He asked them, 'But who do you say that I am?' Peter answered him, 'You are the Messiah.' And he sternly ordered them not to tell anyone about him.

Then he began to teach them that the Son of Man must undergo great suffering, and be rejected by the elders, the chief priests, and the scribes, and be killed, and after three days rise again. He said all this quite openly. And Peter took him aside and began to rebuke him. But turning and looking at his disciples, he rebuked Peter and said, 'Get behind me, Satan! For you are setting your mind not on divine things but on human things.'

- The question that Jesus asks of his disciples, 'But you, who do you say I am?' is one of three key questions that Jesus asks of all his followers. In essence, he is asking, 'What do I mean to you?' The second question he asks is, 'What are you seeking?' He asks this when the two disciples follow after him after John the Baptist has pointed him out to them in John 1:35–37. The third is when Jesus asks Peter by the lake after the resurrection, 'Do you love me?' Let us take any one of these or all of them to prayer.

- Like Peter we constantly see things from our own perspective. We ask to trust in God's love for us as he sees our lives from his higher viewpoint.

Friday 21 February
Mark 8:34—9:1

He called the crowd with his disciples, and said to them, 'If any want to become my followers, let them deny themselves and take up their cross and follow me. For those who want to save their life will lose it, and those who lose their life for my sake, and for the sake of the gospel, will save it. For what will it profit them to gain the whole world and forfeit their life? Indeed, what can they give in return for their life? Those who are ashamed of me and of my words in this adulterous and sinful generation, of them the Son of Man will also be ashamed when he comes in the glory of his Father with the holy angels.' And he said to them, 'Truly I tell you, there are some standing here who will not taste death until they see that the kingdom of God has come with power.'

- A disciple cannot be above their Master. Christ is always the headline for us in how to live our lives. As he took up his cross and accepted whatever life threw at him so must we. There is always a need for us to practise some self-denial if the false self in us is to die. In this way with his grace at work in us we save our real lives. We live to die, and we die to live. This is the true life, both now and for eternity. 'Those who lose their life for my sake will find it' (Matthew 10:39).

- By reminding him of this question, 'What does it profit a person to gain the whole world and lose his/her soul?', St Ignatius of Loyola inspired St Francis Xavier to give his life completely to Christ as a missionary in the Far East.

Saturday 22 February
St Peter's Chair

Matthew 16:13–19

Now when Jesus came into the district of Caesarea Philippi, he asked his disciples, 'Who do people say that the Son of Man is?' And they said, 'Some say John the Baptist, but others Elijah, and still others Jeremiah or one of the prophets.' He said to them, 'But who do you say that I am?' Simon Peter answered, 'You are the Messiah, the Son of the living God.' And Jesus answered him, 'Blessed are you, Simon son of Jonah! For flesh and blood has not revealed this to you, but my Father in heaven. And I tell you, you are Peter, and on this rock I will build my church, and the gates of Hades will not prevail against it. I will give you the keys of the kingdom of heaven, and whatever you bind on earth will be bound in heaven, and whatever you loose on earth will be loosed in heaven.'

- Peter professes his faith in Jesus as the Messiah, who was to come into the world from God. Peter's faith and understanding would need to grow, but it was already enough to become the rock on which Jesus would found his church. Only God can reveal God to us and we ask again and again, 'Lord, that I may see.'

- The church founded by Christ has faced many turbulent times over the centuries, but Christ's promise that the gates of hell would not prevail against it has remained true. Our God is with it and also with each of us at every moment. Let us ask God to reveal this to us more and more.

23 February–1 March 2025

Something to think and pray about each day this week:

There's an inspiring passage from the Book of Habakkuk where the author describes the attitude of a person whose world has come apart—they have lost their livelihood and income, everything! The bottom has fallen out of their world, as happens to countless numbers of people every day, especially in war zones and many other areas of life. Yet the author, faced with such a huge calamity, can still say, 'Yet I will rejoice in the Lord / and exult in God my saviour / The Lord my God is my strength' (Habakkuk 3:18–19). That is just one of the extraordinary acts of trust in God found throughout the Bible. That's the kind of faith involved in 'I believe in God.' At such times many of us may not be able to make such an act of trust as it seems to defy the odds. We simply allow ourselves to be carried along by the prayerful trust of our faith community, as if we're stowaways on their prayers. Experience also confirms that those with a deep trusting faith are supported by their conviction that God can be relied on especially during difficult times, because the Bible reassures us that God is on the side of the broken-hearted.

Jim Maher SJ,
Reimagining Religion: A Jesuit Vision

The Presence of God

I pause for a moment and reflect on God's life-giving presence in every part of my body, in everything around me, in the whole of my life.

Freedom

Many countries are at this moment suffering the agonies of war. I bow my head in thanksgiving for my freedom. I pray for all prisoners and captives.

Consciousness

Knowing that God loves me unconditionally, I look honestly over the past day, its events, and my feelings. Do I have something to be grateful for? Then I give thanks. Is there something I am sorry for? Then I ask forgiveness.

The Word

Now I turn to the Scripture set out for me this day. I read slowly over the words and see if any sentence or sentiment appeals to me. *(Please turn to the Scripture on the following pages. Inspiration points are there, should you need them. When you are ready, return here to continue.)*

Conversation

I know with certainty that there were times when you carried me, Lord. There were times when it was through your strength that I got through the dark times in my life.

Conclusion

Glory be to the Father, and to the Son, and to the Holy Spirit,
As it was in the beginning, is now and ever shall be,
World without end. Amen.

Sunday 23 February
Seventh Sunday in Ordinary Time
Luke 6:27–38

'But I say to you that listen, Love your enemies, do good to those who hate you, bless those who curse you, pray for those who abuse you. If anyone strikes you on the cheek, offer the other also; and from anyone who takes away your coat do not withhold even your shirt. Give to everyone who begs from you; and if anyone takes away your goods, do not ask for them again. Do to others as you would have them do to you.

'If you love those who love you, what credit is that to you? For even sinners love those who love them. If you do good to those who do good to you, what credit is that to you? For even sinners do the same. If you lend to those from whom you hope to receive, what credit is that to you? Even sinners lend to sinners, to receive as much again. But love your enemies, do good, and lend, expecting nothing in return. Your reward will be great, and you will be children of the Most High; for he is kind to the ungrateful and the wicked. Be merciful, just as your Father is merciful.

'Do not judge, and you will not be judged; do not condemn, and you will not be condemned. Forgive, and you will be forgiven; give, and it will be given to you. A good measure, pressed down, shaken together, running over, will be put into your lap; for the measure you give will be the measure you get back.'

- To live the Christian faith is always a challenge and a struggle. We are told to strive to love as the Heavenly Father loves and to aim to be perfect. In particular we are asked to be merciful and never to judge others. It is summed up in the golden rule, which is to treat others as we would want them to treat us. We need the example of Jesus, who prayed on the cross for his executioners, 'Father forgive them.' We have much to reflect upon in our own lives and to talk to the Lord about in prayer.

Monday 24 February
Mark 9:14–29

When they came to the disciples, they saw a great crowd around them, and some scribes arguing with them. When the whole crowd saw him, they were immediately overcome with awe, and they ran forward to greet him. He asked them, 'What are you arguing about with them?' Someone from the crowd answered him, 'Teacher, I brought you my son; he has a spirit that makes him unable to speak; and whenever it seizes him, it dashes him down; and he foams and grinds his teeth and becomes rigid; and I asked your disciples to cast it out, but they could not do so.' He answered them, 'You faithless generation, how much longer must I be among you? How much longer must I put up with you? Bring him to me.' And they brought the boy to him. When the spirit saw him, immediately it threw the boy into convulsions, and he fell on the ground and rolled about, foaming at the mouth. Jesus asked the father, 'How long has this been happening to him?' And he said, 'From childhood. It has often cast him into the fire and into the water, to destroy him; but if you are able to do anything, have pity on us and help us.' Jesus said to him, 'If you are able!—All things can be done for the one who believes.' Immediately the father of the child cried out, 'I believe; help my unbelief!' When Jesus saw that a crowd came running together, he rebuked the unclean spirit, saying to it, 'You spirit that keep this boy from speaking and hearing, I command you, come out of him, and never enter him again!' After crying out and convulsing him terribly, it came out, and the boy was like a corpse, so that most of them said, 'He is dead.' But Jesus took him by the hand and lifted him up, and he was able to stand. When he had entered the house, his disciples asked him privately, 'Why could we not cast it out?' He said to them, 'This kind can come out only through prayer.'

- How often we can say to ourselves, if only my faith were stronger, and we make the prayer of this distraught parent our own: 'I believe; help my unbelief!' Just as our muscles grow stronger by using them so our faith will grow through frequent use. Recalling and being more aware of the times our God has helped us in difficulties will also help. In John 5 we are reminded that God the Father and the son and the Holy Spirit are at work continuously in our lives.

- It has been said that more things are done by prayer than this world dreams of. Let us trust more in the power of prayer, which is made to the Person who loves us most and is always attending to us.

Tuesday 25 February
Mark 9:30–37

They went on from there and passed through Galilee. He did not want anyone to know it; for he was teaching his disciples, saying to them, 'The Son of Man is to be betrayed into human hands, and they will kill him, and three days after being killed, he will rise again.' But they did not understand what he was saying and were afraid to ask him.

Then they came to Capernaum; and when he was in the house he asked them, 'What were you arguing about on the way?' But they were silent, for on the way they had argued with one another about who was the greatest. He sat down, called the twelve, and said to them, 'Whoever wants to be first must be last of all and servant of all.' Then he took a little child and put it among them; and taking it in his arms, he said to them, 'Whoever welcomes one such child in my name welcomes me, and whoever welcomes me welcomes not me but the one who sent me.'

- Jesus had just told his disciples that he would be helpless against his enemies and would be put to death, but all this went over their heads. Human power and greatness was what mattered to them. So Jesus takes and embraces a little child as an example to them to cherish those who are powerless and dependent on others. The Son of Man came not to be served but to serve, and to give his life in service of others.

- One of the great lessons on our Christian journey is the lesson of humility. St Teresa of Ávila wrote, 'Humility is truth.' We all need to grow in the truth of our own littleness and complete dependence on God.

Wednesday 26 February
Mark 9:38–40

John said to him, 'Teacher, we saw someone casting out demons in your name, and we tried to stop him, because he was not following us.' But Jesus said, 'Do not stop him; for no one who does a deed of power in my name will be able soon afterwards to speak evil of me. Whoever is not against us is for us.'

- If someone was working miracles in the name of Jesus then he was certainly on the side of Jesus. We must never be jealous of the gifts that have been given by God to others. Our part is to recognise our own gifts and to serve others by our use of them. And when they don't openly oppose us, let us give others the benefit of the doubt that they are on our side.

Thursday 27 February
Mark 9:41–50

Jesus said to them, 'For truly I tell you, whoever gives you a cup of water to drink because you bear the name of Christ will by no means lose the reward.

'If any of you put a stumbling-block before one of these little ones who believe in me, it would be better for you if a great millstone were hung around your neck and you were thrown into the sea. If your hand causes you to stumble, cut it off; it is better for you to enter life maimed than to have two hands and to go to hell, to the unquenchable fire. And if your foot causes you to stumble, cut it off; it is better for you to enter life lame than to have two feet and to be thrown into hell. And if your eye causes you to stumble, tear it out; it is better for you to enter the kingdom of God with one eye than to have two eyes and to be thrown into hell, where the worm never dies, and the fire is never quenched.

'For everyone will be salted with fire. Salt is good; but if salt has lost its saltiness, how can you season it? Have salt in yourselves, and be at peace with one another.'

- In our living the values of the kingdom of God we must have our priorities. Our God must always come first, even at the cost of our lives. Jesus was never willing to compromise with the truth. When they could not accept his teaching about giving them his own body to eat he simply let them walk away. What are the false gods in my life that try at times to take priority over God?

- Jesus warns us very strongly against leading others astray by our bad example. We all have the responsibility to witness to our faith. Let us pray especially for parents in their task of bringing up their children in the faith.

Friday 28 February
Mark 10:1–12

He left that place and went to the region of Judea and beyond the Jordan. And crowds again gathered around him; and, as was his custom, he again taught them.

Some Pharisees came, and to test him they asked, 'Is it lawful for a man to divorce his wife?' He answered them, 'What did Moses command you?' They said, 'Moses allowed a man to write a certificate of dismissal and to divorce her.' But Jesus said to them, 'Because of your hardness of heart he wrote this commandment for you. But from the beginning of creation, 'God made them male and female.' 'For this reason a man shall leave his father and mother and be joined to his wife, and the two shall become one flesh.' So they are no longer two, but one flesh. Therefore what God has joined together, let no one separate.'

Then in the house the disciples asked him again about this matter. He said to them, 'Whoever divorces his wife and marries another commits adultery against her; and if she divorces her husband and marries another, she commits adultery.'

- Jesus knows that his authority is greater even than that of Moses and so he is free to change the commandments of Moses, which were written for people at a different stage of human development. His teaching here on divorce is clear and direct. In Christian marriage God has joined a man and a woman to become one. We pray to try to live God's way.

- Sometimes when we fail to follow the teachings of Jesus we are tempted to excuse ourselves by saying, 'If Jesus were here today he would change his teaching.' But Jesus is still here and he makes his teachings clear through the authorised voice of his church. Let us pray to be faithful to the teaching of our church.

Saturday 1 March
Mark 10:13–16

People were bringing little children to him in order that he might touch them; and the disciples spoke sternly to them. But when Jesus saw this, he was indignant and said to them, 'Let the little children come to me; do not stop them; for it is to such as these that the kingdom of God belongs.

Truly I tell you, whoever does not receive the kingdom of God as a little child will never enter it.' And he took them up in his arms, laid his hands on them, and blessed them.

- The parents had sensed the compassion and gentleness of Jesus and so they brought their children to him for a blessing. His Father's kingdom is especially for those who, in their own littleness and dependence, know God is their loving Father. In their innocence there is a strong bond between the children and the One who was always without sin. Help us, Lord, to always see ourselves as children of God.

- In this Gospel we have a good example of the One who described himself as 'gentle and humble of heart'. In our prayer we get to meet Jesus Christ who, yesterday and today, is the same for ever.

2–8 March 2025

Something to think and pray about each day this week:

It is no coincidence that Jesus spends forty days in the desert; this is a very particular biblical unit of time. It recalls the Israelites wandering in the desert for forty years before arriving in the Promised Land; the Great Flood lasted forty days; Moses fasted for forty days in the wilderness of Mount Sinai (Deuteronomy 9:18), as did Elijah near Mount Horeb (1 Kings 19:8). We are in good company as we enter into the wilderness, a place where God is revealed. During Lent, it is good for us to remove ourselves from our normal routines, to be still, and to stop and breathe. We need not be afraid of this, for the Gospel shows us that time spent in the wilderness is Spirit-led and we are not alone.

Tríona Doherty and Jane Mellett,
*The Deep End: A Journey with the Sunday Gospels
in the Year of Mark*

The Presence of God

Dear Jesus, today I call on you, but not to ask for anything. I'd like only to dwell in your presence. May my heart respond to your love.

Freedom

God my creator, you gave me life and the gift of freedom. Through your love I exist in this world. May I never take the gift of life for granted. May I always respect others' right to life.

Consciousness

I ask how I am today. Am I particularly tired, stressed or anxious? If any of these characteristics apply, can I try to let go of the concerns that disturb me?

The Word

The word of God comes down to us through the Scriptures. May the Holy Spirit enlighten my mind and my heart to respond to the Gospel teachings. *(Please turn to the Scripture on the following pages. Inspiration points are there, should you need them. When you are ready, return here to continue.)*

Conversation

I begin to talk with Jesus about the Scripture I have just read. What part of it strikes a chord in me? Perhaps the words of a friend—or some story I have heard recently—will rise to the surface in my consciousness. If so, does the story throw light on what the Scripture passage may be saying to me?

Conclusion

Glory be to the Father, and to the Son, and to the Holy Spirit,
As it was in the beginning, is now and ever shall be,
World without end. Amen.

Sunday 2 March
Eighth Sunday in Ordinary Time
Luke 6:39–45

He also told them a parable: 'Can a blind person guide a blind person? Will not both fall into a pit? A disciple is not above the teacher, but everyone who is fully qualified will be like the teacher. Why do you see the speck in your neighbour's eye, but do not notice the log in your own eye? Or how can you say to your neighbour, "Friend, let me take out the speck in your eye", when you yourself do not see the log in your own eye? You hypocrite, first take the log out of your own eye, and then you will see clearly to take the speck out of your neighbour's eye.

'No good tree bears bad fruit, nor again does a bad tree bear good fruit; for each tree is known by its own fruit. Figs are not gathered from thorns, nor are grapes picked from a bramble bush. The good person out of the good treasure of the heart produces good, and the evil person out of evil treasure produces evil; for it is out of the abundance of the heart that the mouth speaks.'

- As a Christian, to pray means to try to pray. We are limited in our understanding and our following of Jesus. So we can never judge others when we are so blind about ourselves. To strive to correct our own faults is a great enough task for a lifetime. 'Lord, help us to see correctly and then we can be a light for others.'

- Love is shown in deeds rather than in words. Let our good deeds speak for themselves.

Monday 3 March
Mark 10:17–27

As he was setting out on a journey, a man ran up and knelt before him, and asked him, 'Good Teacher, what must I do to inherit eternal life?' Jesus said to him, 'Why do you call me good? No one is good but God alone. You know the commandments: "You shall not murder; You shall not commit adultery; You shall not steal; You shall not bear false witness; You shall not defraud; Honour your father and mother."' He said to him, 'Teacher, I have kept all these since my youth.' Jesus, looking at him, loved him and said, 'You lack one thing; go, sell what you own, and give the money to the poor, and you will have treasure in heaven; then come, follow me.' When he heard this, he was shocked and went away grieving, for he had many possessions.

Then Jesus looked around and said to his disciples, 'How hard it will be for those who have wealth to enter the kingdom of God!' And the disciples were perplexed at these words. But Jesus said to them again, 'Children, how hard it is to enter the kingdom of God! It is easier for a camel to go through the eye of a needle than for someone who is rich to enter the kingdom of God.' They were greatly astounded and said to one another, 'Then who can be saved?' Jesus looked at them and said, 'For mortals it is impossible, but not for God; for God all things are possible.'

- The rich young man had many possessions, but in reality it was those things that possessed him and left him unfree to follow the precious invitation from Jesus. Where your treasure is there will your heart be also. What are the things to which we are so attached that they hinder our freedom in living for the kingdom of God?

- Everything is possible for God. Our salvation is his constant concern and is only possible with his grace. Jesus said, 'My Father is still working, and I also am working' (John 5). St Augustine has reminded us that God, who made us without our cooperation, won't save us without our cooperation.

Tuesday 4 March
Mark 10:28–31

Peter began to say to him, 'Look, we have left everything and followed you.' Jesus said, 'Truly I tell you, there is no one who has left house or brothers or sisters or mother or father or children or fields, for my sake and for the sake of the good news, who will not receive a hundredfold now in this age—houses, brothers and sisters, mothers and children, and fields, with persecutions—and in the age to come eternal life. But many who are first will be last, and the last will be first.'

- We can never outdo the Lord in generosity. Whatever we can give to him has already been his gift to us. The hundredfold is nothing in comparison to the gift of our God giving himself to us in love, as he wishes to do for one each of us. In his Spiritual Exercises St Ignatius urges us to ponder this always with 'deep affection'.

- Because of the gift of our free will we can always give joy to the Lord by choosing to say yes to his will. We pray for generosity and discernment and for the grace to make good use of this gift.

Wednesday 5 March
Ash Wednesday
Matthew 6:1–6, 16–18

'Beware of practising your piety before others in order to be seen by them; for then you have no reward from your Father in heaven.

'So whenever you give alms, do not sound a trumpet before you, as the hypocrites do in the synagogues and in the streets, so that they may be praised by others. Truly I tell you, they have received their reward. But when you give alms, do not let your left hand know what your right hand is doing, so that your alms may be done in secret; and your Father who sees in secret will reward you.

'And whenever you pray, do not be like the hypocrites; for they love to stand and pray in the synagogues and at the street corners, so that they may be seen by others. Truly I tell you, they have received their reward. But whenever you pray, go into your room and shut the door and pray to your Father who is in secret; and your Father who sees in secret will reward you. . . .

'And whenever you fast, do not look dismal, like the hypocrites, for they disfigure their faces so as to show others that they are fasting. Truly I tell you, they have received their reward. But when you fast, put oil on your head and wash your face, so that your fasting may be seen not by others but by your Father who is in secret; and your Father who sees in secret will reward you.'

- Our Father, who sees in secret, looks at our hearts, for it is from there that we truly live. In this season of Lent, which can be a kind of spring-cleaning of our souls, let us begin with generosity in giving more time to prayer and making any sacrifices this might entail, for example, less TV or screen time. We pray to place God more and more at the forefront of our lives.

- When you pray, go into your own heart and shut the door to outward distractions and be with him who is present there. 'Now is the time for prayer, now nothing else matters, now no one is important but God!'

Thursday 6 March
Luke 9:21–25

He sternly ordered and commanded them not to tell anyone, saying, 'The Son of Man must undergo great suffering, and be rejected by the elders, chief priests, and scribes, and be killed, and on the third day be raised.'

Then he said to them all, 'If any want to become my followers, let them deny themselves and take up their cross daily and follow me. For those who want to save their life will lose it, and those who lose their life for my sake will save it. What does it profit them if they gain the whole world, but lose or forfeit themselves?'

- Jesus would have been familiar with the account of the suffering servant in Isaiah 52. Knowing that he was destined to suffer and be killed must have been a heavy burden to carry. We can talk to him about this and ask for some of his courage in facing our own crosses.

- A disciple cannot be above his/her Master. As Christ suffered, so will those who follow him, but the suffering will be different and unique to each one. As writer Alan Jones put it, 'Life is about being dispossessed of everything so that we might possess everything.' We have to lose the false life that is centred on our ego. We pray for insight and the courage to accept our crosses.

Friday 7 March
Matthew 9:14–15

Then the disciples of John came to him, saying, 'Why do we and the Pharisees fast often, but your disciples do not fast?' And Jesus said to them, 'The wedding-guests cannot mourn as long as the bridegroom is with them, can they? The days will come when the bridegroom is taken away from them, and then they will fast.'

- New skins for the new wine of the kingdom of God. There is a time for everything under heaven, a time to be joyful, a time to mourn, a time to fast, and a time to refrain from fasting. Fasting can be helpful to our bodies and can train us to be more disciplined in how we live our Christian lives. As we read in the Book of Wisdom, 'The beginning of wisdom is the most sincere desire for instruction.' We pray for the grace to make a decision for God and for the courage to be faithful to it.

Saturday 8 March
Luke 5:27–32

After this he went out and saw a tax-collector named Levi, sitting at the tax booth; and he said to him, 'Follow me.' And he got up, left everything, and followed him.

Then Levi gave a great banquet for him in his house; and there was a large crowd of tax-collectors and others sitting at the table with them. The Pharisees and their scribes were complaining to his disciples, saying, 'Why do you eat and drink with tax-collectors and sinners?' Jesus answered, 'Those who are well have no need of a physician, but those who are sick; I have come to call not the righteous but sinners to repentance.'

- We do not know how often Matthew had listened to Jesus preaching and teaching, but when the call came to him he was ready to respond to it. Let us pray to be open to whatever God calls us to.

- God loves each person with an infinite and unchanging love. Jesus always saw beyond the outward appearance of those he encountered to the deeper yearnings in their hearts. He said, 'I came that they may have life, and have it abundantly.' He loved the sinner but hated the sin. Let us share with him what is deepest in our hearts.

9–15 March 2025

Something to think and pray about each day this week:

There is a Zen proverb, 'Let go or be dragged', and no one wants to be dragged around the place. Lent invites us to embrace this wilderness time. As we fast from things that are not life-giving for us we are also actively making space for God to breathe life and love into our hearts once more. We do this in the trust that God who loves us wants us to choose life and to clear out the blocks that stand in our way. This is 'good news', a true *metanoia* (a change of heart). God's Kingdom is being fulfilled in us and around us, not yet complete, but with every trip into the wilderness we edge closer to that reality. May this Lenten season be a period of grace.

Tríona Doherty and Jane Mellett,
*The Deep End: A Journey with the Sunday Gospels
in the Year of Mark*

The Presence of God
Dear Lord, as I come to you today, fill my heart, my whole being, with the wonder of your presence. Help me remain receptive to you as I put aside the cares of this world. Fill my mind with your peace.

Freedom
Lord, grant me the grace to be free from the excesses of this life. Let me not get caught up with the desire for wealth. Keep my heart and mind free to love and serve you.

Consciousness
I exist in a web of relationships: links to nature, people, God. I trace out these links, giving thanks for the life that flows through them. Some links are twisted or broken; I may feel regret, anger, disappointment. I pray for the gift of acceptance and forgiveness.

The Word
God speaks to each of us individually. I listen attentively to hear what he is saying to me. Read the text a few times, then listen. *(Please turn to the Scripture on the following pages. Inspiration points are there, should you need them. When you are ready, return here to continue.)*

Conversation
Jesus, you speak to me through the words of the Gospels. May I respond to your call today. Teach me to recognise your hand at work in my daily living.

Conclusion
I thank God for these moments we have spent together and for any insights I have been given concerning the text.

Sunday 9 March
First Sunday of Lent

Luke 4:1–13

Jesus, full of the Holy Spirit, returned from the Jordan and was led by the Spirit in the wilderness, where for forty days he was tempted by the devil. He ate nothing at all during those days, and when they were over, he was famished. The devil said to him, 'If you are the Son of God, command this stone to become a loaf of bread.' Jesus answered him, 'It is written, "One does not live by bread alone."'

Then the devil led him up and showed him in an instant all the kingdoms of the world. And the devil said to him, 'To you I will give their glory and all this authority; for it has been given over to me, and I give it to anyone I please. If you, then, will worship me, it will all be yours.' Jesus answered him, 'It is written,

"Worship the Lord your God,
    and serve only him."'

Then the devil took him to Jerusalem, and placed him on the pinnacle of the temple, saying to him, 'If you are the Son of God, throw yourself down from here, for it is written,

"He will command his angels concerning you,
    to protect you",

and

"On their hands they will bear you up,
    so that you will not dash your foot against a stone."'

Jesus answered him, 'It is said, "Do not put the Lord your God to the test."' When the devil had finished every test, he departed from him until an opportune time.

- After his baptism, Jesus, filled with the Holy Spirit, is led into a place of solitude for his final preparation for his mission. We read that Jesus invited his apostles to come apart into a quiet place, which was to be with himself. It is helpful for us regularly to go aside from the busyness of life into a quiet place for reflection and prayer.

- Temptation is always a question of self-identity. We are defined by what we do rather than what we say. As followers of Christ we try to live by a certain moral code but there are certain things we still fail to do. Let us pray for the grace to seek and to do always the will of God for us.

Monday 10 March
Matthew 25:31–46

Jesus said to them, 'When the Son of Man comes in his glory, and all the angels with him, then he will sit on the throne of his glory. All the nations will be gathered before him, and he will separate people one from another as a shepherd separates the sheep from the goats, and he will put the sheep at his right hand and the goats at the left. Then the king will say to those at his right hand, "Come, you that are blessed by my Father, inherit the kingdom prepared for you from the foundation of the world; for I was hungry and you gave me food, I was thirsty and you gave me something to drink, I was a stranger and you welcomed me, I was naked and you gave me clothing, I was sick and you took care of me, I was in prison and you visited me." Then the righteous will answer him, "Lord, when was it that we saw you hungry and gave you food, or thirsty and gave you something to drink? And when was it that we saw you a stranger and welcomed you, or naked and gave you clothing? And when was it that we saw you sick or in prison and visited you?" And the king will answer them, "Truly I tell you, just as you did it to one of the least of these who are members of my family, you did it to me." Then he will say to those at his left hand, "You that are accursed, depart from me into the eternal fire prepared for the devil and his angels; for I was hungry and you gave me no food, I was thirsty and you gave me nothing to drink, I was a stranger and you did not welcome me, naked and you did not give me clothing, sick and in prison and you did not visit me." Then they also will answer, "Lord, when was it that we saw you hungry or thirsty or a stranger or naked or sick or in prison, and did not take care of you?" Then he will answer them, "Truly I tell you, just as you did not do it to one of the least of these, you did not do it to me." And these will go away into eternal punishment, but the righteous into eternal life.'

* Everyone that we meet is always so much more than what we see with our eyes. They are loved into life and held in existence by the infinite love of God for them. St John the Evangelist wrote, 'Those who say, "I love God", and hate their brothers or sisters, are liars; for those who do not love a brother or sister whom they have seen, cannot love God whom they have not seen' (1 John 4:20).

Tuesday 11 March
Matthew 6:7–15

Jesus said to them, 'When you are praying, do not heap up empty phrases as the Gentiles do; for they think that they will be heard because of their many words. Do not be like them, for your Father knows what you need before you ask him.

'Pray then in this way:
Our Father in heaven,
hallowed be your name.
Your kingdom come.
Your will be done,
on earth as it is in heaven.
Give us this day our daily bread.
And forgive us our debts,
as we also have forgiven our debtors.
And do not bring us to the time of trial,
but rescue us from the evil one.

For if you forgive others their trespasses, your heavenly Father will also forgive you; but if you do not forgive others, neither will your Father forgive your trespasses.'

- Prayer is never a mere recitation of words no matter how much we repeat them. It is a disposition of the heart. In Isaiah we read, 'These people draw near with their mouths and honour me with their lips, while their hearts are far from me.' The most important thing we can do in prayer is to love. This can be done even without words in silent adoration. When we find it difficult to know what to say to the Lord in prayer, let us have him say to us, 'I don't need your words. I just want your company and your love.'

- In the Our Father, Jesus teaches us the right attitude to have in prayer, that God has the first place in our lives, that we have forgiveness in our hearts for others, and that we ask him to provide for and protect us. The First Principle in the Spiritual Exercises of St Ignatius begins 'Man is created to praise, reverence and serve God our Lord, and by this means to save his soul.'

Wednesday 12 March
Luke 11:29–32

When the crowds were increasing, he began to say, 'This generation is an evil generation; it asks for a sign, but no sign will be given to it except the sign of Jonah. For just as Jonah became a sign to the people of Nineveh, so the Son of Man will be to this generation. The queen of the South will rise at the judgement with the people of this generation and condemn them, because she came from the ends of the earth to listen to the wisdom of Solomon, and see, something greater than Solomon is here! The people of Nineveh will rise up at the judgement with this generation and condemn it, because they repented at the proclamation of Jonah, and see, something greater than Jonah is here!'

• Today people will still flock to see external signs and wonders, but the true sign for all Christians will always be the figure of Christ on his cross. 'As Moses lifted up the serpent in the wilderness, so must the Son of Man be lifted up' (John 3:14). 'And I, when I am lifted up from the earth, will draw all people to myself' (John 12:32). And this is how Jesus wants us to remember him. When he said at the Last Supper, 'Do this in remembrance of me', he wanted us to recall his life-giving sacrifice on the cross.

• Truly, 'something greater than Solomon is here'. Every time we come to prayer we are being invited to a private audience with someone greater than anyone else on the planet.

Thursday 13 March
Matthew 7:7–12

Jesus said to them, 'Ask, and it will be given to you; search, and you will find; knock, and the door will be opened for you. For everyone who asks receives, and everyone who searches finds, and for everyone who knocks, the door will be opened. Is there anyone among you who, if your child asks for bread, will give a stone? Or if the child asks for a fish, will give a snake? If you then, who are evil, know how to give good gifts to your children, how much more will your Father in heaven give good things to those who ask him!

'In everything do to others as you would have them do to you; for this is the law and the prophets.'

- It is for the deepest desires in our hearts that we should earnestly ask God in prayer. Ask, search, knock at the door. He will always hear these prayers and answer in the way that is best for us. 'When you search for me, you will find me; if you seek me with all your heart' (Jeremiah 29:13). Like a good parent, our Heavenly Father will provide for us.

- 'In everything do to others as you would have them to do to you.' We rightly call this the golden rule, and it reminds us again that our relationship with God is always linked with our relationships with all whom we meet. We are called to live out of our prayer and to pray out of our living.

Friday 14 March
Matthew 5:20–26

Jesus said to them, 'For I tell you, unless your righteousness exceeds that of the scribes and Pharisees, you will never enter the kingdom of heaven.

'You have heard that it was said to those of ancient times, "You shall not murder"; and "whoever murders shall be liable to judgement." But I say to you that if you are angry with a brother or sister, you will be liable to judgement; and if you insult a brother or sister, you will be liable to the council; and if you say, "You fool", you will be liable to the hell of fire. So when you are offering your gift at the altar, if you remember that your brother or sister has something against you, leave your gift there before the altar and go; first be reconciled to your brother or sister, and then come and offer your gift. Come to terms quickly with your accuser while you are on the way to court with him, or your accuser may hand you over to the judge, and the judge to the guard, and you will be thrown into prison. Truly I tell you, you will never get out until you have paid the last penny.'

- Jesus came not to abolish the law but to perfect it. Jesus speaks with a new authority that comes from knowing that the Father had sent him. In the new creation of the kingdom of God the standards of right behaviour are indeed set high. 'Be perfect, therefore, as your heavenly Father is perfect.'

- Jesus came to bring peace and reconciliation to all people. If we do not forgive others we will not be forgiven ourselves. When we come to worship with others we should be at peace with them and reconciled in our hearts with those who have injured us. How aware am I that we go to worship God as a people, and that we are saved as a people?

Saturday 15 March
Matthew 5:43–48

Jesus said, 'You have heard that it was said, "You shall love your neighbour and hate your enemy." But I say to you, Love your enemies and pray for those who persecute you, so that you may be children of your Father in heaven; for he makes his sun rise on the evil and on the good, and sends rain on the righteous and on the unrighteous. For if you love those who love you, what reward do you have? Do not even the tax-collectors do the same? And if you greet only your brothers and sisters, what more are you doing than others? Do not even the Gentiles do the same? Be perfect, therefore, as your heavenly Father is perfect.'

- Human beings are very slow to take things in, and we are still growing in our understanding of revelation. God never stops loving all who exist and we are called to be like our heavenly Father. We pray for the grace to see others more and more as God sees them.

- A story from the East tells us of how a tree leaves its scent even upon the axe that is cutting it down. It is not easy to forgive those who have seriously hurt us, but we have the example of Jesus Christ and the many martyrs. On the cross, Jesus prayed for his executioners, 'Father, forgive them; for they do not know what they are doing.' Let us pray for the grace to forgive others and to recognise our own need for forgiveness.

Something to think and pray about each day this week:

Many legends, stories and traditions have grown up over the centuries regarding Ireland's most famous saint. It is necessary, therefore, to separate the man from the myth by returning to St Patrick's own writings, including what has become known as his *Confession*.

In a simple written account, Patrick's trust in God and his gratitude towards him who had achieved so much through such a weak instrument, shine out. This in no way detracts from the unique light his *Confession* casts on this humble missionary of Christ who brought his Gospel of love to the Irish people. A great missionary looked back on his life and saw the labyrinthine pattern of God's wonderful design.

As he reviews his life journey, which he admits was full of faults and shortcomings, and in the apparently haphazard events of his life, so inexplicable when they occurred, he now sees the hand of God at work in which his hidden plan for the salvation of the Irish is realised. No extraordinary wonders marked his progress throughout Ireland, nevertheless, he touched the hearts of young people who flocked to him and committed their lives to following Christ in the priesthood and religious life.

The essential knowledge about a saint lies not so much in dates and places, but rather in his holiness, his values, what inspired him and his spiritual wrestlings. On these points we are well informed. Patrick sets the record straight regarding his mission and underscores the role God had in it. Often misunderstood in the past, Patrick hoped that his readers would finally grasp how he regarded his long, arduous but ultimately successful mission. His story is one of God's grace that leads to wonder and thanksgiving.

Maurice Hogan SSC,
in the preface to Aidan J. Larkin,
The Spiritual Journey of Saint Patrick

The Presence of God

Dear Jesus, I come to you today longing for your presence. I desire to love you as you love me. May nothing ever separate me from you.

Freedom

Lord, grant me the grace to have freedom of the spirit. Cleanse my heart and soul so that I may live joyously in your love.

Consciousness

Where am I with God? With others? Do I have something to be grateful for? Then I give thanks. Is there something I am sorry for? Then I ask forgiveness.

The Word

The word of God comes down to us through the Scriptures. May the Holy Spirit enlighten my mind and my heart to respond to the Gospel teachings. *(Please turn to the Scripture on the following pages. Inspiration points are there, should you need them. When you are ready, return here to continue.)*

Conversation

How has God's word moved me? Has it left me cold? Has it consoled me or moved me to act in a new way? I imagine Jesus standing or sitting beside me; I turn and share my feelings with him.

Conclusion

I thank God for these moments we have spent together and for any insights I have been given concerning the text.

Sunday 16 March
Second Sunday of Lent
Luke 9:28–36

Now about eight days after these sayings Jesus took with him Peter and John and James, and went up on the mountain to pray. And while he was praying, the appearance of his face changed, and his clothes became dazzling white. Suddenly they saw two men, Moses and Elijah, talking to him. They appeared in glory and were speaking of his departure, which he was about to accomplish at Jerusalem. Now Peter and his companions were weighed down with sleep; but since they had stayed awake, they saw his glory and the two men who stood with him. Just as they were leaving him, Peter said to Jesus, 'Master, it is good for us to be here; let us make three dwellings, one for you, one for Moses, and one for Elijah'—not knowing what he said. While he was saying this, a cloud came and over-shadowed them; and they were terrified as they entered the cloud. Then from the cloud came a voice that said, 'This is my Son, my Chosen; listen to him!' When the voice had spoken, Jesus was found alone. And they kept silent and in those days told no one any of the things they had seen.

- St Luke tells us about Jesus at prayer more than any of the other evangelists. Here, these three apostles are given this extraordinary experience of Jesus transfigured to strengthen them in the face of his coming suffering and death. Years later St Peter recalls in a letter this experience on the mountain. It highlights for us how the divinity of Jesus was hidden in his humanity. We pray for a deeper understanding of the Incarnation.

- In our praying it is always the risen Lord we encounter and we can truly say, 'Master, it is good for us to be here.' Let us have the Father say to us, 'This is my Son, my Chosen; listen to him!' And let us pray like Samuel, 'Speak, Lord, for your servant is listening.'

Monday 17 March
St Patrick, Patron of Ireland
Luke 5:1–11

Once while Jesus was standing beside the lake of Gennesaret, and the crowd was pressing in on him to hear the word of God, he saw two boats there at the shore of the lake; the fishermen had gone out of them and were washing their nets. He got into one of the boats, the one belonging to Simon, and asked him to put out a little way from the shore. Then he sat down and taught the crowds from the boat. When he had finished speaking, he said to Simon, 'Put out into the deep water and let down your nets for a catch.' Simon answered, 'Master, we have worked all night long but have caught nothing. Yet if you say so, I will let down the nets.' When they had done this, they caught so many fish that their nets were beginning to break. So they signalled to their partners in the other boat to come and help them. And they came and filled both boats, so that they began to sink. But when Simon Peter saw it, he fell down at Jesus' knees, saying, 'Go away from me, Lord, for I am a sinful man!' For he and all who were with him were amazed at the catch of fish that they had taken; and so also were James and John, sons of Zebedee, who were partners with Simon. Then Jesus said to Simon, 'Do not be afraid; from now on you will be catching people.' When they had brought their boats to shore, they left everything and followed him.

- St Patrick's call from God to leave his home and kin and go on his mission to Ireland came out of his early experiences as a slave, minding sheep and learning to pray and to depend on God alone. In his *Confession*, what stand out are his faith and his gratitude to God. It is through our own life experiences that God calls us to follow him in faith and in gratitude.

- At Christ's bidding Peter let out the nets. Pope St John Paul II used this same image in his call for a renewal in the church. In whatever mission our God gives to us we will always succeed if we remain attached to Christ, the true vine. Let us pray for the grace of a deeper trust in his help.

Tuesday 18 March
Matthew 23:1–12

Then Jesus said to the crowds and to his disciples, 'The scribes and the Pharisees sit on Moses' seat; therefore, do whatever they teach you and follow it; but do not do as they do, for they do not practise what they teach. They tie up heavy burdens, hard to bear, and lay them on the shoulders of others; but they themselves are unwilling to lift a finger to move them. They do all their deeds to be seen by others; for they make their phylacteries broad and their fringes long. They love to have the place of honour at banquets and the best seats in the synagogues, and to be greeted with respect in the market-places, and to have people call them rabbi. But you are not to be called rabbi, for you have one teacher, and you are all students. And call no one your father on earth, for you have one Father—the one in heaven. Nor are you to be called instructors, for you have one instructor, the Messiah. The greatest among you will be your servant. All who exalt themselves will be humbled, and all who humble themselves will be exalted.'

- We are all called to preach by how we live our faith. The Pharisees showed their own warped attitudes to the God who had revealed himself to their ancestors. In our own pride and lack of understanding we too often seek to make God in our own image and likeness. Let our constant prayer be, 'Lord, let me see again.'

- Humankind has so often been plagued by false prophets. Here Jesus reminds us that we have only one true teacher, Christ himself, who came, as he told Pilate, to witness to the truth. Let us always keep his words and his life before us in the witness of our own lives to the truth of the message of the Gospels. He alone is the way, the truth and the life.

Wednesday 19 March
St Joseph, Husband of the BVM
Matthew 1:18–21, 24

Now the birth of Jesus the Messiah took place in this way. When his mother Mary had been engaged to Joseph, but before they lived together, she was found to be with child from the Holy Spirit. Her husband Joseph, being a righteous man and unwilling to expose her to public disgrace, planned to dismiss her quietly. But just when he had resolved to do this, an angel of the Lord appeared to him in a dream and said, 'Joseph, son of David, do not be afraid to take Mary as your wife, for the child conceived in her is from the Holy Spirit. She will bear a son, and you are to name him Jesus, for he will save his people from their sins.' . . . When Joseph awoke from sleep, he did as the angel of the Lord commanded him; he took her as his wife.

- It can often happen that people who are living good and upright lives can find themselves in difficult circumstances. Joseph here faces a dilemma. In his genuine caring for Mary he did not want her to be shamed in the village, even though it appeared that she had been unfaithful to him. But God never forsakes us. If we continue to trust him he will show us a way out of our difficulties. Let us look back at various crises in our lives and see the hand of God in their resolution, and give him thanks.

Thursday 20 March
Luke 16:19–31

Jesus said to his disciples, 'There was a rich man who was dressed in purple and fine linen and who feasted sumptuously every day. And at his gate lay a poor man named Lazarus, covered with sores, who longed to satisfy his hunger with what fell from the rich man's table; even the dogs would come and lick his sores. The poor man died and was carried away by the angels to be with Abraham. The rich man also died and was buried. In Hades, where he was being tormented, he looked up and saw Abraham far away with Lazarus by his side. He called out, "Father Abraham, have mercy on me, and send Lazarus to dip the tip of his finger in water and cool my tongue; for I am in agony in these flames." But Abraham said, "Child, remember that during your lifetime you received your good things, and Lazarus in like manner evil things; but now he is comforted here, and you are in agony. Besides all this, between you and us a great chasm has been fixed, so that those who might want to pass from here to you cannot do so, and no one can cross from there to us." He said, "Then, father, I beg you to send him to my father's house—for I have five brothers—that he may warn them, so that they will not also come into this place of torment." Abraham replied, "They have Moses and the prophets; they should listen to them." He said, "No, father Abraham; but if someone goes to them from the dead, they will repent." He said to him, "'If they do not listen to Moses and the prophets, neither will they be convinced even if someone rises from the dead.'"

- In this story of rich man, poor man, there is a civility and even kindliness between the rich man and Abraham, whom he calls his father Abraham, and who in turn calls him his child, but still the consequences of the rich man's selfishness and lack of charity remain in place. God respects our free choices and we have to take responsibility for them. In 2 Corinthians 6 St Paul reminds us, 'Now is the acceptable time.' We pray to use our time on earth well and to live our lives guided by the teaching and example of Jesus Christ who is much greater than Moses and the prophets.

- The rich man is concerned for his brothers but they, like all of us, will face judgement on their lives. He wants someone to come from the next world to warn them. We have in Jesus one who did come back from the dead and who lives with us through his Spirit, but so many do not believe this.

Friday 21 March
Matthew 21:33–43, 45–46

Jesus said to them, 'Listen to another parable. There was a landowner who planted a vineyard, put a fence around it, dug a wine press in it, and built a watch-tower. Then he leased it to tenants and went to another country. When the harvest time had come, he sent his slaves to the tenants to collect his produce. But the tenants seized his slaves and beat one, killed another, and stoned another. Again he sent other slaves, more than the first; and they treated them in the same way. Finally he sent his son to them, saying, "They will respect my son." But when the tenants saw the son, they said to themselves, "This is the heir; come, let us kill him and get his inheritance." So they seized him, threw him out of the vineyard, and killed him. Now when the owner of the vineyard comes, what will he do to those tenants?' They said to him, 'He will put those wretches to a miserable death, and lease the vineyard to other tenants who will give him the produce at the harvest time.'

Jesus said to them, 'Have you never read in the scriptures:

"The stone that the builders rejected
    has become the cornerstone;
this was the Lord's doing,
    and it is amazing in our eyes"?

Therefore I tell you, the kingdom of God will be taken away from you and given to a people that produces the fruits of the kingdom.'

When the chief priests and the Pharisees heard his parables, they realised that he was speaking about them. They wanted to arrest him, but they feared the crowds, because they regarded him as a prophet.

- Even the Pharisees, despite their blindness, could see that this parable was about them, but instead of repenting, their only desire is to get rid of the one who was reminding them of their sins. We are all tenants of this earth, which is God's vineyard, and we are tasked with producing the fruits of the kingdom of God by living truly Christian lives, always aided by God's grace. How well do we use our gifts for the good of others and for the good of our earthly environment?

- In this parable we can see Jesus foretelling his own death and the opening up of the kingdom of God to the gentile world. Again and again Jesus faces the hatred of the Jewish religious leaders and seeks to melt their hard hearts. Are there ways that we allow attachments and stubbornness to block the message of Christ from getting through to us and healing our selfishness?

Saturday 22 March
Luke 15:1–3, 11–32

Now all the tax-collectors and sinners were coming near to listen to him. And the Pharisees and the scribes were grumbling and saying, 'This fellow welcomes sinners and eats with them.'

So he told them this parable: . . .

'There was a man who had two sons. The younger of them said to his father, "Father, give me the share of the property that will belong to me." So he divided his property between them. A few days later the younger son gathered all he had and travelled to a distant country, and there he squandered his property in dissolute living. When he had spent everything, a severe famine took place throughout that country, and he began to be in need. So he went and hired himself out to one of the citizens of that country, who sent him to his fields to feed the pigs. He would gladly have filled himself with the pods that the pigs were eating; and no one gave him anything. But when he came to himself he said, "How many of my father's hired hands have bread enough and to spare, but here I am dying of hunger! I will get up and go to my father, and I will say to him, 'Father, I have sinned against heaven and before you; I am no longer worthy to be called your son; treat me like one of your hired hands.'" So he set off and went to his father. But while he was still far off, his father saw him and was filled with compassion; he ran and put his arms around him and kissed him. Then the son said to him, "Father, I have sinned against heaven and before you; I am no longer worthy to be called your son." But the father said to his slaves, "Quickly, bring out a robe—the best one—and put it on him; put a ring on his finger and sandals on his feet. And get the fatted calf and kill it, and let us eat and celebrate; for this son of mine was dead and is alive again; he was lost and is found!" And they began to celebrate.

'Now his elder son was in the field; and when he came and approached the house, he heard music and dancing. He called one of the slaves and asked what was going on. He replied, "Your brother has come, and your father has killed the fatted calf, because he has got him back safe and sound." Then he became angry and refused to go in. His father came out and began to plead with him. But he answered his father, "Listen! For all these years I have been working like a slave for you, and I have never disobeyed your command; yet you have never given me even a young goat so that I might celebrate with my friends. But when this son of yours came back, who has devoured your property with prostitutes, you killed the fatted calf for him!" Then the father said to him, "Son, you are always with me, and all that is mine is yours. But we had to celebrate and rejoice, because this brother of yours was dead and has come to life; he was lost and has been found."'

- Our God is a God of mercy. The famous painting by Rembrandt of the prodigal son kneeling at the feet of his father, whose hand is gently laid upon him, speaks volumes of the loving and forgiving nature of our heavenly Father. When Pope Francis declared a year of mercy he sought to emphasise this aspect of God. The prophet Hosea wrote, 'What I want is mercy, not sacrifice.' Recognising our own sinfulness, let us place all our trust in the loving mercy of our Father.

- Despite all his years of living with his father, the elder brother did not really know him. His attitude was a legal one of being obedient to the rules and commands of his father but his heart was not with his father. He had only to ask and he could have had a party for himself and his friends at any time, because his father wanted to give him everything. How well do we know this infinitely loving and generous Father who longs to give himself entirely to each of us? St Ignatius advises us 'to ponder with deep affection, how the Lord wishes to give himself to us'.

Something to think and pray about each day this week:

The Annunciation brings us back to the source of Lent: the announcement of the Incarnation and Mary saying 'yes' to her part in it. It is the announcement of heaven that God's son will soon be born on earth. The mystery that comes to a close in Lent now begins.

The Incarnation is full of people: Mary, Joseph and Elizabeth and the two unborn babies, in the wombs of their mothers, as we all began. God's son would not come on earth without human origins. He had a mother like all of us. We are remembering our beginnings.

Maybe Lent can be about people rather than rituals. We can give time to enjoying family life, putting the emphasis on giving to family and community rather than on wondering what we can get. Lent can be a time to share with those who are needy, a time to meet some of the needs of the wider world. During Lent we can volunteer our time and personal gifts to others. Lent can be a time to listen, to God's word and to one another.

Donal Neary SJ,
The Sacred Heart Messenger,
April 2023

The Presence of God
As I sit here, the beating of my heart, the ebb and flow of my breath-ing, the movements of my mind are all signs of God's ongoing creation of me. I pause for a moment and become aware of this presence of God within me.

Freedom
I will ask God's help to be free from my own preoccupations, to be open to God in this time of prayer, to come to know, love and serve God more.

Consciousness
At this moment, Lord, I turn my thoughts to you. I will leave aside my chores and preoccupations. I will take rest and refreshment in your presence.

The Word
Now I turn to the Scripture set out for me this day. I read slowly over the words and see if any sentence or sentiment appeals to me. *(Please turn to the Scripture on the following pages. Inspiration points are there, should you need them. When you are ready, return here to continue.)*

Conversation
Begin to talk to Jesus about the Scripture you have just read. What part of it strikes a chord in you? Perhaps the words of a friend—or some story you have heard recently—will slowly rise to the surface of your conscious-ness. If so, does the story throw light on what the Scripture passage may be saying to you?

Conclusion
Glory be to the Father, and to the Son, and to the Holy Spirit,
As it was in the beginning, is now and ever shall be,
World without end. Amen.

Sunday 23 March
Third Sunday of Lent
Luke 13:1–9

At that very time there were some present who told him about the Galileans whose blood Pilate had mingled with their sacrifices. He asked them, 'Do you think that because these Galileans suffered in this way they were worse sinners than all other Galileans? No, I tell you; but unless you repent, you will all perish as they did. Or those eighteen who were killed when the tower of Siloam fell on them—do you think that they were worse offenders than all the others living in Jerusalem? No, I tell you; but unless you repent, you will all perish just as they did.'

Then he told this parable: 'A man had a fig tree planted in his vineyard; and he came looking for fruit on it and found none. So he said to the gardener, "See here! For three years I have come looking for fruit on this fig tree, and still I find none. Cut it down! Why should it be wasting the soil?" He replied, "Sir, let it alone for one more year, until I dig round it and put manure on it. If it bears fruit next year, well and good; but if not, you can cut it down."'

- During Lent we are invited to reflect on the really important things in life. Our allotted life span is always an unknown. Only God sees the bigger picture of our lives. Our time on earth is indeed a time of grace to prepare for an eternity of happiness, but this time is made up of a series of nows, of moments, none of which will ever come again. 'Carpe diem!—Seize the day!' In the Gospels we are frequently called to watch and pray! Let us do so now.

- The sudden death of friends and the experience of life-threatening illnesses and accidents are all reminders that our sojourn on earth is temporary. Both Jesus and his Father are continually at work in our lives. Let us make good use of the opportunities that are being given to us.

Monday 24 March
Luke 4:24–30

And he said, 'Truly I tell you, no prophet is accepted in the prophet's home town. But the truth is, there were many widows in Israel in the time of Elijah, when the heaven was shut up for three years and six months, and there was a severe famine over all the land; yet Elijah was sent to none of them except to a widow at Zarephath in Sidon. There were also many lepers in Israel in the time of the prophet Elisha, and none of them was cleansed except Naaman the Syrian.' When they heard this, all in the synagogue were filled with rage. They got up, drove him out of the town, and led him to the brow of the hill on which their town was built, so that they might hurl him off the cliff. But he passed through the midst of them and went on his way.

- Is it pride or blindness that blocks us from accepting the truth from other human beings? It has been said, 'There are none so blind as those who will not see.' In this Gospel we also see great anger and resentment in the Nazarenes against the one who had grown up among them, and they try to destroy him. We too are human beings. What are the dark parts in our own hearts?

- Jesus lived a fully human life, with all its ups and downs, joys and sorrows. Let us be with Jesus as he is driven out of his home village by the townspeople, and talk to him about his feelings and great disappointment.

Tuesday 25 March
The Annunciation of the Lord
Luke 1:26–38

In the sixth month the angel Gabriel was sent by God to a town in Galilee called Nazareth, to a virgin engaged to a man whose name was Joseph, of the house of David. The virgin's name was Mary. And he came to her and said, 'Greetings, favoured one! The Lord is with you.' But she was much perplexed by his words and pondered what sort of greeting this might be. The angel said to her, 'Do not be afraid, Mary, for you have found favour with God. And now, you will conceive in your womb and bear a son, and you will name him Jesus. He will be great, and will be called the Son of the Most High, and the Lord God will give to him the throne of his ancestor David. He will reign over the house of Jacob for ever, and of his kingdom there will be no end.' Mary said to the angel, 'How can this be, since I am a virgin?' The angel said to her, 'The Holy Spirit will come upon you, and the power of the Most High will overshadow you;

therefore the child to be born will be holy; he will be called Son of God. And now, your relative Elizabeth in her old age has also conceived a son; and this is the sixth month for her who was said to be barren. For nothing will be impossible with God.' Then Mary said, 'Here am I, the servant of the Lord; let it be with me according to your word.' Then the angel departed from her.

- Mary did not understand all that was being asked of her, and Luke tells us she pondered over many things as they unfolded around her. Her 'yes' to God's message was a blanket acceptance in faith of whatever would come in her life. Our own faith and trust in God has to be like that. We will never in this life come to understand the reason for all that happens to us. Our 'yes' to God is a commitment of mind and heart to God. Let us pray to renew our own commitment and to live it.

Wednesday 26 March
Matthew 5:17–19

Jesus said to his disciples, 'Do not think that I have come to abolish the law or the prophets; I have come not to abolish but to fulfil. For truly I tell you, until heaven and earth pass away, not one letter, not one stroke of a letter, will pass from the law until all is accomplished. Therefore, whoever breaks one of the least of these commandments, and teaches others to do the same, will be called least in the kingdom of heaven; but whoever does them and teaches them will be called great in the kingdom of heaven.'

- God's revelation about himself and what he was asking of us came only gradually over a very long period. The keeping of the law and the prophets could never be enough to redeem and save us. Christ alone could do this, but by living according to the law and prophets the people of God were being prepared for the later acceptance of the teaching of Jesus, who came with a new and unique authority to complete and to fulfil the law. It is Christ that we now look to in our seeking to live what God is asking of us.

- Lord Jesus, help us to live according to your teachings and your example and to practise what we profess in our faith.

Thursday 27 March

Luke 11:14–23

Now he was casting out a demon that was mute; when the demon had gone out, the one who had been mute spoke, and the crowds were amazed. But some of them said, 'He casts out demons by Beelzebul, the ruler of the demons.' Others, to test him, kept demanding from him a sign from heaven. But he knew what they were thinking and said to them, 'Every kingdom divided against itself becomes a desert, and house falls on house. If Satan also is divided against himself, how will his kingdom stand?—for you say that I cast out the demons by Beelzebul. Now if I cast out the demons by Beelzebul, by whom do your exorcists cast them out? Therefore they will be your judges. But if it is by the finger of God that I cast out the demons, then the kingdom of God has come to you. When a strong man, fully armed, guards his castle, his property is safe. But when one stronger than he attacks him and overpowers him, he takes away his armour in which he trusted and divides his plunder. Whoever is not with me is against me, and whoever does not gather with me scatters.'

- The sheer logic of Christ's argument should have been enough to make his opponents reflect on their position. However, for their own selfish reasons they did not want to be with him. Let us pray to grasp more deeply our own littleness and lack of understanding.

- In the Gospels Jesus cast out many evil spirits. Pope Francis has agreed that we can change the translation at the end of the Our Father, so I now find it more helpful to say, 'And lead us in time of temptation and deliver us from the evil one.' The image of our God leading us by the hand can be very helpful in our prayer. It is mentioned in Psalms 63 and 73, and in Mark 8:23, when Jesus leads the blind man by the hand out of the village at Bethsaida.

Friday 28 March

Mark 12:28–34

One of the scribes came near and heard them disputing with one another, and seeing that he answered them well, he asked him, 'Which commandment is the first of all?' Jesus answered, 'The first is, "Hear, O Israel: the Lord our God, the Lord is one; you shall love the Lord your God with all your heart, and with all your soul, and with all your mind, and with all your strength." The second is this, "You shall love your neighbour as yourself." There is no other commandment greater than these.' Then the scribe said to him, 'You are right, Teacher; you have truly said that "he is one, and besides him there is no other"; and "to love him with all the heart, and with all the understanding, and with all the strength", and "to love one's neighbour as oneself",—this is much more important than all whole burnt-offerings and sacrifices.' When Jesus saw that he answered wisely, he said to him, 'You are not far from the kingdom of God.' After that no one dared to ask him any question.

- It is very rare in the Gospels to find our Lord praising one of the scribes. It can be said that our Lord reduced all the commandments to two, namely love God and love your neighbour. They are really two parts of the one great commandment to love, as it is out of a loving heart that we love both God and neighbour. In the order of things God must always come first. Do I always put God in the first place in my life? He can never take second place.

Saturday 29 March
Luke 18:9–14

He also told this parable to some who trusted in themselves that they were righteous and regarded others with contempt: 'Two men went up to the temple to pray, one a Pharisee and the other a tax-collector. The Pharisee, standing by himself, was praying thus, "God, I thank you that I am not like other people: thieves, rogues, adulterers, or even like this tax-collector. I fast twice a week; I give a tenth of all my income." But the tax-collector, standing far off, would not even look up to heaven, but was beating his breast and saying, "God, be merciful to me, a sinner!" I tell you, this man went down to his home justified rather than the other; for all who exalt themselves will be humbled, but all who humble themselves will be exalted.'

- Here Jesus gives a very important lesson about prayer. For our prayers to be heard we must always pray with humility before our God. Humility is truth, the truth of our own littleness and complete dependence on God. It is in this attitude that we come now before God to pray from our hearts.

- In his prayer the Pharisee focused on himself and all he had done. The tax collector focused on God and his great mercy. St Teresa of Ávila taught that real prayer is more about loving than thinking. There is a lot of truth in the statement that when we are thinking in prayer we are with ourselves, and when we are loving in prayer we are with God. Prayer is all about a relationship. Do I go to prayer just to ask for things for myself and others, or do I spend most of my time staying with the Lord, sharing with him and listening to him?

Fourth Week of Lent
30 March–5 April 2025

Something to think and pray about each day this week:

'What are you giving up for Lent?' 'Sweets!' Childish? Of course. As a child, though, to go forty days without sweets was a serious commitment. St Patrick's Day was the only light in a seemingly endless journey of sweet deprivation.

There is so much more to Lent. The child in us may give up sweets, but the faithful part of us is called to a place of reflection and repentance, where we take stock and accept what we find, a storeroom from which is brought out the old and the new, where we might find memories of more faith-filled and innocent days, when going to church and blessing our face came naturally.

As well as 'giving up' for Lent is there a place for 'taking up' too? Taking up a more positive outlook, taking up again the call to Sunday Mass? Is there room on the Lenten journey for a bit of social justice, outreach, charity, volunteerism? Space to make a difference in the lives of others? Maybe, if we can forgive a little, love a lot, share more, pray sincerely, be involved, we will find that instead of giving up sweets, a spiritual sweetness, a true sense of wellness, will envelop us.

Vincent Sherlock,
The Sacred Heart Messenger,
February 2023

The Presence of God

'Be still, and know that I am God!' Lord, your words lead us to the calmness and greatness of your presence.

Freedom

God is not foreign to my freedom. The Spirit breathes life into my most intimate desires, gently nudging me towards all that is good. I ask for the grace to let myself be enfolded by the Spirit.

Consciousness

Where do I sense hope, encouragement and growth in my life? By looking back over the past few months, I may be able to see which activities and occasions have produced rich fruit. If I do notice such areas, I will determine to give those areas both time and space in the future.

The Word

The word of God comes down to us through the Scriptures. May the Holy Spirit enlighten my mind and my heart to respond to the Gospel teachings. *(Please turn to the Scripture on the following pages. Inspiration points are there, should you need them. When you are ready, return here to continue.)*

Conversation

What is stirring in me as I pray? Am I consoled, troubled, left cold? I imagine Jesus standing or sitting at my side, and I share my feelings with him.

Conclusion

Glory be to the Father, and to the Son, and to the Holy Spirit,
As it was in the beginning, is now and ever shall be,
World without end. Amen.

Sunday 30 March
Fourth Sunday of Lent
Luke 15:1–3, 11–32

Now all the tax-collectors and sinners were coming near to listen to him. And the Pharisees and the scribes were grumbling and saying, 'This fellow welcomes sinners and eats with them.'

So he told them this parable: . . . 'There was a man who had two sons. The younger of them said to his father, "Father, give me the share of the property that will belong to me." So he divided his property between them. A few days later the younger son gathered all he had and travelled to a distant country, and there he squandered his property in dissolute living. When he had spent everything, a severe famine took place throughout that country, and he began to be in need. So he went and hired himself out to one of the citizens of that country, who sent him to his fields to feed the pigs. He would gladly have filled himself with the pods that the pigs were eating; and no one gave him anything. But when he came to himself he said, "How many of my father's hired hands have bread enough and to spare, but here I am dying of hunger! I will get up and go to my father, and I will say to him, 'Father, I have sinned against heaven and before you; I am no longer worthy to be called your son; treat me like one of your hired hands.'" So he set off and went to his father. But while he was still far off, his father saw him and was filled with compassion; he ran and put his arms around him and kissed him. Then the son said to him, "Father, I have sinned against heaven and before you; I am no longer worthy to be called your son." But the father said to his slaves, "Quickly, bring out a robe—the best one—and put it on him; put a ring on his finger and sandals on his feet. And get the fatted calf and kill it, and let us eat and celebrate; for this son of mine was dead and is alive again; he was lost and is found!" And they began to celebrate.

'Now his elder son was in the field; and when he came and approached the house, he heard music and dancing. He called one of the slaves and asked what was going on. He replied, "Your brother has come, and your father has killed the fatted calf, because he has got him back safe and sound." Then he became angry and refused to go in. His father came out and began to plead with him. But he answered his father, "Listen! For all these years I have been working like a slave for you, and I have never disobeyed your command; yet you have never given me even a young goat so that I might celebrate with my friends. But when this son of yours came back, who has devoured your property with prostitutes, you killed the fatted calf for him!" Then the father said to him, "Son, you are always with me, and all that is mine is yours. But we had to celebrate and rejoice, because this brother of yours was dead and has come to life; he was lost and has been found."'

- The marginalised and sinners found something very attractive in Jesus and they came in droves to listen to him. They sensed his love and compassion for them. This beautiful story of the father and his wayward son epitomises these qualities in Jesus. Jesus came to reveal the Father to us. Our God is a God of infinite love and compassion. In this season of Lent, when we reflect on our own waywardness, let us kneel at his feet and acknowledge our need for his mercy and help.

- The elder brother, while keeping all the rules, had closed his heart to the call to be compassionate and forgiving. Are there attitudes in my life that block me from hearing this same call to me?

Monday 31 March
John 4:43–54

When the two days were over, he went from that place to Galilee (for Jesus himself had testified that a prophet has no honour in the prophet's own country). When he came to Galilee, the Galileans welcomed him, since they had seen all that he had done in Jerusalem at the festival; for they too had gone to the festival.

Then he came again to Cana in Galilee where he had changed the water into wine. Now there was a royal official whose son lay ill in Capernaum. When he heard that Jesus had come from Judea to Galilee, he went and begged him to come down and heal his son, for he was at the point of death. Then Jesus said to him, 'Unless you see signs and wonders you will not believe.' The official said to him, 'Sir, come down before my little boy dies.' Jesus said to him, 'Go; your son will live.' The man believed the word that Jesus spoke to him and started on his way. As he was going down, his slaves met him and told him that his child was alive. So he asked them the hour when he began to recover, and they said to him, 'Yesterday at one in the afternoon the fever left him.' The father realised that this was the hour when Jesus had said to him, 'Your son will live.' So he himself believed, along with his whole household. Now this was the second sign that Jesus did after coming from Judea to Galilee.

- St John's Gospel has been called the book of signs—this is the second sign Jesus gave of his divinity. The royal official immediately took Jesus at his word and believed that his son would be cured. Too often we are like 'doubting Thomas', who said he would not believe unless he could see the mark of the nails and could touch the risen Jesus. Let us pray to be among those who are blessed because although they have not seen, yet they believe.

Tuesday 1 April
John 5:1–3, 5–16

After this there was a festival of the Jews, and Jesus went up to Jerusalem.

Now in Jerusalem by the Sheep Gate there is a pool, called in Hebrew Beth-zatha, which has five porticoes. In these lay many invalids—blind, lame, and paralysed. . . . One man was there who had been ill for thirty-eight years. When Jesus saw him lying there and knew that he had been there a long time, he said to him, 'Do you want to be made well?' The sick man answered him, 'Sir, I have no one to put me into the pool when the water is stirred up; and while I am making my way, someone else steps down ahead of me.' Jesus said to him, 'Stand up, take your mat and walk.' At once the man was made well, and he took up his mat and began to walk.

Now that day was a sabbath. So the Jews said to the man who had been cured, 'It is the sabbath; it is not lawful for you to carry your mat.' But he answered them, 'The man who made me well said to me, "Take up your mat and walk."' They asked him, 'Who is the man who said to you, "Take it up and walk"?' Now the man who had been healed did not know who it was, for Jesus had disappeared in the crowd that was there. Later Jesus found him in the temple and said to him, 'See, you have been made well! Do not sin any more, so that nothing worse happens to you.' The man went away and told the Jews that it was Jesus who had made him well. Therefore the Jews started persecuting Jesus, because he was doing such things on the sabbath.

- The fact that Jesus asked the invalid if he wanted to be cured showed great sensitivity. An invalid for almost forty years, he would face many big changes in his life if suddenly made well again. We should be careful with what we ask for in prayer. The request of Jesus in the garden of Gethsemane was followed each time with, 'Yet, not my will but yours be done.' Let us ask God to give us whatever he knows is best for us.

- The Jewish religious leaders made many laws that they claimed were to honour God but in reality were to give themselves authority and control over people's lives. Jesus, knowing their hypocrisy, ignored these laws. Our human laws should always be motivated by love and compassion for the welfare of all. In my dealings with others do I put human laws above the good of others? Do I season justice with mercy?

Wednesday 2 April
John 5:17–30

But Jesus answered them, 'My Father is still working, and I also am working.' For this reason the Jews were seeking all the more to kill him, because he was not only breaking the sabbath, but was also calling God his own Father, thereby making himself equal to God.

Jesus said to them, 'Very truly, I tell you, the Son can do nothing on his own, but only what he sees the Father doing; for whatever the Father does, the Son does likewise. The Father loves the Son and shows him all that he himself is doing; and he will show him greater works than these, so that you will be astonished. Indeed, just as the Father raises the dead and gives them life, so also the Son gives life to whomsoever he wishes. The Father judges no one but has given all judgement to the Son, so that all may honour the Son just as they honour the Father. Anyone who does not honour the Son does not honour the Father who sent him. Very truly, I tell you, anyone who hears my word and believes him who sent me has eternal life, and does not come under judgement, but has passed from death to life.

'Very truly, I tell you, the hour is coming, and is now here, when the dead will hear the voice of the Son of God, and those who hear will live. For just as the Father has life in himself, so he has granted the Son also to have life in himself; and he has given him authority to execute judgement, because he is the Son of Man. Do not be astonished at this; for the hour is coming when all who are in their graves will hear his voice and will come out—those who have done good, to the resurrection of life, and those who have done evil, to the resurrection of condemnation.

'I can do nothing on my own. As I hear, I judge; and my judgement is just, because I seek to do not my own will but the will of him who sent me.'

- St John's Gospel, written after the other three Gospels, is unequalled in making clear the divinity of Jesus and his close relationship with his Father in heaven. At the end of chapter 20 he states that this Gospel was written that we may come to believe that Jesus is the Messiah and the Son of God. Jesus told us he sought always to do the will of his Father. As followers of Jesus this should always be our aim.

- Without God holding us in existence every moment of our lives, we simply would cease to exist. This working in us is the work of the whole Trinity, Father, Son and Holy Spirit. As we read in Luke 12:7, every hair on our heads is counted. Let us pray to have complete trust in the unchanging love of God for every one of us.

Thursday 3 April
John 5:31–47

Jesus said to them, 'If I testify about myself, my testimony is not true. There is another who testifies on my behalf, and I know that his testimony to me is true. You sent messengers to John, and he testified to the truth. Not that I accept such human testimony, but I say these things so that you may be saved. He was a burning and shining lamp, and you were willing to rejoice for a while in his light. But I have a testimony greater than John's. The works that the Father has given me to complete, the very works that I am doing, testify on my behalf that the Father has sent me. And the Father who sent me has himself testified on my behalf. You have never heard his voice or seen his form, and you do not have his word abiding in you, because you do not believe him whom he has sent.

'You search the scriptures because you think that in them you have eternal life; and it is they that testify on my behalf. Yet you refuse to come to me to have life. I do not accept glory from human beings. But I know that you do not have the love of God in you. I have come in my Father's name, and you do not accept me; if another comes in his own name, you will accept him. How can you believe when you accept glory from one another and do not seek the glory that comes from the one who alone is God? Do not think that I will accuse you before the Father; your accuser is Moses, on whom you have set your hope. If you believed Moses, you would believe me, for he wrote about me. But if you do not believe what he wrote, how will you believe what I say?'

- What we do defines who and what we are more than any words we may use. Jesus told Pilate that he had come to witness to the truth. He did this not only through what he preached but even more by what he did. 'The very works that I am doing, testify on my behalf.' Jesus told us that his disciples are those who do the will of his Father, not those who call out, 'Lord, Lord.' We ask God to help us to be true to the name of his Son and to ourselves by how we live.

- In his love for his enemies Jesus tried hard to save them but they deliberately closed their ears and hearts to him. To reject Jesus Christ is to reject the One who sent him. Here Jesus tells them, 'I know that you do not have the love of God in you.' Let us pray for a greater love of God.

Friday 4 April
John 7:1–2, 10, 25–30

After this Jesus went about in Galilee. He did not wish to go about in Judea because the Jews were looking for an opportunity to kill him. Now the Jewish festival of Booths was near. . . .

But after his brothers had gone to the festival, then he also went, not publicly but as it were in secret. . . .

Now some of the people of Jerusalem were saying, 'Is not this the man whom they are trying to kill? And here he is, speaking openly, but they say nothing to him! Can it be that the authorities really know that this is the Messiah? Yet we know where this man is from; but when the Messiah comes, no one will know where he is from.' Then Jesus cried out as he was teaching in the temple, 'You know me, and you know where I am from. I have not come on my own. But the one who sent me is true, and you do not know him. I know him, because I am from him, and he sent me.' Then they tried to arrest him, but no one laid hands on him, because his hour had not yet come.

- Jesus, knowing the bloodthirsty nature of his opponents, walked a tightrope. He knew he was destined to suffer and be killed but that would only be in the fullness of time. For now he would continue to carry out his mission from his Father, which was to spread the Good News of the kingdom at whatever cost to himself. In the end he paid a heavy price. Are we willing to take up our cross each day and witness to our faith, despite ridicule and even persecution?

Saturday 5 April

John 7:40–52

When they heard these words, some in the crowd said, 'This is really the prophet.' Others said, 'This is the Messiah.' But some asked, 'Surely the Messiah does not come from Galilee, does he? Has not the scripture said that the Messiah is descended from David and comes from Bethlehem, the village where David lived?' So there was a division in the crowd because of him. Some of them wanted to arrest him, but no one laid hands on him.

Then the temple police went back to the chief priests and Pharisees, who asked them, 'Why did you not arrest him?' The police answered, 'Never has anyone spoken like this!' Then the Pharisees replied, 'Surely you have not been deceived too, have you? Has any one of the authorities or of the Pharisees believed in him? But this crowd, which does not know the law—they are accursed.' Nicodemus, who had gone to Jesus before, and who was one of them, asked, 'Our law does not judge people without first giving them a hearing to find out what they are doing, does it?' They replied, 'Surely you are not also from Galilee, are you? Search and you will see that no prophet is to arise from Galilee.'

- A closed mind is a great affliction, all the more so when it is reinforced by pride. These so-called 'learned men' were so convinced of their own rightness in interpreting the Scriptures, nothing that Jesus said or did could get through to them. St John Henry Newman said, 'To live is to change, and to live well is to change often.' How willing am I to let go of the addictions and selfishness that block God's working in me?

- Even the police, sent to arrest him, acknowledged that 'Never has anyone spoken like this!' Let us open ourselves to the teachings of Jesus and say to him, 'Speak, Lord, for your servant is listening.'

Fifth Week of Lent
6–12 April 2025

Something to think and pray about each day this week:

Lent is a time to respond to that hunger which lies at the core of our being, the hunger for a deeper connection with the Creator, the hunger to experience freshness in our lives, the hunger for what we truly long for. What better place to work all of this out than 'the wilderness'? From time to time, we are landed in the wilderness. Sometimes it is an unpleasant experience and at other times we crave it, in response to a deep desire to step back from the day-to-day and make space in our lives for reflection.

Tríona Doherty and Jane Mellett,
The Deep End: A Journey with the Sunday Gospels
in the Year of Mark

The Presence of God

'Come to me, all you that are weary and are carrying heavy burdens, and I will give you rest.' Here I am, Lord. I come to seek your presence. I long for your healing power.

Freedom

By God's grace I was born to live in freedom. Free to enjoy the pleasures he created for me. Dear Lord, grant that I may live as you intended, with complete confidence in your loving care.

Consciousness

Knowing that God loves me unconditionally, I look honestly over the past day, its events, and my feelings. Do I have something to be grateful for? Then I give thanks. Is there something I am sorry for? Then I ask forgiveness.

The Word

God speaks to each of us individually. I listen attentively to hear what he is saying to me. Read the text a few times, then listen. *(Please turn to the Scripture on the following pages. Inspiration points are there, should you need them. When you are ready, return here to continue.)*

Conversation

I know with certainty that there were times when you carried me, Lord. There were times when it was through your strength that I got through the dark times in my life.

Conclusion

Glory be to the Father, and to the Son, and to the Holy Spirit,
As it was in the beginning, is now and ever shall be,
World without end. Amen.

Sunday 6 April
Fifth Sunday of Lent

John 8:1–11

Then each of them went home, while Jesus went to the Mount of Olives. Early in the morning he came again to the temple. All the people came to him and he sat down and began to teach them. The scribes and the Pharisees brought a woman who had been caught in adultery; and making her stand before all of them, they said to him, 'Teacher, this woman was caught in the very act of committing adultery. Now in the law Moses commanded us to stone such women. Now what do you say?' They said this to test him, so that they might have some charge to bring against him. Jesus bent down and wrote with his finger on the ground. When they kept on questioning him, he straightened up and said to them, 'Let anyone among you who is without sin be the first to throw a stone at her.' And once again he bent down and wrote on the ground. When they heard it, they went away, one by one, beginning with the elders; and Jesus was left alone with the woman standing before him. Jesus straightened up and said to her, 'Woman, where are they? Has no one condemned you?' She said, 'No one, sir.' And Jesus said, 'Neither do I condemn you. Go your way, and from now on do not sin again.'

• During this last week of his life, when his hearers went home to their houses, Jesus spent his nights at the foot of the Mount of Olives in the garden of Gethsemane, praying and sleeping. Early each morning he set out for the temple for his day's work of preaching and teaching, at daily risk of arrest. In our meeting with him now in prayer we can dialogue with him about what this last week was like.

• Jesus always loved the sinner and not the sin. 'Neither do I condemn you. Go your way, and from now on do not sin again.' The Gospel of John says elsewhere that God did not send the Son to condemn the world but to save it. Let us pray to imitate him in his great mercy.

Monday 7 April

John 8:12–20

Again Jesus spoke to them, saying, 'I am the light of the world. Whoever follows me will never walk in darkness but will have the light of life.' Then the Pharisees said to him, 'You are testifying on your own behalf;

your testimony is not valid.' Jesus answered, 'Even if I testify on my own behalf, my testimony is valid because I know where I have come from and where I am going, but you do not know where I come from or where I am going. You judge by human standards; I judge no one. Yet even if I do judge, my judgement is valid; for it is not I alone who judge, but I and the Father who sent me. In your law it is written that the testimony of two witnesses is valid. I testify on my own behalf, and the Father who sent me testifies on my behalf.' Then they said to him, 'Where is your Father?' Jesus answered, 'You know neither me nor my Father. If you knew me, you would know my Father also.' He spoke these words while he was teaching in the treasury of the temple, but no one arrested him, because his hour had not yet come.

- 'You know neither me nor my Father.' We cannot love someone we do not know. Our God wants us to come to know him, and knowing him will inevitably lead us to love him who is infinitely loveable. 'For I desire steadfast love and not sacrifice, the knowledge of God rather than burnt-offerings.' (Hosea 6:6). Let us pray to be open to our God revealing himself to us as Jesus promised that he would in John 14:21.

Tuesday 8 April
John 8:21–30

Again he said to them, 'I am going away, and you will search for me, but you will die in your sin. Where I am going, you cannot come.' Then the Jews said, 'Is he going to kill himself? Is that what he means by saying, "Where I am going, you cannot come"?' He said to them, 'You are from below, I am from above; you are of this world, I am not of this world. I told you that you would die in your sins, for you will die in your sins unless you believe that I am he.' They said to him, 'Who are you?' Jesus said to them, 'Why do I speak to you at all? I have much to say about you and much to condemn; but the one who sent me is true, and I declare to the world what I have heard from him.' They did not understand that he was speaking to them about the Father. So Jesus said, 'When you have lifted up the Son of Man, then you will realise that I am he, and that I do nothing on my own, but I speak these things as the Father instructed me. And the one who sent me is with me; he has not left me alone, for I always do what is pleasing to him.' As he was saying these things, many believed in him.

- At his trial Jesus told Pilate that his kingdom was not of this world. Here Jesus speaks of how he has come from his Father and speaks what his Father wants him to speak. Jesus is the fullness of God's revelation to us. Let us pray to learn how to listen to him and to place him always at the centre of our lives.

Wednesday 9 April
John 8:31–42

Then Jesus said to the Jews who had believed in him, 'If you continue in my word, you are truly my disciples; and you will know the truth, and the truth will make you free.' They answered him, 'We are descendants of Abraham and have never been slaves to anyone. What do you mean by saying, 'You will be made free'?'

Jesus answered them, 'Very truly, I tell you, everyone who commits sin is a slave to sin. The slave does not have a permanent place in the household; the son has a place there for ever. So if the Son makes you free, you will be free indeed. I know that you are descendants of Abraham; yet you look for an opportunity to kill me, because there is no place in you for my word. I declare what I have seen in the Father's presence; as for you, you should do what you have heard from the Father.'

They answered him, 'Abraham is our father.' Jesus said to them, 'If you were Abraham's children, you would be doing what Abraham did, but now you are trying to kill me, a man who has told you the truth that I heard from God. This is not what Abraham did. You are indeed doing what your father does.' They said to him, 'We are not illegitimate children; we have one father, God himself.' Jesus said to them, 'If God were your Father, you would love me, for I came from God and now I am here. I did not come on my own, but he sent me.'

- In their blindness and pride the Jews could not see their own wrongdoing and lack of compassion. Despite the witness of his deeds they refused to accept the words of Jesus when he told them he had been sent by the Father. Our faith is a commitment we make to God without having all the answers to our many questions. We grow in this faith by using it and, especially, by spending time in real prayer from our hearts. 'Lord, we believe. Help Thou our unbelief.'

Thursday 10 April
John 8:51–59

Jesus said to them, 'Very truly, I tell you, whoever keeps my word will never see death.' The Jews said to him, 'Now we know that you have a demon. Abraham died, and so did the prophets; yet you say, "Whoever keeps my word will never taste death." Are you greater than our father Abraham, who died? The prophets also died. Who do you claim to be?' Jesus answered, 'If I glorify myself, my glory is nothing. It is my Father who glorifies me, he of whom you say, "He is our God", though you do not know him. But I know him; if I were to say that I do not know him, I would be a liar like you. But I do know him and I keep his word. Your ancestor Abraham rejoiced that he would see my day; he saw it and was glad.' Then the Jews said to him, 'You are not yet fifty years old, and have you seen Abraham?' Jesus said to them, 'Very truly, I tell you, before Abraham was, I am.' So they picked up stones to throw at him, but Jesus hid himself and went out of the temple.

- Yet again, in this Gospel we see the two levels at work. When Jesus speaks of life he is speaking about the life of the soul that goes on for eternity. But for the Jews it is the earthly life of the body that is uppermost in their minds, hence the references to Abraham being dead and the age of Jesus. We have to put on the mind of Christ and give priority to the life of the soul. Let us speak to the Lord about this, asking for a greater understanding.

Friday 11 April
John 10:31–42

The Jews took up stones again to stone him. Jesus replied, 'I have shown you many good works from the Father. For which of these are you going to stone me?' The Jews answered, 'It is not for a good work that we are going to stone you, but for blasphemy, because you, though only a human being, are making yourself God.' Jesus answered, 'Is it not written in your law, "I said, you are gods"? If those to whom the word of God came were called "gods"—and the scripture cannot be annulled—can you say that the one whom the Father has sanctified and sent into the world is blaspheming because I said, "I am God's Son"? If I am not doing the works of my Father, then do not believe me. But if I do them, even though you do not believe me, believe the works, so that you may know and understand that the Father is in me and I am in the Father.' Then they tried to arrest him again, but he escaped from their hands.

He went away again across the Jordan to the place where John had been baptizing earlier, and he remained there. Many came to him, and they were saying, 'John performed no sign, but everything that John said about this man was true.' And many believed in him there.

- Jesus appeals to his hearers to judge the truth of his words by the witness of his doing the good works of his Father. 'You will know them by their fruits.' This is too much for the Scribes and Pharisees in their hardness of heart. 'Unless you change and become like children you will never enter the kingdom of heaven.' Let us pray for the gift of humility and to recognise the truth of our own littleness.

Saturday 12 April
John 11:45–56

Many of the Jews therefore, who had come with Mary and had seen what Jesus did, believed in him. But some of them went to the Pharisees and told them what he had done. So the chief priests and the Pharisees called a meeting of the council, and said, 'What are we to do? This man is performing many signs. If we let him go on like this, everyone will believe in him, and the Romans will come and destroy both our holy place and our nation.' But one of them, Caiaphas, who was high priest that year, said to them, 'You know nothing at all! You do not understand that it is better for you to have one man die for the people than to have the whole nation destroyed.' He did not say this on his own, but being high priest that year he prophesied that Jesus was about to die for the nation, and not for the nation only, but to gather into one the dispersed children of God. So from that day on they planned to put him to death.

Jesus therefore no longer walked about openly among the Jews, but went from there to a town called Ephraim in the region near the wilderness; and he remained there with the disciples.

Now the Passover of the Jews was near, and many went up from the country to Jerusalem before the Passover to purify themselves. They were looking for Jesus and were asking one another as they stood in the temple, 'What do you think? Surely he will not come to the festival, will he?'

- The members of the Sanhedrin were aware of the signs Jesus was performing but they failed to see where they were pointing to. Let us pray to be able to read the signs of our times, and to see our need for God.

- The Jewish religious leaders could find only one solution to the problem of Jesus and that was to kill him. Even though it failed for them, many human beings have continued down the centuries to apply this same solution to rid themselves of problems. That there is a darkness in the heart of humankind is undoubted. Let us pray that the light of Christ and the illumination of the Holy Spirit will transform the hearts of all.

Holy Week
13–19 April 2025

There are two bowls of water in the story of the Passion. One is Pilate's, used to scrub himself of all responsibility. The other is the one with which Jesus bathes others, soaking them in lavish love.

The two bowls are always before us in life. Jesus shows us that when you take the side of the dispossessed, your spirit deepens and grows. When your self-obsession is reduced, your life expands and your horizon enlarges. To pick up the towel is not to become a doormat. We are called, not to serve people's wants, but their needs. We serve others in the name of Christ. We share what we have, but, more importantly, who we are, especially with people who are rejected and alienated. They are the life presence that transforms us by showing us the heart of God, the prophets, preachers and provocative witnesses of the Gospel. They challenge us with questions that disturb and disquiet us, as they lead us into looking at the Passion and Easter with new eyes and hearts.

Easter invites us to remember the Lord when we gather as a community for the Eucharist. He entrusts his future in the world to us in the Church.

John Cullen,
The Sacred Heart Messenger,
April 2022

The Presence of God
'Be still, and know that I am God!' Lord, your words lead us to the calmness and greatness of your presence.

Freedom
Leave me here freely all alone. / In cell where never sunlight shone. / Should no one ever speak to me. / This golden silence makes me free!
     —Part of a poem by Bl Titus Brandsma,
    written while he was a prisoner at Dachau concentration camp

Consciousness
Knowing that God loves me unconditionally, I can afford to be honest about how I am. How has the day been, and how do I feel now? I share my feelings openly with the Lord.

The Word
I take my time to read the word of God slowly, a few times, allowing myself to dwell on anything that strikes me. *(Please turn to the Scripture on the following pages. Inspiration points are there, should you need them. When you are ready, return here to continue.)*

Conversation
Sometimes I wonder what I might say if I were to meet you in person, Lord. I think I might say, 'Thank you', because you are always there for me.

Conclusion
I thank God for these moments we have spent together and for any insights I have been given concerning the text.

Sunday 13 April
Palm Sunday of the Passion of the Lord
Luke 22:14—23:56

When the hour came, he took his place at the table, and the apostles with him. He said to them, 'I have eagerly desired to eat this Passover with you before I suffer; for I tell you, I will not eat it until it is fulfilled in the kingdom of God.' Then he took a cup, and after giving thanks he said, 'Take this and divide it among yourselves; for I tell you that from now on I will not drink of the fruit of the vine until the kingdom of God comes.' Then he took a loaf of bread, and when he had given thanks, he broke it and gave it to them, saying, 'This is my body, which is given for you. Do this in remembrance of me.' And he did the same with the cup after supper, saying, 'This cup that is poured out for you is the new covenant in my blood. But see, the one who betrays me is with me, and his hand is on the table. For the Son of Man is going as it has been determined, but woe to that one by whom he is betrayed!' Then they began to ask one another which one of them it could be who would do this.

A dispute also arose among them as to which one of them was to be regarded as the greatest. But he said to them, 'The kings of the Gentiles lord it over them; and those in authority over them are called benefactors. But not so with you; rather the greatest among you must become like the youngest, and the leader like one who serves. For who is greater, the one who is at the table or the one who serves? Is it not the one at the table? But I am among you as one who serves.

'You are those who have stood by me in my trials; and I confer on you, just as my Father has conferred on me, a kingdom, so that you may eat and drink at my table in my kingdom, and you will sit on thrones judging the twelve tribes of Israel.

'Simon, Simon, listen! Satan has demanded to sift all of you like wheat, but I have prayed for you that your own faith may not fail; and you, when once you have turned back, strengthen your brothers.' And he said to him, 'Lord, I am ready to go with you to prison and to death!' Jesus said, 'I tell you, Peter, the cock will not crow this day, until you have denied three times that you know me.'

He said to them, 'When I sent you out without a purse, bag, or sandals, did you lack anything?' They said, 'No, not a thing.' He said to them,

'But now, the one who has a purse must take it, and likewise a bag. And the one who has no sword must sell his cloak and buy one. For I tell you, this scripture must be fulfilled in me, "And he was counted among the lawless"; and indeed what is written about me is being fulfilled.' They said, 'Lord, look, here are two swords.' He replied, 'It is enough.'

He came out and went, as was his custom, to the Mount of Olives; and the disciples followed him. When he reached the place, he said to them, 'Pray that you may not come into the time of trial.' Then he withdrew from them about a stone's throw, knelt down, and prayed, 'Father, if you are willing, remove this cup from me; yet, not my will but yours be done.' [Then an angel from heaven appeared to him and gave him strength. In his anguish he prayed more earnestly, and his sweat became like great drops of blood falling down on the ground.] When he got up from prayer, he came to the disciples and found them sleeping because of grief, and he said to them, 'Why are you sleeping? Get up and pray that you may not come into the time of trial.'

While he was still speaking, suddenly a crowd came, and the one called Judas, one of the twelve, was leading them. He approached Jesus to kiss him; but Jesus said to him, 'Judas, is it with a kiss that you are betraying the Son of Man?' When those who were around him saw what was coming, they asked, 'Lord, should we strike with the sword?' Then one of them struck the slave of the high priest and cut off his right ear. But Jesus said, 'No more of this!' And he touched his ear and healed him. Then Jesus said to the chief priests, the officers of the temple police, and the elders who had come for him, 'Have you come out with swords and clubs as if I were a bandit? When I was with you day after day in the temple, you did not lay hands on me. But this is your hour, and the power of darkness!'

Then they seized him and led him away, bringing him into the high priest's house. But Peter was following at a distance. When they had kindled a fire in the middle of the courtyard and sat down together, Peter sat among them. Then a servant-girl, seeing him in the firelight, stared at him and said, 'This man also was with him.' But he denied it, saying, 'Woman, I do not know him.' A little later someone else, on seeing him, said, 'You also are one of them.' But Peter said, 'Man, I am not!' Then about an hour later yet another kept insisting, 'Surely this man also was with him; for he is a Galilean.' But Peter said, 'Man, I do not know what you are talking about!' At that moment, while he was still speaking, the cock crowed. The Lord turned and looked at Peter. Then Peter remembered the word of the Lord, how he had said to him, 'Before the cock crows today, you will deny me three times.' And he went out and wept bitterly.

Now the men who were holding Jesus began to mock him and beat him; they also blindfolded him and kept asking him, 'Prophesy! Who is it that struck you?' They kept heaping many other insults on him.

When day came, the assembly of the elders of the people, both chief priests and scribes, gathered together, and they brought him to their council. They said, 'If you are the Messiah, tell us.' He replied, 'If I tell you, you will not believe; and if I question you, you will not answer. But from now on the Son of Man will be seated at the right hand of the power of God.' All of them asked, 'Are you, then, the Son of God?' He said to them, 'You say that I am.' Then they said, 'What further testimony do we need? We have heard it ourselves from his own lips!'

Then the assembly rose as a body and brought Jesus before Pilate. They began to accuse him, saying, 'We found this man perverting our nation, forbidding us to pay taxes to the emperor, and saying that he himself is the Messiah, a king.' Then Pilate asked him, 'Are you the king of the Jews?' He answered, 'You say so.' Then Pilate said to the chief priests and the crowds, 'I find no basis for an accusation against this man.' But they were insistent and said, 'He stirs up the people by teaching throughout all Judea, from Galilee where he began even to this place.'

When Pilate heard this, he asked whether the man was a Galilean. And when he learned that he was under Herod's jurisdiction, he sent him off to Herod, who was himself in Jerusalem at that time. When Herod saw Jesus, he was very glad, for he had been wanting to see him for a long time, because he had heard about him and was hoping to see him perform some sign. He questioned him at some length, but Jesus gave him no answer. The chief priests and the scribes stood by, vehemently accusing him. Even Herod with his soldiers treated him with contempt and mocked him; then he put an elegant robe on him, and sent him back to Pilate. That same day Herod and Pilate became friends with each other; before this they had been enemies.

Pilate then called together the chief priests, the leaders, and the people, and said to them, 'You brought me this man as one who was perverting the people; and here I have examined him in your presence and have not found this man guilty of any of your charges against him. Neither has Herod, for he sent him back to us. Indeed, he has done nothing to deserve death. I will therefore have him flogged and release him.'

Then they all shouted out together, 'Away with this fellow! Release Barabbas for us!' (This was a man who had been put in prison for an insurrection that had taken place in the city, and for murder.) Pilate, wanting to release Jesus, addressed them again; but they kept shouting, 'Crucify, crucify him!' A third time he said to them, 'Why, what evil has he done? I have found in him no ground for the sentence of death; I will therefore have him flogged and then release him.' But they kept urgently demanding with loud shouts that he should be crucified; and their voices prevailed. So Pilate gave his verdict that their demand should be granted. He released the man they asked for, the one who had been put in prison for insurrection and murder, and he handed Jesus over as they wished.

As they led him away, they seized a man, Simon of Cyrene, who was coming from the country, and they laid the cross on him, and made him carry it behind Jesus. A great number of the people followed him, and among them were women who were beating their breasts and wailing for him. But Jesus turned to them and said, 'Daughters of Jerusalem, do not weep for me, but weep for yourselves and for your children. For the days are surely coming when they will say, "Blessed are the barren, and the wombs that never bore, and the breasts that never nursed." Then they will begin to say to the mountains, "Fall on us"; and to the hills, "Cover us." For if they do this when the wood is green, what will happen when it is dry?'

Two others also, who were criminals, were led away to be put to death with him. When they came to the place that is called The Skull, they crucified Jesus there with the criminals, one on his right and one on his left. [Then Jesus said, 'Father, forgive them; for they do not know what they are doing.'] And they cast lots to divide his clothing. And the people stood by, watching; but the leaders scoffed at him, saying, 'He saved others; let him save himself if he is the Messiah of God, his chosen one!' The soldiers also mocked him, coming up and offering him sour wine, and saying, 'If you are the King of the Jews, save yourself!' There was also an inscription over him, 'This is the King of the Jews.'

One of the criminals who were hanged there kept deriding him and saying, 'Are you not the Messiah? Save yourself and us!' But the other rebuked him, saying, 'Do you not fear God, since you are under the same sentence of condemnation? And we indeed have been condemned justly, for we are getting what we deserve for our deeds, but this man has done nothing wrong.' Then he said, 'Jesus, remember me when you come into your kingdom.' He replied, 'Truly I tell you, today you will be with me in Paradise.'

It was now about noon, and darkness came over the whole land until three in the afternoon, while the sun's light failed; and the curtain of the temple was torn in two. Then Jesus, crying with a loud voice, said, 'Father, into your hands I commend my spirit.' Having said this, he breathed his last. When the centurion saw what had taken place, he praised God and said, 'Certainly this man was innocent.' And when all the crowds who had gathered there for this spectacle saw what had taken place, they returned home, beating their breasts. But all his acquaintances, including the women who had followed him from Galilee, stood at a distance, watching these things.

Now there was a good and righteous man named Joseph, who, though a member of the council, had not agreed to their plan and action. He came from the Jewish town of Arimathea, and he was waiting expectantly for the kingdom of God. This man went to Pilate and asked for the body of Jesus. Then he took it down, wrapped it in a linen cloth, and laid it in a rock-hewn tomb where no one had ever been laid. It was the day of Preparation, and the sabbath was beginning. The women who had come with him from Galilee followed, and they saw the tomb and how his body was laid. Then they returned, and prepared spices and ointments.

On the sabbath they rested according to the commandment.

- Our praying on the Passion can be a most unselfish prayer as we focus not on our own needs but on the sufferings of our Saviour. For prayer we can take any of the Gospel accounts, or the Stations of the Cross, or the sorrowful mysteries of the Rosary.

- What was it like as a human being to feel the pain of being crucified? 'Father, forgive them; for they do not know what they are doing.' Jesus never stopped loving those who crucified him.

Monday 14 April
John 12:1–11

Six days before the Passover Jesus came to Bethany, the home of Lazarus, whom he had raised from the dead. There they gave a dinner for him. Martha served, and Lazarus was one of those at the table with him. Mary took a pound of costly perfume made of pure nard, anointed Jesus' feet, and wiped them with her hair. The house was filled with the fragrance of the perfume. But Judas Iscariot, one of his disciples (the one who was about to betray him), said, 'Why was this perfume not sold for three hundred denarii and the money given to the poor?' (He said this not because he cared about the poor, but because he was a thief; he kept the common purse and used to steal what was put into it.) Jesus said, 'Leave her alone. She bought it so that she might keep it for the day of my burial. You always have the poor with you, but you do not always have me.'

When the great crowd of the Jews learned that he was there, they came not only because of Jesus but also to see Lazarus, whom he had raised from the dead. So the chief priests planned to put Lazarus to death as well, since it was on account of him that many of the Jews were deserting and were believing in Jesus.

- In the home of Martha and Mary Jesus found a great welcome and a reverence which drew him back to visit them. Let us pray for the grace to make him welcome in our hearts, and to be enabled to make our home in him, as he has invited us to do.

- Despite being called to the inner circle of Jesus' apostles, Judas in his selfishness had not taken his opportunities to come to know and love him. Now is the acceptable time for each of us to come to know and love and follow Jesus our Lord and Master.

Tuesday 15 April
John 13:21–33, 36–38

After saying this Jesus was troubled in spirit, and declared, 'Very truly, I tell you, one of you will betray me.' The disciples looked at one another, uncertain of whom he was speaking. One of his disciples—the one whom Jesus loved—was reclining next to him; Simon Peter therefore motioned to him to ask Jesus of whom he was speaking. So while reclining next to Jesus, he asked him, 'Lord, who is it?' Jesus answered, 'It is the one to whom I give this piece of bread when I have dipped it in the dish.' So when he had dipped the piece of bread, he gave it to Judas son of Simon Iscariot. After he received the piece of bread, Satan entered into him. Jesus said to him, 'Do quickly what you are going to do.' Now no one at the table knew why he said this to him. Some thought that, because Judas had the common purse, Jesus was telling him, 'Buy what we need for the festival'; or, that he should give something to the poor. So, after receiving the piece of bread, he immediately went out. And it was night.

When he had gone out, Jesus said, 'Now the Son of Man has been glorified, and God has been glorified in him. If God has been glorified in him, God will also glorify him in himself and will glorify him at once. Little children, I am with you only a little longer. You will look for me; and as I said to the Jews so now I say to you, 'Where I am going, you cannot come.' . . .

Simon Peter said to him, 'Lord, where are you going?' Jesus answered, 'Where I am going, you cannot follow me now; but you will follow afterwards.' Peter said to him, 'Lord, why can I not follow you now? I will lay down my life for you.' Jesus answered, 'Will you lay down your life for me? Very truly, I tell you, before the cock crows, you will have denied me three times.'

- To know that one of his own close companions was about to betray him to his enemies must have been a great sadness for Jesus. In Psalm 55:13–15 we read of the treachery of one who had walked in harmony with him in the house of God.

- That Peter too would so soon deny even knowing him, despite saying he would lay down his life for him, would also be a source of sadness for Jesus. So often we, like St Peter, profess our faith and, indeed, our love for Jesus, but fail to live this in our lives. We ask for a deep sorrow for our fickleness and our failure to be true to him.

Wednesday 16 April
Matthew 26:14–25

Then one of the twelve, who was called Judas Iscariot, went to the chief priests and said, 'What will you give me if I betray him to you?' They paid him thirty pieces of silver. And from that moment he began to look for an opportunity to betray him.

On the first day of Unleavened Bread the disciples came to Jesus, saying, 'Where do you want us to make the preparations for you to eat the Passover?' He said, 'Go into the city to a certain man, and say to him, "The Teacher says, My time is near; I will keep the Passover at your house with my disciples."' So the disciples did as Jesus had directed them, and they prepared the Passover meal.

When it was evening, he took his place with the twelve; and while they were eating, he said, 'Truly I tell you, one of you will betray me.' And they became greatly distressed and began to say to him one after another, 'Surely not I, Lord?' He answered, 'The one who has dipped his hand into the bowl with me will betray me. The Son of Man goes as it is written of him, but woe to that one by whom the Son of Man is betrayed! It would have been better for that one not to have been born.' Judas, who betrayed him, said, 'Surely not I, Rabbi?' He replied, 'You have said so.'

• We are told that Judas used to steal from the common purse. Now his greed has increased and he wants even more money. It is frightening, especially for those consecrated to God in religious life or the priesthood, that despite his privileged call Judas could still sin so grievously. St Paul in Philippians 2 tells his converts to 'work out your own salvation with fear and trembling'. We are all sinners, always in need of God's mercy and grace.

Thursday 17 April
Holy Thursday
John 13:1–15

Now before the festival of the Passover, Jesus knew that his hour had come to depart from this world and go to the Father. Having loved his own who were in the world, he loved them to the end. The devil had already put it into the heart of Judas son of Simon Iscariot to betray him. And during supper Jesus, knowing that the Father had given all things into his hands, and that he had come from God and was going to God, got up from the table, took off his outer robe, and tied a towel around himself. Then he poured water into a basin and began to wash the disciples' feet and to wipe them with the towel that was tied around him. He came to Simon Peter, who said to him, 'Lord, are you going to wash my feet?' Jesus answered, 'You do not know now what I am doing, but later you will understand.' Peter said to him, 'You will never wash my feet.' Jesus answered, 'Unless I wash you, you have no share with me.' Simon Peter said to him, 'Lord, not my feet only but also my hands and my head!' Jesus said to him, 'One who has bathed does not need to wash, except for the feet, but is entirely clean. And you are clean, though not all of you.' For he knew who was to betray him; for this reason he said, 'Not all of you are clean.'

After he had washed their feet, had put on his robe, and had returned to the table, he said to them, 'Do you know what I have done to you? You call me Teacher and Lord—and you are right, for that is what I am. So if I, your Lord and Teacher, have washed your feet, you also ought to wash one another's feet. For I have set you an example, that you also should do as I have done to you.'

• Actions speak louder than words. Not only the teaching but also the example of Jesus, our Lord and Master, is always the headline for all his followers. He told us that he came not to be served but to serve and here he shows it. And he said that the greatest among us are those who serve the weakest. Lord, help us to see that whatever kindness and help we show to others you take it as done to you.

Friday 18 April
Good Friday
John 18:1—19:42

After Jesus had spoken these words, he went out with his disciples across the Kidron valley to a place where there was a garden, which he and his disciples entered. Now Judas, who betrayed him, also knew the place, because Jesus often met there with his disciples. So Judas brought a detachment of soldiers together with police from the chief priests and the Pharisees, and they came there with lanterns and torches and weapons. Then Jesus, knowing all that was to happen to him, came forward and asked them, 'For whom are you looking?' They answered, 'Jesus of Nazareth.' Jesus replied, 'I am he.' Judas, who betrayed him, was standing with them. When Jesus said to them, 'I am he', they stepped back and fell to the ground. Again he asked them, 'For whom are you looking?' And they said, 'Jesus of Nazareth.' Jesus answered, 'I told you that I am he. So if you are looking for me, let these men go.' This was to fulfil the word that he had spoken, 'I did not lose a single one of those whom you gave me.' Then Simon Peter, who had a sword, drew it, struck the high priest's slave, and cut off his right ear. The slave's name was Malchus. Jesus said to Peter, 'Put your sword back into its sheath. Am I not to drink the cup that the Father has given me?'

So the soldiers, their officer, and the Jewish police arrested Jesus and bound him. First they took him to Annas, who was the father-in-law of Caiaphas, the high priest that year. Caiaphas was the one who had advised the Jews that it was better to have one person die for the people.

Simon Peter and another disciple followed Jesus. Since that disciple was known to the high priest, he went with Jesus into the courtyard of the high priest, but Peter was standing outside at the gate. So the other disciple, who was known to the high priest, went out, spoke to the woman who guarded the gate, and brought Peter in. The woman said to Peter, 'You are not also one of this man's disciples, are you?' He said, 'I am not.' Now the slaves and the police had made a charcoal fire because it was cold, and they were standing round it and warming themselves. Peter also was standing with them and warming himself.

Then the high priest questioned Jesus about his disciples and about his teaching. Jesus answered, 'I have spoken openly to the world; I have always taught in synagogues and in the temple, where all the Jews come together. I have said nothing in secret. Why do you ask me? Ask those who heard what I said to them; they know what I said.' When he had said this, one of the police standing nearby struck Jesus on the face, saying, 'Is that how you answer the high priest?' Jesus answered, 'If I have spoken wrongly, testify to the wrong. But if I have spoken rightly, why do you strike me?' Then Annas sent him bound to Caiaphas the high priest.

Now Simon Peter was standing and warming himself. They asked him, 'You are not also one of his disciples, are you?' He denied it and said, 'I am not.' One of the slaves of the high priest, a relative of the man whose ear Peter had cut off, asked, 'Did I not see you in the garden with him?' Again Peter denied it, and at that moment the cock crowed.

Then they took Jesus from Caiaphas to Pilate's headquarters. It was early in the morning. They themselves did not enter the headquarters, so as to avoid ritual defilement and to be able to eat the Passover. So Pilate went out to them and said, 'What accusation do you bring against this man?' They answered, 'If this man were not a criminal, we would not have handed him over to you.' Pilate said to them, 'Take him yourselves and judge him according to your law.' The Jews replied, 'We are not permitted to put anyone to death.' (This was to fulfil what Jesus had said when he indicated the kind of death he was to die.)

Then Pilate entered the headquarters again, summoned Jesus, and asked him, 'Are you the King of the Jews?' Jesus answered, 'Do you ask this on your own, or did others tell you about me?' Pilate replied, 'I am not a Jew, am I? Your own nation and the chief priests have handed you over to me. What have you done?' Jesus answered, 'My kingdom is not from this world. If my kingdom were from this world, my followers would be fighting to keep me from being handed over to the Jews. But as it is, my kingdom is not from here.' Pilate asked him, 'So you are a king?' Jesus answered, 'You say that I am a king. For this I was born, and for this I came into the world, to testify to the truth. Everyone who belongs to the truth listens to my voice.' Pilate asked him, 'What is truth?'

After he had said this, he went out to the Jews again and told them, 'I find no case against him. But you have a custom that I release someone for you at the Passover. Do you want me to release for you the King of the Jews?' They shouted in reply, 'Not this man, but Barabbas!' Now Barabbas was a bandit.

Then Pilate took Jesus and had him flogged. And the soldiers wove a crown of thorns and put it on his head, and they dressed him in a purple robe. They kept coming up to him, saying, 'Hail, King of the Jews!' and striking him on the face. Pilate went out again and said to them, 'Look, I am bringing him out to you to let you know that I find no case against him.' So Jesus came out, wearing the crown of thorns and the purple robe. Pilate said to them, 'Here is the man!' When the chief priests and the police saw him, they shouted, 'Crucify him! Crucify him!' Pilate said to them, 'Take him yourselves and crucify him; I find no case against him.' The Jews answered him, 'We have a law, and according to that law he ought to die because he has claimed to be the Son of God.'

Now when Pilate heard this, he was more afraid than ever. He entered his headquarters again and asked Jesus, 'Where are you from?' But Jesus gave him no answer. Pilate therefore said to him, 'Do you refuse to speak to me? Do you not know that I have power to release you, and power to crucify you?' Jesus answered him, 'You would have no power over me unless it had been given you from above; therefore the one who handed me over to you is guilty of a greater sin.' From then on Pilate tried to release him, but the Jews cried out, 'If you release this man, you are no friend of the emperor. Everyone who claims to be a king sets himself against the emperor.'

When Pilate heard these words, he brought Jesus outside and sat on the judge's bench at a place called The Stone Pavement, or in Hebrew Gabbatha. Now it was the day of Preparation for the Passover; and it was about noon. He said to the Jews, 'Here is your King!' They cried out, 'Away with him! Away with him! Crucify him!' Pilate asked them, 'Shall I crucify your King?' The chief priests answered, 'We have no king but the emperor.' Then he handed him over to them to be crucified.

So they took Jesus; and carrying the cross by himself, he went out to what is called The Place of the Skull, which in Hebrew is called Golgotha. There they crucified him, and with him two others, one on either side, with Jesus between them. Pilate also had an inscription written and put on the cross. It read, 'Jesus of Nazareth, the King of the Jews.' Many of the Jews read this inscription, because the place where Jesus was crucified was near the city; and it was written in Hebrew, in Latin, and in Greek. Then the chief priests of the Jews said to Pilate, 'Do not write, "The King of the Jews", but, "This man said, I am King of the Jews."' Pilate answered, 'What I have written I have written.' When the soldiers had crucified Jesus, they took his clothes and divided them into four parts, one for each soldier. They also took his tunic; now the tunic was seamless, woven in one piece from the top. So they said to one another, 'Let us not tear it, but cast lots for it to see who will get it.' This was to fulfil what the scripture says,

'They divided my clothes among themselves,
    and for my clothing they cast lots.'
And that is what the soldiers did.

Meanwhile, standing near the cross of Jesus were his mother, and his mother's sister, Mary the wife of Clopas, and Mary Magdalene. When Jesus saw his mother and the disciple whom he loved standing beside her, he said to his mother, 'Woman, here is your son.' Then he said to the disciple, 'Here is your mother.' And from that hour the disciple took her into his own home.

After this, when Jesus knew that all was now finished, he said (in order to fulfil the scripture), 'I am thirsty.' A jar full of sour wine was standing there. So they put a sponge full of the wine on a branch of hyssop and held it to his mouth. When Jesus had received the wine, he said, 'It is finished.' Then he bowed his head and gave up his spirit.

Since it was the day of Preparation, the Jews did not want the bodies left on the cross during the sabbath, especially because that sabbath was a day of great solemnity. So they asked Pilate to have the legs of the crucified men broken and the bodies removed. Then the soldiers came and broke the legs of the first and of the other who had been crucified with him. But when they came to Jesus and saw that he was already dead, they did not break his legs. Instead, one of the soldiers pierced his side with a spear, and at once blood and water came out. (He who saw this has testified so that you also may believe. His testimony is true, and he knows that he tells the truth.) These things occurred so that the scripture might be fulfilled, 'None of his bones shall be broken.' And again another passage of scripture says, 'They will look on the one whom they have pierced.'

After these things, Joseph of Arimathea, who was a disciple of Jesus, though a secret one because of his fear of the Jews, asked Pilate to let him take away the body of Jesus. Pilate gave him permission; so he came and removed his body. Nicodemus, who had at first come to Jesus by night, also came, bringing a mixture of myrrh and aloes, weighing about a hundred pounds. They took the body of Jesus and wrapped it with the spices in linen cloths, according to the burial custom of the Jews. Now there was a garden in the place where he was crucified, and in the garden there was a new tomb in which no one had ever been laid. And so, because it was the Jewish day of Preparation, and the tomb was nearby, they laid Jesus there.

- The gospel story of the life, death and resurrection of Jesus is truly the story of a life given up for others. At the Last Supper he said, 'This is my body, which is given *for you*,' and, 'This cup that is poured out *for you* is the new covenant in my blood.' Let us consider any part of the Passion now, and ask for a deep compassion with Jesus in his suffering and to accompany him in it.

- Fr Pedro Arrupe SJ, a former father general of the Society of Jesus, wrote that we cannot be fair-weather friends of Jesus. We must be willing to enter with him into the cloud of Calvary and to watch and pray with him.

Saturday 19 April
Holy Saturday
Luke 24:1–12

But on the first day of the week, at early dawn, they came to the tomb, taking the spices that they had prepared. They found the stone rolled away from the tomb, but when they went in, they did not find the body. While they were perplexed about this, suddenly two men in dazzling clothes stood beside them. The women were terrified and bowed their faces to the ground, but the men said to them, 'Why do you look for the living among the dead? He is not here, but has risen. Remember how he told you, while he was still in Galilee, that the Son of Man must be handed over to sinners, and be crucified, and on the third day rise again.' Then they remembered his words, and returning from the tomb, they told all this to the eleven and to all the rest. Now it was Mary Magdalene, Joanna, Mary the mother of James, and the other women with them who told this to the apostles. But these words seemed to them an idle tale, and they did not believe them. But Peter got up and ran to the tomb; stooping and looking in, he saw the linen cloths by themselves; then he went home, amazed at what had happened.

- The first Holy Saturday must have been a day of stunned silence for the mother of Jesus and for his disciples. In the Jewish understanding, a person's end was an indication of how they had lived. In the Book of Wisdom 2:16–17 we read, 'He . . . boasts that God is his Father . . . let us test what will happen at the end of his life.' Let us spend some time now in prayer with Mary and the apostles, sharing in the mood of sombreness and waiting for the dawn of Easter Sunday.

20–26 April 2025

Something to think and pray about each day this week:

The first Easter shattered all the disciples' expectations. Easter continues to shatter our expectations. The risen Lord continues to take us by surprise. He stands among us even when all hope seems lost; he touches us with his presence when we are least expecting it. When we are most aware of our failure to follow him, he speaks his word of peace to us, because even when we are faithless, he remains faithful. Easter announces that the story of our relationship with the Lord never ends, because his relationship with us never ends. He continues to stand among us, assuring us of his presence, offering us his gift of peace and sending us out as his messengers of hope.

Martin Hogan,
The Word Is Near You, on Your Lips and in Your Heart

The Presence of God

'Come to me, all you that are weary and are carrying heavy burdens, and I will give you rest.' Here I am, Lord. I come to seek your presence. I long for your healing power.

Freedom

By God's grace I was born to live in freedom. Free to enjoy the pleasures he created for me. Dear Lord, grant that I may live as you intended, with complete confidence in your loving care.

Consciousness

Knowing that God loves me unconditionally, I look honestly over the past day, its events, and my feelings. Do I have something to be grateful for? Then I give thanks. Is there something I am sorry for? Then I ask forgiveness.

The Word

God speaks to each of us individually. I listen attentively to hear what he is saying to me. Read the text a few times, then listen. *(Please turn to the Scripture on the following pages. Inspiration points are there, should you need them. When you are ready, return here to continue.)*

Conversation

I know with certainty that there were times when you carried me, Lord. There were times when it was through your strength that I got through the dark times in my life.

Conclusion

Glory be to the Father, and to the Son, and to the Holy Spirit,
As it was in the beginning, is now and ever shall be,
World without end. Amen.

Sunday 20 April
Easter Sunday of the Resurrection of the Lord
John 20:1–9

Early on the first day of the week, while it was still dark, Mary Magdalene came to the tomb and saw that the stone had been removed from the tomb. So she ran and went to Simon Peter and the other disciple, the one whom Jesus loved, and said to them, 'They have taken the Lord out of the tomb, and we do not know where they have laid him.' Then Peter and the other disciple set out and went towards the tomb. The two were running together, but the other disciple outran Peter and reached the tomb first. He bent down to look in and saw the linen wrappings lying there, but he did not go in. Then Simon Peter came, following him, and went into the tomb. He saw the linen wrappings lying there, and the cloth that had been on Jesus' head, not lying with the linen wrappings but rolled up in a place by itself. Then the other disciple, who reached the tomb first, also went in, and he saw and believed; for as yet they did not understand the scripture, that he must rise from the dead.

- 'Enough! The Resurrection. A heart's-clarion! Away grief's gasping, / joyless days, dejection. Across my foundering deck shone a beacon, an eternal beam.' So wrote the poet Gerard Manley Hopkins SJ about the comfort of the Resurrection. The darkness of sin and death is forever shattered by the 'eternal beam' of Easter morning. We open our hearts to the joy of Christ's victory, and we give immense thanks to God.

- Jesus had foretold his rising from the dead and now everything has changed. He is vindicated in his triumph over those who opposed him. We all share in the victory of Jesus, our Brother, and all the graces that we could ever need have been won for us. Like the apostles who ran to the tomb, let us allow the enormity of this event to seep into our souls as we now meet our Saviour in prayer.

Monday 21 April
Matthew 28:8–15

So they left the tomb quickly with fear and great joy, and ran to tell his disciples. Suddenly Jesus met them and said, 'Greetings!' And they came to him, took hold of his feet, and worshipped him. Then Jesus said to them, 'Do not be afraid; go and tell my brothers to go to Galilee; there they will see me.'

While they were going, some of the guard went into the city and told the chief priests everything that had happened. After the priests had assembled with the elders, they devised a plan to give a large sum of money to the soldiers, telling them, 'You must say, "His disciples came by night and stole him away while we were asleep." If this comes to the governor's ears, we will satisfy him and keep you out of trouble.' So they took the money and did as they were directed. And this story is still told among the Jews to this day.

- To suddenly meet the risen Lord alive after the terrible events of the previous Friday must have been a huge shock to the women. In fear and joy all they can think of is to hurry to tell his friends. We all love to hear good news and wish to share it with others. Let us now in our prayer enter into the mood of joyful celebration with deep gratitude.

- Let us be willing to share the Good News with others.

Tuesday 22 April
John 20:11–18

But Mary stood weeping outside the tomb. As she wept, she bent over to look into the tomb; and she saw two angels in white, sitting where the body of Jesus had been lying, one at the head and the other at the feet. They said to her, 'Woman, why are you weeping?' She said to them, 'They have taken away my Lord, and I do not know where they have laid him.' When she had said this, she turned round and saw Jesus standing there, but she did not know that it was Jesus. Jesus said to her, 'Woman, why are you weeping? For whom are you looking?' Supposing him to be the gardener, she said to him, 'Sir, if you have carried him away, tell me where you have laid him, and I will take him away.' Jesus said to her, 'Mary!' She turned and said to him in Hebrew, 'Rabbouni!' (which means Teacher). Jesus said to her, 'Do not hold on to me, because I have not yet ascended to the Father. But go to my brothers and say to them, "I am ascending to my Father and your Father, to my God and your God."' Mary Magdalene went and announced to the disciples, 'I have seen the Lord'; and she told them that he had said these things to her.

- It has been said that our voices are the last part of us that changes. When Jesus called Mary of Magdalene by her name, she instantly recognised his voice. In John 10:4 we read that Jesus said that his sheep follow him for they recognise his voice. Let us, using our imagination in prayer, have him now call us by our name. 'I have inscribed you on the palms of my hands' (Isaiah 49:16).

- It was the women followers of Jesus that were the first to see the risen Lord. Mary Magdalene was rewarded for her great love for the Lord and she must have been filled with an extraordinary joy. The goal of all prayer is union with our God and, with St John of the Cross, we strive to grow in a loving attentiveness to his presence within us.

Wednesday 23 April
Luke 24:13–35

Now on that same day two of them were going to a village called Emmaus, about seven miles from Jerusalem, and talking with each other about all these things that had happened. While they were talking and discussing, Jesus himself came near and went with them, but their eyes were kept from recognising him. And he said to them, 'What are you discussing with each other while you walk along?' They stood still, looking sad. Then one of them, whose name was Cleopas, answered him, 'Are you the only stranger in Jerusalem who does not know the things that have taken place there in these days?' He asked them, 'What things?' They replied, 'The things about Jesus of Nazareth, who was a prophet mighty in deed and word before God and all the people, and how our chief priests and leaders handed him over to be condemned to death and crucified him. But we had hoped that he was the one to redeem Israel. Yes, and besides all this, it is now the third day since these things took place. Moreover, some women of our group astounded us. They were at the tomb early this morning, and when they did not find his body there, they came back and told us that they had indeed seen a vision of angels who said that he was alive. Some of those who were with us went to the tomb and found it just as the women had said; but they did not see him.' Then he said to them, 'Oh, how foolish you are, and how slow of heart to believe all that the prophets have declared! Was it not necessary that the Messiah should suffer these things and then enter into his glory?' Then beginning with

Moses and all the prophets, he interpreted to them the things about himself in all the scriptures.

As they came near the village to which they were going, he walked ahead as if he were going on. But they urged him strongly, saying, 'Stay with us, because it is almost evening and the day is now nearly over.' So he went in to stay with them. When he was at the table with them, he took bread, blessed and broke it, and gave it to them. Then their eyes were opened, and they recognised him; and he vanished from their sight. They said to each other, 'Were not our hearts burning within us while he was talking to us on the road, while he was opening the scriptures to us?' That same hour they got up and returned to Jerusalem; and they found the eleven and their companions gathered together. They were saying, 'The Lord has risen indeed, and he has appeared to Simon!' Then they told what had happened on the road, and how he had been made known to them in the breaking of the bread.

- This encounter of the two disciples with the risen Lord is a great example for our own prayer. The Christ we meet in our prayer is, of course, always the risen Lord, and in our encounters with him we enter into a dialogue with him. Here we see this dialogue at work as Jesus asks what is troubling them, and then they answer and he listens. Then he answers them by speaking through the Scriptures, which are the word of God. We know that this experience set their hearts on fire as we are told they said, 'Were not our hearts burning within us while he was talking to us on the road?' We ask to learn how to listen to the Lord in our own dialogues with him.

- The language of God in prayer is silence and love. In our listening we attend with our hearts to his loving presence. As Fr Karl Rahner wrote, 'He has veiled his love in the stillness of his silence, so that our love might reveal itself in faith.'

Thursday 24 April
Luke 24:35–48

Then they told what had happened on the road, and how he had been made known to them in the breaking of the bread.

While they were talking about this, Jesus himself stood among them and said to them, 'Peace be with you.' They were startled and terrified, and thought that they were seeing a ghost. He said to them, 'Why are you frightened, and why do doubts arise in your hearts? Look at my hands and my feet; see that it is I myself. Touch me and see; for a ghost does not have flesh and bones as you see that I have.' And when he had said this, he showed them his hands and his feet. While in their joy they were disbelieving and still wondering, he said to them, 'Have you anything here to eat?' They gave him a piece of broiled fish, and he took it and ate in their presence.

Then he said to them, 'These are my words that I spoke to you while I was still with you—that everything written about me in the law of Moses, the prophets, and the psalms must be fulfilled.' Then he opened their minds to understand the scriptures, and he said to them, 'Thus it is written, that the Messiah is to suffer and to rise from the dead on the third day, and that repentance and forgiveness of sins is to be proclaimed in his name to all nations, beginning from Jerusalem. You are witnesses of these things.'

• The apostles will now go out as witnesses of the Resurrection from Jerusalem to the whole world. As followers of Jesus we too are called to go and be witnesses to the truth of his resurrection.

Friday 25 April
John 21:1–14

After these things Jesus showed himself again to the disciples by the Sea of Tiberias; and he showed himself in this way. Gathered there together were Simon Peter, Thomas called the Twin, Nathanael of Cana in Galilee, the sons of Zebedee, and two others of his disciples. Simon Peter said to them, 'I am going fishing.' They said to him, 'We will go with you.' They went out and got into the boat, but that night they caught nothing.

Just after daybreak, Jesus stood on the beach; but the disciples did not know that it was Jesus. Jesus said to them, 'Children, you have no fish, have you?' They answered him, 'No.' He said to them, 'Cast the net to the right side of the boat, and you will find some.' So they cast it, and now they were not able to haul it in because there were so many fish. That disciple whom Jesus loved said to Peter, 'It is the Lord!' When Simon Peter heard that it was the Lord, he put on some clothes, for he was naked, and jumped into the lake. But the other disciples came in the boat, dragging the net full of fish, for they were not far from the land, only about a hundred yards off.

When they had gone ashore, they saw a charcoal fire there, with fish on it, and bread. Jesus said to them, 'Bring some of the fish that you have just caught.' So Simon Peter went aboard and hauled the net ashore, full of large fish, a hundred and fifty-three of them; and though there were so many, the net was not torn. Jesus said to them, 'Come and have breakfast.' Now none of the disciples dared to ask him, 'Who are you?' because they knew it was the Lord. Jesus came and took the bread and gave it to them, and did the same with the fish. This was now the third time that Jesus appeared to the disciples after he was raised from the dead.

- The meeting of the risen Jesus with his friends by the lakeshore is one of the most intimate scenes in the Gospels. In his humanity Jesus knows they will be tired and hungry and disappointed after their night of fruitless fishing. He has prepared breakfast for them. He is still their Lord and Master and he will be their companion for ever. This holds good for each of us too. Let us be with him now in our prayer.

- Jesus asks Simon Peter, 'Do you love me?' in John 21:15. This is the third question Jesus asks of all his followers, the other two being, 'What are you looking for? (John 1:38), and 'Who do you say that I am?' (Luke 9:20). This third question is the most important and it can include the other two. Let us allow the Lord to ask each of us these three questions now.

Saturday 26 April
Mark 16:9–15

And all that had been commanded them they told briefly to those around Peter. And afterwards Jesus himself sent out through them, from east to west, the sacred and imperishable proclamation of eternal salvation.

Now after he rose early on the first day of the week, he appeared first to Mary Magdalene, from whom he had cast out seven demons. She went out and told those who had been with him, while they were mourning and weeping. But when they heard that he was alive and had been seen by her, they would not believe it.

After this he appeared in another form to two of them, as they were walking into the country. And they went back and told the rest, but they did not believe them.

Later he appeared to the eleven themselves as they were sitting at the table; and he upbraided them for their lack of faith and stubbornness, because they had not believed those who saw him after he had risen. And he said to them, 'Go into all the world and proclaim the good news to the whole creation.'

- In the Fourth Week of his Spiritual Exercises St Ignatius of Loyola gives us prayer points for the Resurrection. In these the whole mood is one of rejoicing with Jesus in his great victory and in his joy at now having won everything for us. Jesus is seen as the great Consoler. Let us enter into that mood of rejoicing with Jesus and ask for the gift of his consolation as we continue on our own pilgrim way.

- Jesus complains to his disciples about their lack of faith and their stubbornness. In the encounter on the road to Emmaus he also says to the two disciples, 'Oh, how foolish you are, and how slow of heart to believe all that the prophets have declared! Was it not necessary that the Messiah should suffer these things and then enter into his glory?' Let us acknowledge our own slowness of heart to believe.

Something to think and pray about each day this week:

What is the Kingdom of God? This is not an easy question to answer. Once it was described in terms of somebody witnessing a downpour in a busy city on a crowded shopping day. The rain caught people off guard, and as people huddled together for shelter, it was noticed that young lads walked towards a boy in a wheelchair and helped his mother get him in out of the rain. Another man held his jacket over his wife's head as the icy rain soaked through his shirt and inched its way down his back. A girl stood from her sheltered and cherished doorway to offer the space to an elderly woman. A young mother wrapped her coat around her little children to shield and protect them.

All so simple, but for the one observing, every act spoke of God's Kingdom fully alive; it's about putting the other first. The Kingdom of God is not a geographical location nor is it a walled garden. It's not somewhere to be reached but a reality to be lived. It is not about a future address but living life in the now, living it fully and alive, living it freely and cheerfully, living it for others and with others so that God's glory can reveal itself again and again, even in a winter's cloudburst.

Vincent Sherlock,
Let Advent Be Advent

The Presence of God

'I am standing at the door, knocking,' says the Lord. What a wonderful privilege that the Lord of all creation desires to come to me. I welcome his presence.

Freedom

Everything has the potential to draw forth from me a fuller love and life. Yet my desires are often fixed, caught, on illusions of fulfilment. I ask that God, through my freedom, may orchestrate my desires in a vibrant loving melody rich in harmony.

Consciousness

To be conscious about something is to be aware of it. Dear Lord, help me to remember that you gave me life. Thank you for the gift of life. Teach me to slow down, to be still and enjoy the pleasures created for me. To be aware of the beauty that surrounds me: the marvel of mountains, the calmness of lakes, the fragility of a flower petal. I need to remember that all these things come from you.

The Word

I read the word of God slowly, a few times over, and I listen to what God is saying to me. *(Please turn to the Scripture on the following pages. Inspiration points are there, should you need them. When you are ready, return here to continue.)*

Conversation

What feelings are rising in me as I pray and reflect on God's word? I imagine Jesus himself sitting or standing near me, and I open my heart to him.

Conclusion

I thank God for these moments we have spent together and for any insights I have been given concerning the text.

Sunday 27 April
Divine Mercy Sunday (Second Sunday of Easter)
John 20:19–31

When it was evening on that day, the first day of the week, and the doors of the house where the disciples had met were locked for fear of the Jews, Jesus came and stood among them and said, 'Peace be with you.' After he said this, he showed them his hands and his side. Then the disciples rejoiced when they saw the Lord. Jesus said to them again, 'Peace be with you. As the Father has sent me, so I send you.' When he had said this, he breathed on them and said to them, 'Receive the Holy Spirit. If you forgive the sins of any, they are forgiven them; if you retain the sins of any, they are retained.'

But Thomas (who was called the Twin), one of the twelve, was not with them when Jesus came. So the other disciples told him, 'We have seen the Lord.' But he said to them, 'Unless I see the mark of the nails in his hands, and put my finger in the mark of the nails and my hand in his side, I will not believe.'

A week later his disciples were again in the house, and Thomas was with them. Although the doors were shut, Jesus came and stood among them and said, 'Peace be with you.' Then he said to Thomas, 'Put your finger here and see my hands. Reach out your hand and put it in my side. Do not doubt but believe.' Thomas answered him, 'My Lord and my God!' Jesus said to him, 'Have you believed because you have seen me? Blessed are those who have not seen and yet have come to believe.'

Now Jesus did many other signs in the presence of his disciples, which are not written in this book. But these are written so that you may come to believe that Jesus is the Messiah, the Son of God, and that through believing you may have life in his name.

- Here Jesus shows great understanding and compassion for our weakness and slowness of heart to believe. It appears that he came especially for the sake of Doubting Thomas, but of course it was for us too. On this Divine Mercy Sunday he shows that he is always a God of forgiveness and love.

- This was originally intended to be the final chapter, but the writer states that the whole purpose of this book is to show that Jesus is the Messiah and the Son of God. We pray to grow in our faith and in our understanding of the revelation of God in this Gospel.

Monday 28 April
John 3:1–8

Now there was a Pharisee named Nicodemus, a leader of the Jews. He came to Jesus by night and said to him, 'Rabbi, we know that you are a teacher who has come from God; for no one can do these signs that you do apart from the presence of God.' Jesus answered him, 'Very truly, I tell you, no one can see the kingdom of God without being born from above.' Nicodemus said to him, 'How can anyone be born after having grown old? Can one enter a second time into the mother's womb and be born?' Jesus answered, 'Very truly, I tell you, no one can enter the kingdom of God without being born of water and Spirit. What is born of the flesh is flesh, and what is born of the Spirit is spirit. Do not be astonished that I said to you, "You must be born from above." The wind blows where it chooses, and you hear the sound of it, but you do not know where it comes from or where it goes. So it is with everyone who is born of the Spirit.'

- Our baptism is our first real birthday into the new life of grace. We become the temple of the Holy Spirit, sharing in the very life of God himself. The floodgates of all the graces Christ has won for us are opened to us. But, like the life of our bodies, it takes time and nurturing for this new life to grow in us. We give thanks for this great sacrament of initiation when so many millions have never even heard of Christ.

- It is so easy for us to forget that the life of the soul is so much more important than the life of the body. Jesus said in John 6:63, 'It is the spirit that gives life; the flesh is useless. The words that I have spoken to you are spirit and life.' It is through water and the Spirit at our baptism that we first receive the new life of grace. Let us pray for a greater appreciation of the gift we received at our baptism.

Tuesday 29 April
John 3:7–15

Jesus said, 'Do not be astonished that I said to you, "You must be born from above." The wind blows where it chooses, and you hear the sound of it, but you do not know where it comes from or where it goes. So it is with everyone who is born of the Spirit.' Nicodemus said to him, 'How can these things be?' Jesus answered him, 'Are you a teacher of Israel, and yet you do not understand these things?

'Very truly, I tell you, we speak of what we know and testify to what we have seen; yet you do not receive our testimony. If I have told you about earthly things and you do not believe, how can you believe if I tell you about heavenly things? No one has ascended into heaven except the one who descended from heaven, the Son of Man. And just as Moses lifted up the serpent in the wilderness, so must the Son of Man be lifted up, that whoever believes in him may have eternal life.'

• Nicodemus, a Pharisee, knowing that his fellow leaders did not see things as he saw them, came to Jesus by night. He acknowledges that Jesus has come from God and that the signs he has given show God's presence. He is seeking the truth and wants to be on God's side. In living our faith we will often have to go against the tide of secularism that prevails in our world. Let us be genuine seekers of the truth and pray for the courage to live it.

Wednesday 30 April
John 3:16–21

'For God so loved the world that he gave his only Son, so that everyone who believes in him may not perish but may have eternal life.

'Indeed, God did not send the Son into the world to condemn the world, but in order that the world might be saved through him. Those who believe in him are not condemned; but those who do not believe are condemned already, because they have not believed in the name of the only Son of God. And this is the judgement, that the light has come into the world, and people loved darkness rather than light because their deeds were evil. For all who do evil hate the light and do not come to the light, so that their deeds may not be exposed. But those who do what is true come to the light, so that it may be clearly seen that their deeds have been done in God.'

- In John's Gospel we often see this contrast between light and darkness. Evil deeds are done in the dark and 'those who do what is true' act in the light. After Judas went out from the Last Supper to betray Jesus, there is a simple sentence: 'It was night.' From our daily newspapers we see the evidence of the darkness that is at the heart of humanity. Let us pray to follow Christ, who is the light of the world, so that we too might fulfil St Paul's urging, 'as lights in the world so you are to shine'.

Thursday 1 May
John 3:31–36

John said to his disciples, 'The one who comes from above is above all; the one who is of the earth belongs to the earth and speaks about earthly things. The one who comes from heaven is above all. He testifies to what he has seen and heard, yet no one accepts his testimony. Whoever has accepted his testimony has certified this, that God is true. He whom God has sent speaks the words of God, for he gives the Spirit without measure. The Father loves the Son and has placed all things in his hands. Whoever believes in the Son has eternal life; whoever disobeys the Son will not see life, but must endure God's wrath.'

- It was God the Father's plan to save us through his beloved Son whom he sent to us. We can never bypass Jesus Christ to get to the Father. Nor should we want to, since he has shared in our humanity and become our brother. Lord, help us to learn how to listen to you and to share our lives with you.

Friday 2 May
John 6:1–15

After this Jesus went to the other side of the Sea of Galilee, also called the Sea of Tiberias. A large crowd kept following him, because they saw the signs that he was doing for the sick. Jesus went up the mountain and sat down there with his disciples. Now the Passover, the festival of the Jews, was near. When he looked up and saw a large crowd coming towards him, Jesus said to Philip, 'Where are we to buy bread for these people to eat?' He said this to test him, for he himself knew what he was going to do.

Philip answered him, 'Six months' wages would not buy enough bread for each of them to get a little.' One of his disciples, Andrew, Simon Peter's brother, said to him, 'There is a boy here who has five barley loaves and two fish. But what are they among so many people?' Jesus said, 'Make the people sit down.' Now there was a great deal of grass in the place; so they sat down, about five thousand in all. Then Jesus took the loaves, and when he had given thanks, he distributed them to those who were seated; so also the fish, as much as they wanted. When they were satisfied, he told his disciples, 'Gather up the fragments left over, so that nothing may be lost.' So they gathered them up, and from the fragments of the five barley loaves, left by those who had eaten, they filled twelve baskets. When the people saw the sign that he had done, they began to say, 'This is indeed the prophet who is to come into the world.'

When Jesus realised that they were about to come and take him by force to make him king, he withdrew again to the mountain by himself.

* In this miracle of the feeding of the five thousand by the multiplication of the loaves and fishes, Jesus prefigures the much greater miracle of the feeding of the multitudes with his own body and blood down through the ages. It was Jesus who, on seeing the crowd, asks how to feed all these people. God knows that we have need of food for both our bodies and souls. Let us pray to trust him more to look after us.

* Our God is a generous God. For thousands of years our seas, without any input from us, have provided food for billions of creatures, including ourselves. Jesus tells us that the very hairs on our heads are counted. We give thanks for God's providential care for us.

Saturday 3 May
Ss Philip and James, Apostles
John 14:6–14

Jesus said to him, 'I am the way, and the truth, and the life. No one comes to the Father except through me. If you know me, you will know my Father also. From now on you do know him and have seen him.'

Philip said to him, 'Lord, show us the Father, and we will be satisfied.' Jesus said to him, 'Have I been with you all this time, Philip, and you still do not know me? Whoever has seen me has seen the Father. How can you say, "Show us the Father"? Do you not believe that I am in the Father and the Father is in me? The words that I say to you I do not speak on my own; but the Father who dwells in me does his works. Believe me that I am in the Father and the Father is in me; but if you do not, then believe me because of the works themselves. Very truly, I tell you, the one who believes in me will also do the works that I do and, in fact, will do greater works than these, because I am going to the Father. I will do whatever you ask in my name, so that the Father may be glorified in the Son. If in my name you ask me for anything, I will do it.'

- Only God can reveal God to us and he has done this by sending his Son Jesus to us in his human nature. We no longer have the physical presence of Jesus among us but he is still with us through his Spirit. We can see him through the eyes of faith and we truly meet him in prayer. He is now more available to each of us than when he walked this earth. This is now all mediated to us by our faith. Let us pray for a deeper faith.

Something to think and pray about each day this week:

Most weekends I say Mass in one of our local prisons. Usually about 10 to 15 per cent of the prisoners come to Mass, much more than you would expect. They divide roughly into three groups: the first are the 'cradle Catholics', the people who are meant to be there and the only ones who ever give any trouble; the second are members of various reformed traditions who didn't make it out of bed in time for the Anglican service; the third are people who look like they may never have been inside a church in their lives. Maybe the third group come out of curiosity, just to have something to do. They have no idea where they are or how to behave, but they are also the ones who listen the hardest.

I used to wonder why until one of them, Kolo, a Ghanaian, said to me, 'Father, coming into prison is a pretty clear sign in anyone's life that Plan A isn't really working. And if you have a Plan B that might work, they may or may not believe you, they may or may not agree with you, but they'll always give you a fair hearing.' That's the moment when I thought to myself, 'Yes, that's why I got up this morning. I knew there was a reason.' There is something very humbling in knowing that the people you are preaching to may well be hearing the Gospel for the very first time.

The men's task, no different from our own, is to be the presence of Christ within the place they live and work. I do not think there is any church that could not learn something from the Catholic Christian communities of the 'inside'.

Paul O'Reilly SJ,
Hope in All Things

The Presence of God

'Be still, and know that I am God!' Lord, your words lead us to the calmness and greatness of your presence.

Freedom

God is not foreign to my freedom. The Spirit breathes life into my most intimate desires, gently nudging me towards all that is good. I ask for the grace to let myself be enfolded by the Spirit.

Consciousness

Where do I sense hope, encouragement and growth in my life? By looking back over the past few months, I may be able to see which activities and occasions have produced rich fruit. If I do notice such areas, I will determine to give those areas both time and space in the future.

The Word

The word of God comes down to us through the Scriptures. May the Holy Spirit enlighten my mind and my heart to respond to the Gospel teachings. *(Please turn to the Scripture on the following pages. Inspiration points are there, should you need them. When you are ready, return here to continue.)*

Conversation

What is stirring in me as I pray? Am I consoled, troubled, left cold? I imagine Jesus standing or sitting at my side, and I share my feelings with him.

Conclusion

Glory be to the Father, and to the Son, and to the Holy Spirit,
As it was in the beginning, is now and ever shall be,
World without end. Amen.

Sunday 4 May
Third Sunday of Easter
John 21:1–19

After these things Jesus showed himself again to the disciples by the Sea of Tiberias; and he showed himself in this way. Gathered there together were Simon Peter, Thomas called the Twin, Nathanael of Cana in Galilee, the sons of Zebedee, and two others of his disciples. Simon Peter said to them, 'I am going fishing.' They said to him, 'We will go with you.' They went out and got into the boat, but that night they caught nothing.

Just after daybreak, Jesus stood on the beach; but the disciples did not know that it was Jesus. Jesus said to them, 'Children, you have no fish, have you?' They answered him, 'No.' He said to them, 'Cast the net to the right side of the boat, and you will find some.' So they cast it, and now they were not able to haul it in because there were so many fish. That disciple whom Jesus loved said to Peter, 'It is the Lord!' When Simon Peter heard that it was the Lord, he put on some clothes, for he was naked, and jumped into the lake. But the other disciples came in the boat, dragging the net full of fish, for they were not far from the land, only about a hundred yards off.

When they had gone ashore, they saw a charcoal fire there, with fish on it, and bread. Jesus said to them, 'Bring some of the fish that you have just caught.' So Simon Peter went aboard and hauled the net ashore, full of large fish, a hundred and fifty-three of them; and though there were so many, the net was not torn. Jesus said to them, 'Come and have breakfast.' Now none of the disciples dared to ask him, 'Who are you?' because they knew it was the Lord. Jesus came and took the bread and gave it to them, and did the same with the fish. This was now the third time that Jesus appeared to the disciples after he was raised from the dead.

When they had finished breakfast, Jesus said to Simon Peter, 'Simon son of John, do you love me more than these?' He said to him, 'Yes, Lord; you know that I love you.' Jesus said to him, 'Feed my lambs.' A second time he said to him, 'Simon son of John, do you love me?' He said to him, 'Yes, Lord; you know that I love you.' Jesus said to him, 'Tend my sheep.' He said to him the third time, 'Simon son of John, do you love me?' Peter felt hurt because he said to him the third time, 'Do you love me?' And he said to him, 'Lord, you know everything; you know that I love you.'

Jesus said to him, 'Feed my sheep. Very truly, I tell you, when you were younger, you used to fasten your own belt and to go wherever you wished. But when you grow old, you will stretch out your hands, and someone else will fasten a belt around you and take you where you do not wish to go.' (He said this to indicate the kind of death by which he would glorify God.) After this he said to him, 'Follow me.'

- We read here that Peter felt hurt that Jesus asked him a third time, 'Do you love me?' We know that Peter had already met Jesus alive and there had been a reconciliation, hence Peter's eagerness to jump out of the boat to come to Jesus. We too have been reconciled with God through his forgiveness of our sins. Let us be eager to meet him now in prayer.

- Peter said, 'Lord, you know everything.' We can say, 'Lord, you know too my lack of love, but you know that I want to love you.'

Monday 5 May
John 6:22–29
The next day the crowd that had stayed on the other side of the lake saw that there had been only one boat there. They also saw that Jesus had not got into the boat with his disciples, but that his disciples had gone away alone. Then some boats from Tiberias came near the place where they had eaten the bread after the Lord had given thanks. So when the crowd saw that neither Jesus nor his disciples were there, they themselves got into the boats and went to Capernaum looking for Jesus.

When they found him on the other side of the lake, they said to him, 'Rabbi, when did you come here?' Jesus answered them, 'Very truly, I tell you, you are looking for me, not because you saw signs, but because you ate your fill of the loaves. Do not work for the food that perishes, but for the food that endures for eternal life, which the Son of Man will give you. For it is on him that God the Father has set his seal.' Then they said to him, 'What must we do to perform the works of God?' Jesus answered them, 'This is the work of God, that you believe in him whom he has sent.'

- There is a selfishness in all of us. As children our prayers were filled with asking for things, but with maturity we recognise that we have different needs. We trust more and more in the love of our Father for us and that he will give us what is best for us. All prayer is about a relationship and our prayer time helps us to grow in this relationship. Our encounter with our Friend should be an experience of quiet joy and peace.

Tuesday 6 May
John 6:30–35

So they said to him, 'What sign are you going to give us then, so that we may see it and believe you? What work are you performing? Our ancestors ate the manna in the wilderness; as it is written, "He gave them bread from heaven to eat."' Then Jesus said to them, 'Very truly, I tell you, it was not Moses who gave you the bread from heaven, but it is my Father who gives you the true bread from heaven. For the bread of God is that which comes down from heaven and gives life to the world.' They said to him, 'Sir, give us this bread always.'

Jesus said to them, 'I am the bread of life. Whoever comes to me will never be hungry, and whoever believes in me will never be thirsty.'

- God fed his people in the wilderness for forty years with manna but those people are all dead. Although our bodies will die, the bread that Jesus gives us is himself and this bread will lead to eternal life, as it is the food of our souls. God the Father still feeds his people as we journey on our pilgrim way, by giving us his Son.
- In his Spiritual Exercises St Ignatius advises us continually to 'ponder with deep affection, how the Lord our God wishes to give himself to me'.

Wednesday 7 May
John 6:35–40

Jesus said to them, 'I am the bread of life. Whoever comes to me will never be hungry, and whoever believes in me will never be thirsty. But I said to you that you have seen me and yet do not believe. Everything that the Father gives me will come to me, and anyone who comes to me I will never drive away; for I have come down from heaven, not to do my own will, but the will of him who sent me. And this is the will of him who sent me, that I should lose nothing of all that he has given me, but raise it up on the last day. This is indeed the will of my Father, that all who see the Son and believe in him may have eternal life; and I will raise them up on the last day.'

- Jesus longs to draw all people to himself and to find life in him. This is what the Father wants too and it is why he sent his Son to us. It is again a call to believe in Jesus, and is the main reason John wrote his Gospel. It was Peter who said, 'Lord, to whom can we go? You have the words of eternal life. We have come to believe and know that you are the Holy One of God' (John 6:68–69). We pray to grow in our faith.

Thursday 8 May
John 6:44–51

Jesus said to them, 'No one can come to me unless drawn by the Father who sent me; and I will raise that person up on the last day. It is written in the prophets, "And they shall all be taught by God." Everyone who has heard and learned from the Father comes to me. Not that anyone has seen the Father except the one who is from God; he has seen the Father. Very truly, I tell you, whoever believes has eternal life. I am the bread of life. Your ancestors ate the manna in the wilderness, and they died. This is the bread that comes down from heaven, so that one may eat of it and not die. I am the living bread that came down from heaven. Whoever eats of this bread will live for ever; and the bread that I will give for the life of the world is my flesh.'

- In teaching us that Jesus is the bread of life St John emphasises that it is because Jesus has come from heaven, from his Father, that he is this bread of life. If his hearers don't accept his claim to come from God, then they won't accept that he can give them his flesh to eat. The question of who Jesus is becomes central here, as does the question about his divinity, with which people struggled in past centuries. Jesus continues to challenge us with, 'But who do you say that I am?' We can tell him again in prayer what he means to us.

Friday 9 May
John 6:52–59

The Jews then disputed among themselves, saying, 'How can this man give us his flesh to eat?' So Jesus said to them, 'Very truly, I tell you, unless you eat the flesh of the Son of Man and drink his blood, you have no life in you. Those who eat my flesh and drink my blood have eternal life, and I will raise them up on the last day; for my flesh is true food and my blood is true drink. Those who eat my flesh and drink my blood abide in me, and I in them. Just as the living Father sent me, and I live because of the Father, so whoever eats me will live because of me. This is the bread that came down from heaven, not like that which your ancestors ate, and they died. But the one who eats this bread will live for ever.' He said these things while he was teaching in the synagogue at Capernaum.

• For the Jews to be told that they must eat this man's flesh if they are to have life in the hereafter must have been, for many of them, a bridge too far. Jesus tells them that he will raise them up on the last day. But only God could do this, so in their eyes he is a blasphemer. Only faith in who Jesus is can enable us to receive his body and blood in the Eucharist.

• Our souls need to be nourished with the real food and drink of Christ's body and blood if they are to have his life in us. Our God always longs to give himself to us.

Saturday 10 May
John 6:60–69

When many of his disciples heard it, they said, 'This teaching is difficult; who can accept it?' But Jesus, being aware that his disciples were complaining about it, said to them, 'Does this offend you? Then what if you were to see the Son of Man ascending to where he was before? It is the spirit that gives life; the flesh is useless. The words that I have spoken to you are spirit and life. But among you there are some who do not believe.' For Jesus knew from the first who were the ones that did not believe, and who was the one that would betray him. And he said, 'For this reason I have told you that no one can come to me unless it is granted by the Father.'

Because of this many of his disciples turned back and no longer went about with him. So Jesus asked the twelve, 'Do you also wish to go away?' Simon Peter answered him, 'Lord, to whom can we go? You have the words of eternal life. We have come to believe and know that you are the Holy One of God.'

- The disciples of Jesus had seen him work many miracles, even raising the dead to life, and still found it difficult to have that complete trust in his words. For this man to claim that he was divine is indeed astonishing, but this is in fact is what Jesus was claiming. The church's later struggles over the divinity of Jesus show how difficult it was. Faith is a gift granted to us by God.

- Despite the opposition from the Jews and even his own disciples, Jesus never backed down from his statement about eating his body if we are to have life. Let us renew our faith in his divinity and his teaching.

Something to think and pray about each day this week:

Somebody was asked once, 'Why do you bother staying in the Church?' The answer, 'I've no other spiritual home.' We'll hear the word and return, often during Lent. We stray away from God in small journeys or big ones. We might not feel like returning, but when we do, we know we're home.

Church is home because it is where Jesus lives—not in the building only but in the people. Jesus lives with each of us, as 'he makes his home with us'. He lives also among us in community, 'wherever two or three are gathered in my name'.

We need to make the building and the spirit of our gatherings a home-coming. In our Church home we can hear each week of different needs and celebrations of the parish. We remember especially the sick, the dying and the ones gone before us.

Everyone helps build a home. The priest cannot do it alone. Can we ensure that every parish has a welcoming group, a group that keeps in touch with locals and plans future events?

Donal Neary SJ,
The Sacred Heart Messenger,
February 2023

The Presence of God
As I sit here, the beating of my heart, the ebb and flow of my breathing, the movements of my mind are all signs of God's ongoing creation of me. I pause for a moment and become aware of this presence of God within me.

Freedom
I will ask God's help to be free from my own preoccupations, to be open to God in this time of prayer, to come to know, love, and serve God more.

Consciousness
At this moment, Lord, I turn my thoughts to you. I will leave aside my chores and preoccupations. I will take rest and refreshment in your presence.

The Word
Now I turn to the Scripture set out for me this day. I read slowly over the words and see if any sentence or sentiment appeals to me. *(Please turn to the Scripture on the following pages. Inspiration points are there, should you need them. When you are ready, return here to continue.)*

Conversation
Begin to talk to Jesus about the Scripture you have just read. What part of it strikes a chord in you? Perhaps the words of a friend—or some story you have heard recently—will slowly rise to the surface of your consciousness. If so, does the story throw light on what the Scripture passage may be saying to you?

Conclusion
Glory be to the Father, and to the Son, and to the Holy Spirit,
As it was in the beginning, is now and ever shall be,
World without end. Amen.

Sunday 11 May
Fourth Sunday of Easter
John 10:27–30

Jesus answered, 'My sheep hear my voice. I know them, and they follow me. I give them eternal life, and they will never perish. No one will snatch them out of my hand. What my Father has given me is greater than all else, and no one can snatch it out of the Father's hand. The Father and I are one.'

- In both the Old Testament and the New, the image and theme of God as the shepherd is very common. The relationship between us and Jesus our Shepherd is very close. He will never forsake us and he will lead us to eternal life. Let us spend some time now in his company, and ask for complete trust in him.

Monday 12 May
John 10:1–10

Jesus said to them, 'Very truly, I tell you, anyone who does not enter the sheepfold by the gate but climbs in by another way is a thief and a bandit. The one who enters by the gate is the shepherd of the sheep. The gatekeeper opens the gate for him, and the sheep hear his voice. He calls his own sheep by name and leads them out. When he has brought out all his own, he goes ahead of them, and the sheep follow him because they know his voice. They will not follow a stranger, but they will run from him because they do not know the voice of strangers.' Jesus used this figure of speech with them, but they did not understand what he was saying to them.

So again Jesus said to them, 'Very truly, I tell you, I am the gate for the sheep. All who came before me are thieves and bandits; but the sheep did not listen to them. I am the gate. Whoever enters by me will be saved, and will come in and go out and find pasture. The thief comes only to steal and kill and destroy. I came that they may have life, and have it abundantly.'

- Jesus alone is the true gate of the sheepfold. There have been many other false prophets and false messiahs as Jesus prophesied there would be. Through fidelity to him in our prayer and in how we live our Christian lives we come gradually to recognise his voice in our hearts.

The language of God is silence and love, and we have to learn how to listen to him within us. It is all about being present to his Presence with us.

Tuesday 13 May
John 10:22–30

At that time the festival of the Dedication took place in Jerusalem. It was winter, and Jesus was walking in the temple, in the portico of Solomon. So the Jews gathered around him and said to him, 'How long will you keep us in suspense? If you are the Messiah, tell us plainly.' Jesus answered, 'I have told you, and you do not believe. The works that I do in my Father's name testify to me; but you do not believe, because you do not belong to my sheep. My sheep hear my voice. I know them, and they follow me. I give them eternal life, and they will never perish. No one will snatch them out of my hand. What my Father has given me is greater than all else, and no one can snatch it out of the Father's hand. The Father and I are one.'

• When the Jews question Jesus about his actions and teaching, it is clearly in the context of their own ideas of the Messiah. They ask him to tell them plainly if he is the Messiah. But when he tells them that he and the Father are one and backs this up by his miracles they refuse to believe in him. What of our own faith in his words? We can acknowledge he is God with our heads, but this has to make the long journey to our hearts, for it is out of our hearts that we live.

Wednesday 14 May
St Matthias, Apostle
John 15:9–17

Jesus said to them, 'As the Father has loved me, so I have loved you; abide in my love. If you keep my commandments, you will abide in my love, just as I have kept my Father's commandments and abide in his love. I have said these things to you so that my joy may be in you, and that your joy may be complete.

'This is my commandment, that you love one another as I have loved you. No one has greater love than this, to lay down one's life for one's friends. You are my friends if you do what I command you. I do not call you servants any longer, because the servant does not know what the master is doing; but I have called you friends, because I have made known to you everything that I have heard from my Father. You did not choose me but I chose you. And I appointed you to go and bear fruit, fruit that will last, so that the Father will give you whatever you ask him in my name. I am giving you these commands so that you may love one another.'

- Real love is proved in deeds rather than in words. Our Lord reduced all the commandments to two, and even these are really the one great commandment to love. It is out of the one heart that we love both God and neighbour. This is what our lives on earth are all about, namely to develop our own individual God-given capacity to love, so that in the end we can merge with God, who is Love.

- Jesus invites all of us into an intimate friendship with him. In this relationship he will reveal himself to us and he will share with us, as he did with his apostles, what he has learned from his Father. Prayer is always an invitation and it is up to us to respond to it.

Thursday 15 May
John 13:16–20

Jesus said to them, 'Very truly, I tell you, servants are not greater than their master, nor are messengers greater than the one who sent them. If you know these things, you are blessed if you do them. I am not speaking of all of you; I know whom I have chosen. But it is to fulfil the scripture, "The one who ate my bread has lifted his heel against me." I tell you this now, before it occurs, so that when it does occur, you may believe that I am he. Very truly, I tell you, whoever receives one whom I send receives me; and whoever receives me receives him who sent me.'

- It is one thing to know the truth and another thing to live it, but Jesus tells us we are blessed if we do. We have only one teacher, namely the Christ. Jesus our Master and Guide is always the headline for us. In the Second Week of the Spiritual Exercises the prayer that is repeated in every meditation is, 'Lord help me to know you more, so that I may love you more and follow you more closely in my life.'

Friday 16 May
John 14:1–6

Jesus said to them, 'Do not let your hearts be troubled. Believe in God, believe also in me. In my Father's house there are many dwelling-places. If it were not so, would I have told you that I go to prepare a place for you? And if I go and prepare a place for you, I will come again and will take you to myself, so that where I am, there you may be also. And you know the way to the place where I am going.' Thomas said to him, 'Lord, we do not know where you are going. How can we know the way?' Jesus said to him, 'I am the way, and the truth, and the life. No one comes to the Father except through me.'

• At the end of our life Jesus says he will come to take us home because the one who loves wants the beloved to be with them. In the meantime we strive to come to know and love this Friend we will have for all eternity.

Saturday 17 May
John 14:7–14

Jesus said to them, 'If you know me, you will know my Father also. From now on you do know him and have seen him.'

Philip said to him, 'Lord, show us the Father, and we will be satisfied.' Jesus said to him, 'Have I been with you all this time, Philip, and you still do not know me? Whoever has seen me has seen the Father. How can you say, 'Show us the Father'? Do you not believe that I am in the Father and the Father is in me? The words that I say to you I do not speak on my own; but the Father who dwells in me does his works. Believe me that I am in the Father and the Father is in me; but if you do not, then believe me because of the works themselves. Very truly, I tell you, the one who believes in me will also do the works that I do and, in fact, will do greater works than these, because I am going to the Father. I will do whatever you ask in my name, so that the Father may be glorified in the Son. If in my name you ask me for anything, I will do it.'

- In Jesus our God has come to be with us and to help us to come to know him. We read in Hosea 6:6, 'For I desire steadfast love and not sacrifice, the knowledge of God rather than burnt-offerings.' As human beings we come to know *about* a person by reading about them, but we only know a person by personally meeting them. This why the encounter with God in prayer is so important.

- It is always God who does the work in prayer by revealing himself to us. Our part is to come before him in faith and give him our time and attention as best we can. We leave the rest to him.

Something to think and pray about each day this week:

Most people carry burdens of one kind or another, very often imposed by others. Jesus is clear that our relationship with God is not intended to be another burden on a burdened people. Among the burdens Jesus carried was that imposed by those who were hostile to all he stood for. He was at his most burdened as he hung from the cross. He carried that burden so that he could help us to carry our own burdens. Through his life, death and resurrection, he released into the world the power of God's love, the power of the Holy Spirit, a lifegiving, enabling power. Saint Paul was burdened as he wrote to the church in Philippi from his prison cell. Yet he could say, 'I can do all things through him who strengthens me' (Philippians 4:13). The Lord strengthens us to carry our burdens so that we can help to carry those of others. As Paul writes to the churches of Galatia, 'Bear one another's burdens, and in this way you will fulfil the law of Christ' (Galatians 6:2). The law of Christ, which is the law of love, the fruit of the Spirit, is not about imposing burdens but about lifting them.

Martin Hogan,
The Word Is Near You, on Your Lips and in Your Heart

The Presence of God

At any time of the day or night we can call on Jesus. He is always waiting, listening for our call. What a wonderful blessing. No phone needed, no e-mails, just a whisper.

Freedom

If God were trying to tell me something, would I know? If God were reassuring me or challenging me, would I notice? I ask for the grace to be free of my own preoccupations and open to what God may be saying to me.

Consciousness

Help me, Lord, become more conscious of your presence. Teach me to recognise your presence in others. Fill my heart with gratitude for the times your love has been shown to me through the care of others.

The Word

In this expectant state of mind, please turn to the text for the day with confidence. Believe that the Holy Spirit is present and may reveal whatever the passage has to say to you. Read reflectively, listening with a third ear to what may be going on in your heart. *(Please turn to the Scripture on the following pages. Inspiration points are there, should you need them. When you are ready, return here to continue.)*

Conversation

Conversation requires talking and listening. As I talk to Jesus, may I also learn to pause and listen. I picture the gentleness in his eyes and the love in his smile. I can be totally honest with Jesus as I tell him my worries and cares. I will open my heart to Jesus as I tell him my fears and doubts. I will ask him to help me place myself fully in his care, knowing that he always desires good for me.

Conclusion

I thank God for these moments we have spent together and for any insights I have been given concerning the text.

Sunday 18 May
Fifth Sunday of Easter
John 13:31–35

When he had gone out, Jesus said, 'Now the Son of Man has been glorified, and God has been glorified in him. If God has been glorified in him, God will also glorify him in himself and will glorify him at once. Little children, I am with you only a little longer. You will look for me; and as I said to the Jews so now I say to you, "Where I am going, you cannot come." I give you a new commandment, that you love one another. Just as I have loved you, you also should love one another. By this everyone will know that you are my disciples, if you have love for one another.'

- The time is approaching for Jesus to finish his mission on earth and return to the Father who sent him. His apostles must remain behind but they will follow him later. His final instruction to them is that they should love one another just as he has loved them. This will be how Christians are to be recognised in the future. If we were to be on trial as Christians, would we be convicted on this score?

Monday 19 May
John 14:21–26

Jesus said, 'They who have my commandments and keep them are those who love me; and those who love me will be loved by my Father, and I will love them and reveal myself to them.' Judas (not Iscariot) said to him, 'Lord, how is it that you will reveal yourself to us, and not to the world?' Jesus answered him, 'Those who love me will keep my word, and my Father will love them, and we will come to them and make our home with them. Whoever does not love me does not keep my words; and the word that you hear is not mine, but is from the Father who sent me.

'I have said these things to you while I am still with you. But the Advocate, the Holy Spirit, whom the Father will send in my name, will teach you everything, and remind you of all that I have said to you.'

- Those who love Jesus by keeping his commandments will be loved by the Father, and both Jesus and his Father will come and live in us. Wherever the Father and Jesus are, there also is the Holy Spirit. I often think this must be one of the best-kept secrets in our Catholic religion, namely that the Trinity live in and make their home in us. We find it so difficult to live in some awareness of this. Let us ask God to reveal this to us more and more.

Tuesday 20 May
John 14:27–31

Jesus said to them, 'Peace I leave with you; my peace I give to you. I do not give to you as the world gives. Do not let your hearts be troubled, and do not let them be afraid. You heard me say to you, "I am going away, and I am coming to you." If you loved me, you would rejoice that I am going to the Father, because the Father is greater than I. And now I have told you this before it occurs, so that when it does occur, you may believe. I will no longer talk much with you, for the ruler of this world is coming. He has no power over me; but I do as the Father has commanded me, so that the world may know that I love the Father. Rise, let us be on our way.'

- From our daily news it would appear that our world has never been in more need of peace. We all long for it, but the world will only find it in Christ. It is his special gift to his followers and it will take away distress and fear from their lives. Let us pray for this peace now.

- We should be happy for Jesus and rejoice with him that he is now about to go home to his beloved Father. For him to have left heaven and come to walk our human journey for our sake showed extraordinary love. We give him thanks in prayer and ask for some of his courage and love.

Wednesday 21 May
John 15:1–8

Jesus said to them, 'I am the true vine, and my Father is the vine-grower. He removes every branch in me that bears no fruit. Every branch that bears fruit he prunes to make it bear more fruit. You have already been cleansed by the word that I have spoken to you. Abide in me as I abide in you. Just as the branch cannot bear fruit by itself unless it abides in the vine, neither can you unless you abide in me. I am the vine, you are the branches. Those who abide in me and I in them bear much fruit, because apart from me you can do nothing. Whoever does not abide in me is thrown away like a branch and withers; such branches are gathered, thrown into the fire, and burned. If you abide in me, and my words abide in you, ask for whatever you wish, and it will be done for you. My Father is glorified by this, that you bear much fruit and become my disciples.'

- We are called to bear much fruit and so to become his disciples. Without the branches there will be no fruit on the vine. Like those in the parable of the talents, we are expected by God to use our gifts for the benefit of others and so to be fruitful. Christ needs his apostles and his followers to grow the kingdom of God on earth. Let us pray not to be found wanting in this work.

- One doesn't have to be a gardener to appreciate that the image of the vine and the branches is one of the most powerful for those who seek to have Christ at the centre of their lives. Every breath we take, every step, is only because of God, who holds everything in existence. We ask in humility for a deep appreciation of this and for gratitude.

Thursday 22 May
John 15:9–11

Jesus said to his disciples, 'As the Father has loved me, so I have loved you; abide in my love. If you keep my commandments, you will abide in my love, just as I have kept my Father's commandments and abide in his love. I have said these things to you so that my joy may be in you, and that your joy may be complete.'

- Jesus Christ, yesterday, today, the same for ever! That Jesus loves us with the same infinite love that his Father had for him should be a source of great joy and hope for us. We were made for joy and too often in the past our religion became a killjoy. Jesus found all of his joy in his Father and he wants us to share in this joy. Teilhard de Chardin SJ wrote, 'Joy is an infallible sign of the presence of God.' Where do we find our joy and what blocks us from it?

Friday 23 May
John 15:12–17

Jesus said to them, 'This is my commandment, that you love one another as I have loved you. No one has greater love than this, to lay down one's life for one's friends. You are my friends if you do what I command you. I do not call you servants any longer, because the servant does not know what the master is doing; but I have called you friends, because I have made known to you everything that I have heard from my Father. You did not choose me but I chose you. And I appointed you to go and bear fruit, fruit that will last, so that the Father will give you whatever you ask him in my name. I am giving you these commands so that you may love one another.'

- In our call to love one another, we are invited by the words and example of Jesus to be willing to give up even our lives for our brothers and sisters. In human history there are countless men and women who have done this, the greatest act of love. I am not thinking primarily of the multitude of martyrs but of the unknown men and women who died for the sake of others. Let us pray for the courage to love as they did.

Saturday 24 May
John 15:18–21

Jesus said to his disciples, 'If the world hates you, be aware that it hated me before it hated you. If you belonged to the world, the world would love you as its own. Because you do not belong to the world, but I have chosen you out of the world—therefore the world hates you. Remember the word that I said to you, "Servants are not greater than their master." If they persecuted me, they will persecute you; if they kept my word, they will keep yours also. But they will do all these things to you on account of my name, because they do not know him who sent me.'

- If the world loves and praises you, be very much on your guard, because the world does not see as God sees. It is both fickle and false and not particularly interested in the truth. From the beginning of Christianity the world has persecuted Christ and all who belong to him because they live by different values. We are called to help make it a different world and to grow God's kingdom on earth.

Something to think and pray about each day this week:

For the Church, Mary is a model of faith, charity and discipleship. In the Magnificat, there is a fourth quality that underpins each of the others. Mary is seen as a model of desire: she helps us to recognise what it is that we want.

The Magnificat begins: 'My soul proclaims the greatness of the Lord and my spirit rejoices in God my Saviour' (Luke 1:46–47). We note that Mary does not say that she is happy. Happiness might be a contentment that we find for a time in life, whereas joy has a restless quality, a longing. There is an expectation of what we seek, an aching, wonderful anticipation. It's a bit like the experience of children on Christmas Eve, waiting to see what Father Christmas will bring. I can recall this experience of anticipation much more sharply than any present I ever opened.

I imagine that Mary was telling Elizabeth of a Christmas Eve experience much more intense and fuller than that of children waiting for presents. That's because she longs for what she bears in her womb: God. She welcomes her mission to bring the Saviour to birth. Now she desires always what her Son and God our Father desire in her life, and through her for the life of God's people.

Every time we reach a milestone or get our hands on something we've been after for some time, the afterglow of satisfaction doesn't last long. Something else always comes along to entice us. The reason this happens is that we don't just want beautiful things, we want beauty itself; we don't want this or that good thing, we want goodness itself. In short, we want God. God is our deepest desire.

Eamonn Walls SJ,
The Sacred Heart Messenger,
May 2023

The Presence of God
Dear Jesus, as I call on you today, I realise that often I come asking for favours. Today I'd like just to be in your presence. Draw my heart in response to your love.

Freedom
It is so easy to get caught up with the trappings of wealth in this life. Grant, O Lord, that I may be free from greed and selfishness. Remind me that the best things in life are free: love, laughter, caring and sharing.

Consciousness
How am I really feeling? Lighthearted? Heavyhearted? I may be very much at peace, happy to be here. Equally, I may be frustrated, worried or angry. I acknowledge how I really am. It is the real me whom the Lord loves.

The Word
Lord Jesus, you became human to communicate with me. You walked and worked on this earth. You endured the heat and struggled with the cold. All your time on this earth was spent in caring for humanity. You healed the sick, you raised the dead. Most important of all, you saved me from death. *(Please turn to the Scripture on the following pages. Inspiration points are there, should you need them. When you are ready, return here to continue.)*

Conversation
Do I notice myself reacting as I pray with the word of God? Do I feel challenged, comforted, angry? Imagining Jesus sitting or standing by me, I speak out my feelings, as one trusted friend to another.

Conclusion
Glory be to the Father, and to the Son, and to the Holy Spirit,
As it was in the beginning, is now and ever shall be,
World without end. Amen.

Sunday 25 May
Sixth Sunday of Easter
John 14:23–29

Jesus answered him, 'Those who love me will keep my word, and my Father will love them, and we will come to them and make our home with them. Whoever does not love me does not keep my word; and the word that you hear is not mine, but is from the Father who sent me.

'I have said these things to you while I am still with you. But the Advocate, the Holy Spirit, whom the Father will send in my name, will teach you everything, and remind you of all that I have said to you. Peace I leave with you; my peace I give to you. I do not give to you as the world gives. Do not let your hearts be troubled, and do not let them be afraid. You heard me say to you, "I am going away, and I am coming to you." If you loved me, you would rejoice that I am going to the Father, because the Father is greater than I. And now I have told you this before it occurs, so that when it does occur, you may believe.'

• Jesus tells his disciples that he is about to go away but that he will come back to them. It is through the sending of the Holy Spirit that he will come back to be with them. Help us, Lord, to know how to listen to your Spirit, who is within us.

• More than forty times in the Gospels Jesus tells us not to be afraid. The gift of his peace is to help ease our troubled hearts.

Monday 26 May
John 15:26—16:4

Jesus said, 'When the Advocate comes, whom I will send to you from the Father, the Spirit of truth who comes from the Father, he will testify on my behalf. You also are to testify because you have been with me from the beginning.

'I have said these things to you to keep you from stumbling. They will put you out of the synagogues. Indeed, an hour is coming when those who kill you will think that by doing so they are offering worship to God. And they will do this because they have not known the Father or me. But I have said these things to you so that when their hour comes you may remember that I told you about them.

'I did not say these things to you from the beginning, because I was with you.'

- Jesus foretells the persecution that his followers will endure at the hands of those who do not know God. The Holy Spirit will help his disciples and all of us to witness to Jesus, and he will give us whatever words are needed for this. We see this again and again in the lives of the martyrs. Let us pray for the courage to persevere in our faith.

Tuesday 27 May
John 16:5–11

He said to them, 'But now I am going to him who sent me; yet none of you asks me, "Where are you going?" But because I have said these things to you, sorrow has filled your hearts. Nevertheless, I tell you the truth: it is to your advantage that I go away, for if I do not go away, the Advocate will not come to you; but if I go, I will send him to you. And when he comes, he will prove the world wrong about sin and righteousness and judgement: about sin, because they do not believe in me; about righteousness, because I am going to the Father and you will see me no longer; about judgement, because the ruler of this world has been condemned.'

- Jesus is about to return to the One who sent him. He knows his disciples will miss him and be sorrowful, but together with his Father he will send them the Holy Spirit who will support and comfort them. It is through faith that we know him now and can truly meet our risen Lord in prayer.

Wednesday 28 May
John 16:12–15

Jesus said to his disciples, 'I still have many things to say to you, but you cannot bear them now. When the Spirit of truth comes, he will guide you into all the truth; for he will not speak on his own, but will speak whatever he hears, and he will declare to you the things that are to come. He will glorify me, because he will take what is mine and declare it to you. All that the Father has is mine. For this reason I said that he will take what is mine and declare it to you.'

- The first disciples of Jesus were largely simple, uneducated men. That they found it hard to take in what Jesus was saying to them is an understatement. Even today we still find it difficult; it has taken centuries of study and brilliant minds to help us grow in our understanding of Jesus' words. We need the guarantee of the Holy Spirit that our church will not err in what it teaches. We give thanks for the gift of the Holy Spirit and pray to be open to his leading us in the truth.

Thursday 29 May
John 16:16–20

Jesus said to them, 'A little while, and you will no longer see me, and again a little while, and you will see me.' Then some of his disciples said to one another, 'What does he mean by saying to us, "A little while, and you will no longer see me, and again a little while, and you will see me"; and "Because I am going to the Father"?' They said, 'What does he mean by this "a little while"? We do not know what he is talking about.' Jesus knew that they wanted to ask him, so he said to them, 'Are you discussing among yourselves what I meant when I said, "A little while, and you will no longer see me, and again a little while, and you will see me"? Very truly, I tell you, you will weep and mourn, but the world will rejoice; you will have pain, but your pain will turn into joy.'

- The suffering and death of Jesus on the cross was truly a shattering experience for his disciples. In the Jewish understanding at that time it meant that God had abandoned Jesus and thus refuted all that Jesus had done and taught. The Resurrection changed all that and transformed their mourning and their confusion into joy and the courage to go out and proclaim him. For the Christian the norm in our lives should be a quiet joy and confidence in the God who loves and accompanies us on our pilgrim way. Let us find this now in our prayer time with him.

Friday 30 May
John 16:20–23

Jesus said to them, 'Very truly, I tell you, you will weep and mourn, but the world will rejoice; you will have pain, but your pain will turn into joy. When a woman is in labour, she has pain, because her hour has come.

But when her child is born, she no longer remembers the anguish because of the joy of having brought a human being into the world. So you have pain now; but I will see you again, and your hearts will rejoice, and no one will take your joy from you. On that day you will ask nothing of me. Very truly, I tell you, if you ask anything of the Father in my name, he will give it to you.'

• In our temporal world nothing remains the same and all things are passing. Because we live in time, every moment and every moment of pain will pass, never to return. There will, of course, be new moments and new pain. Jesus promises, through his resurrection, that we will see him again and this will lead to rejoicing and, in the end, a permanent happiness.

Saturday 31 May
The Visitation of the BVM
Luke 1:39–56

In those days Mary set out and went with haste to a Judean town in the hill country, where she entered the house of Zechariah and greeted Elizabeth. When Elizabeth heard Mary's greeting, the child leapt in her womb. And Elizabeth was filled with the Holy Spirit and exclaimed with a loud cry, 'Blessed are you among women, and blessed is the fruit of your womb. And why has this happened to me, that the mother of my Lord comes to me? For as soon as I heard the sound of your greeting, the child in my womb leapt for joy. And blessed is she who believed that there would be a fulfilment of what was spoken to her by the Lord.'

MARY'S SONG OF PRAISE
  And Mary said,
  'My soul magnifies the Lord,
      and my spirit rejoices in God my Saviour,
  for he has looked with favour on the lowliness of his servant.
      Surely, from now on all generations will call me blessed;
  for the Mighty One has done great things for me,
      and holy is his name.
  His mercy is for those who fear him
      from generation to generation.

He has shown strength with his arm;
> he has scattered the proud in the thoughts of their hearts.

He has brought down the powerful from their thrones,
> and lifted up the lowly;

he has filled the hungry with good things,
> and sent the rich away empty.

He has helped his servant Israel,
> in remembrance of his mercy,

according to the promise he made to our ancestors,
> to Abraham and to his descendants for ever.'

And Mary remained with her for about three months and then returned to her home.

- Mary in her kindness goes to be of help to her aged cousin Elizabeth who is pregnant. Elizabeth, inspired by the Holy Spirit, praises Mary for her believing in the words of the message brought to her from God by the angel Gabriel. Mary is our great model of faith as she accepts whatever will happen to her.

- Mary is also a model of gratitude to God as she acknowledges that all comes from the hands of God. 'For the Mighty One has done great things for me.' She prays in a great spirit of humility, recognising her own littleness. 'Mary, our Mother, help us to learn from you and to follow your Son Jesus Christ in faith and humility.'

Something to think and pray about each day this week:

All of us are wounded, damaged, broken and troubled; everyone needs healing. The healing required isn't always physical. Sometimes it can be emotional scarring, hurt feelings, grief, and the healing of relationships and memories. It's fascinating how fragile, weak and vulnerable we are.

Many people experience low self-esteem, feelings of inferiority, no self-worth and no confidence. They feel they are no good. The way to healing of this kind is through words of praise, encouragement and affirmation.

Wherever you go today, plant words of encouragement and just watch what happens. The greatest healing therapy of all is friendship. There is more healing done among friends over a cup of tea than in many counselling rooms. We need to take care of one another.

The secret is to learn to live with and cope with the pain and realise it is okay not to be okay. It is not what happens to us but how we deal with what happens. When life hands you a lemon turn it into lemonade. A little bit of encouragement, a kind word and a listening ear can heal.

Terence Harrington OFMCap,
The Sacred Heart Messenger,
December 2023

The Presence of God
Dear Jesus, I come to you today longing for your presence. I desire to love you as you love me. May nothing ever separate me from you.

Freedom
Lord, grant me the grace to have freedom of the Spirit. Cleanse my heart and soul so that I may live joyously in your love.

Consciousness
Where am I with God? With others? Do I have something to be grateful for? Then I give thanks. Is there something I am sorry for? Then I ask forgiveness.

The Word
The word of God comes down to us through the Scriptures. May the Holy Spirit enlighten my mind and my heart to respond to the Gospel teachings. *(Please turn to the Scripture on the following pages. Inspiration points are there, should you need them. When you are ready, return here to continue.)*

Conversation
How has God's word moved me? Has it left me cold? Has it consoled me or moved me to act in a new way? I imagine Jesus standing or sitting beside me; I turn and share my feelings with him.

Conclusion
I thank God for these moments we have spent together and for any insights I have been given concerning the text.

Sunday 1 June
The Ascension of the Lord
Luke 24:46–53

And he said to them, 'Thus it is written, that the Messiah is to suffer and to rise from the dead on the third day, and that repentance and forgiveness of sins is to be proclaimed in his name to all nations, beginning from Jerusalem. You are witnesses of these things. And see, I am sending upon you what my Father promised; so stay here in the city until you have been clothed with power from on high.'

Then he led them out as far as Bethany, and, lifting up his hands, he blessed them. While he was blessing them, he withdrew from them and was carried up into heaven. And they worshipped him, and returned to Jerusalem with great joy; and they were continually in the temple blessing God.

- St Augustine reminds us that Jesus came to earth without leaving heaven and he returned to heaven without leaving our earth. As God, Jesus was always in heaven, but truly walked this earth, like us in all things but sin.

- After Jesus was taken up into heaven the disciples who saw this were filled with joy. In a new way, through all that Jesus achieved, heaven has become joined to earth and his presence remains the source of our joy and consolation.

Monday 2 June
John 16:29–33

His disciples said, 'Yes, now you are speaking plainly, not in any figure of speech! Now we know that you know all things, and do not need to have anyone question you; by this we believe that you came from God.' Jesus answered them, 'Do you now believe? The hour is coming, indeed it has come, when you will be scattered, each one to his home, and you will leave me alone. Yet I am not alone because the Father is with me. I have said this to you, so that in me you may have peace. In the world you face persecution. But take courage; I have conquered the world!'

- By his victory over sin and death Christ has overcome every obstacle and difficulty that we can encounter on this earth. He has won every grace that we can ever need. We share fully in his victory and we already know that where he has gone we will go too, if we remain faithful to him. In this is the source of our peace and our courage.

Tuesday 3 June
John 17:1–11

After Jesus had spoken these words, he looked up to heaven and said, 'Father, the hour has come; glorify your Son so that the Son may glorify you, since you have given him authority over all people, to give eternal life to all whom you have given him. And this is eternal life, that they may know you, the only true God, and Jesus Christ whom you have sent. I glorified you on earth by finishing the work that you gave me to do. So now, Father, glorify me in your own presence with the glory that I had in your presence before the world existed.

'I have made your name known to those whom you gave me from the world. They were yours, and you gave them to me, and they have kept your word. Now they know that everything you have given me is from you; for the words that you gave to me I have given to them, and they have received them and know in truth that I came from you; and they have believed that you sent me. I am asking on their behalf; I am not asking on behalf of the world, but on behalf of those whom you gave me, because they are yours. All mine are yours, and yours are mine; and I have been glorified in them. And now I am no longer in the world, but they are in the world, and I am coming to you. Holy Father, protect them in your name that you have given me, so that they may be one, as we are one.'

- This chapter in John has been called the priestly prayer of Jesus as he prays to his Father for his own who have believed in him. In Luke 22:32 we read that Jesus had prayed for Peter that his faith would not fail. Jesus shows by his example that we should make intercessory prayer for ourselves and others. Let us ask him now for our own needs and the needs of others.

- Our asking in faith is an acknowledgment that everything comes from God and so this too is praise of God.

Wednesday 4 June
John 17:11–19

Jesus said, 'And now I am no longer in the world, but they are in the world, and I am coming to you. Holy Father, protect them in your name that you have given me, so that they may be one, as we are one. While I was with them, I protected them in your name that you have given me. I guarded them, and not one of them was lost except the one destined to be lost, so that the scripture might be fulfilled. But now I am coming to you, and I speak these things in the world so that they may have my joy made complete in themselves. I have given them your word, and the world has hated them because they do not belong to the world, just as I do not belong to the world. I am not asking you to take them out of the world, but I ask you to protect them from the evil one. They do not belong to the world, just as I do not belong to the world. Sanctify them in the truth; your word is truth. As you have sent me into the world, so I have sent them into the world. And for their sakes I sanctify myself, so that they also may be sanctified in truth.'

- Jesus prays for the spirit of unity and joy among his brethren. He has already told them that he does not call them servants, but friends, because he has shared with them everything his Father has taught him. If he is their friend, then they should be friends with one another. How united are we with those we live with and meet? Do we live in a spirit of unity and joy?

- Jesus asks his Father to protect his disciples from the evil one. At the end of the Our Father we can pray, 'Do not bring us to the time of trial, but rescue us from the evil one.'

Thursday 5 June
John 17:20–26

Jesus said to the Father, 'I ask not only on behalf of these, but also on behalf of those who will believe in me through their word, that they may all be one. As you, Father, are in me and I am in you, may they also be in us, so that the world may believe that you have sent me. The glory that you have given me I have given them, so that they may be one, as we are one, I in them and you in me, that they may become completely one, so that the world may know that you have sent me and have loved them even as you have loved me. Father, I desire that those also, whom you have given me, may be with me where I am, to see my glory, which you have given me because you loved me before the foundation of the world.

'Righteous Father, the world does not know you, but I know you; and these know that you have sent me. I made your name known to them, and I will make it known, so that the love with which you have loved me may be in them, and I in them.'

- In this section Jesus prays for all of us who have come to believe in him through the teaching of his apostles. The theme of unity among his followers is stressed and it is to be the sign to others that Jesus was truly sent by the Father. Sadly, this unity was shattered by the various schisms that have taken place, and instead we have the scandal of our disunity. Let us pray for unity among us and in our church.

- The unity of Jesus and his Father comes from their dwelling in each other through the Holy Spirit of Love uniting them. The source of our unity should come from our attachment to Christ who loves us and has made his home in us. Our love for him should include a love for all that he loves. Let us pray in humility for this grace.

Friday 6 June
John 21:15–19

When they had finished breakfast, Jesus said to Simon Peter, 'Simon son of John, do you love me more than these?' He said to him, 'Yes, Lord; you know that I love you.' Jesus said to him, 'Feed my lambs.' A second time he said to him, 'Simon son of John, do you love me?' He said to him, 'Yes, Lord; you know that I love you.' Jesus said to him, 'Tend my sheep.' He said to him the third time, 'Simon son of John, do you love me?' Peter felt hurt because he said to him the third time, 'Do you love me?' And he said to him, 'Lord, you know everything; you know that I love you.' Jesus said to him, 'Feed my sheep. Very truly, I tell you, when you were younger, you used to fasten your own belt and to go wherever you wished. But when you grow old, you will stretch out your hands, and someone else will fasten a belt around you and take you where you do not wish to go.' (He said this to indicate the kind of death by which he would glorify God.) After this he said to him, 'Follow me.'

- After Jesus asks Peter the third time, 'Do you love me?' Peter changes his reply. This time he says, 'Lord, you know everything; you know that I love you.' And included in this can be, 'Lord, you know also my lack of love; but you know too that I want to love you.' Our own situation can be like this before the Lord.

- Peter felt hurt that Jesus asked him a third time, 'Do you love me?' We know that Peter had already met Jesus after the Resurrection and there had been a reconciliation, hence Peter's eagerness to jump out of the boat to come to Jesus. We too have been reconciled with God through his forgiveness of our sins. Let us be eager to meet him now in prayer with grateful hearts.

Saturday 7 June
John 20:21–25

Jesus said to them again, 'Peace be with you. As the Father has sent me, so I send you.' When he had said this, he breathed on them and said to them, 'Receive the Holy Spirit. If you forgive the sins of any, they are forgiven them; if you retain the sins of any, they are retained.'

But Thomas (who was called the Twin), one of the twelve, was not with them when Jesus came. So the other disciples told him, 'We have seen the Lord.' But he said to them, 'Unless I see the mark of the nails in his hands, and put my finger in the mark of the nails and my hand in his side, I will not believe.'

- Only God can forgive sins, but in his public life and mission Jesus showed that he had authority from his Father to forgive sins. He now gives this same authority to his apostles who act in his name. In the sacrament of reconciliation it is important that we hear clearly the words of absolution used by the priest, who acts in the name of the Father and the Son and the Holy Spirit. This can be a moment of awe for us and of deep gratitude for God's forgiveness.

Something to think and pray about each day this week:

In any year there are thirty-three or thirty-four Sundays in Ordinary Time, depending on the date of Easter. The term 'ordinary' in English means something that is not special or distinctive. Yet Ordinary Time makes up most of the liturgical year, and in our Church calendar is far from unimportant and uninteresting. The time is called 'ordinary' because it is numbered. The Latin word *'ordinalis'* refers to numbers in a series. The weeks of Ordinary Time represent the ordered life of the Church, when we are not feasting or fasting. Ordinary Time follows the Christmas season and ends when Lent begins. A second portion begins after Pentecost and leads us into Advent.

The story of the life, mission, message and ministry of Jesus unfolds for us during Ordinary Time: miracles, parables, the calling of the Twelve, the Sermon on the Mount, the gift of the Bread of Life, all connect us to the Gospel way that we are invited to follow.

Like all the liturgical seasons, Ordinary Time is meant to be lived! We are not passive receptors of the liturgy or the Christian life. We are called to be full, active participants in the varied life of Jesus, bringing the ordinariness of our lives to our liturgy.

Ordinary Time is anything but ordinary or run-of-the-mill time. It is the time that God does extraordinary things in the lives of ordinary people. It is a time when we become more aware that the everyday moments of our ordinary lives are charged with God's presence.

We all try to follow that Gospel way in the ordinariness of the here and now, in the muddle, the mess, the mystery and the mundane. This is where God is.

John Cullen,
The Sacred Heart Messenger,
June 2023

The Presence of God

Dear Jesus, today I call on you, but not to ask for anything. I'd like only to dwell in your presence. May my heart respond to your love.

Freedom

God my creator, you gave me life and the gift of freedom. Through your love I exist in this world. May I never take the gift of life for granted. May I always respect others' right to life.

Consciousness

I ask how I am today. Am I particularly tired, stressed or anxious? If any of these characteristics apply, can I try to let go of the concerns that disturb me?

The Word

The word of God comes down to us through the Scriptures. May the Holy Spirit enlighten my mind and my heart to respond to the Gospel teachings. *(Please turn to the Scripture on the following pages. Inspiration points are there, should you need them. When you are ready, return here to continue.)*

Conversation

I begin to talk with Jesus about the Scripture I have just read. What part of it strikes a chord in me? Perhaps the words of a friend—or some story I have heard recently—will rise to the surface in my consciousness. If so, does the story throw light on what the Scripture passage may be saying to me?

Conclusion

Glory be to the Father, and to the Son, and to the Holy Spirit,
As it was in the beginning, is now and ever shall be,
World without end. Amen.

Sunday 8 June
Pentecost Sunday
John 14:15–16, 23–26

Jesus said to his disciples, 'If you love me, you will keep my commandments. And I will ask the Father, and he will give you another Advocate, to be with you for ever.' . . . Jesus answered him [Philip], 'Those who love me will keep my word, and my Father will love them, and we will come to them and make our home with them. Whoever does not love me does not keep my words; and the word that you hear is not mine, but is from the Father who sent me.

'I have said these things to you while I am still with you. But the Advocate, the Holy Spirit, whom the Father will send in my name, will teach you everything, and remind you of all that I have said to you.'

• Jesus understands our humanity so well and knows how poor our memories can be, especially when, like the apostles, we grow older. To guide his church and preserve her in the truth, he promises to send the gift of the Holy Spirit. The Holy Spirit will lead us into all truth, but we need to trust in this promise of our Lord and be faithful to the teaching of the church.

Monday 9 June
Mary, Mother of the Church
John 19:25–34

Meanwhile, standing near the cross of Jesus were his mother, and his mother's sister, Mary the wife of Clopas, and Mary Magdalene. When Jesus saw his mother and the disciple whom he loved standing beside her, he said to his mother, 'Woman, here is your son.' Then he said to the disciple, 'Here is your mother.' And from that hour the disciple took her into his own home.

After this, when Jesus knew that all was now finished, he said (in order to fulfil the scripture), 'I am thirsty.' A jar full of sour wine was standing there. So they put a sponge full of the wine on a branch of hyssop and held it to his mouth. When Jesus had received the wine, he said, 'It is finished.' Then he bowed his head and gave up his spirit.

Since it was the day of Preparation, the Jews did not want the bodies left on the cross during the sabbath, especially because that sabbath was a day of great solemnity. So they asked Pilate to have the legs of the crucified men broken and the bodies removed. Then the soldiers came and broke the legs of the first and of the other who had been crucified with him. But when they came to Jesus and saw that he was already dead, they did not break his legs. Instead, one of the soldiers pierced his side with a spear, and at once blood and water came out.

- At that moment, as Mary stood by the cross, to lose her only Son and to take on being the Mother of all his brothers and sisters must have been a huge ask. As in all of her life, she accepted this willingly. As mother of the church she was there with the infant church, gathered in prayer just after the ascension of her Son to heaven. Let us pray with her now for the church.

- In the various apparitions of Mary down through the centuries she has shown an extraordinary care and love for all people and not just those who are believers.

Tuesday 10 June
Matthew 5:13–16

Jesus taught them, saying, 'You are the salt of the earth; but if salt has lost its taste, how can its saltiness be restored? It is no longer good for anything, but is thrown out and trampled under foot.

'You are the light of the world. A city built on a hill cannot be hidden. No one after lighting a lamp puts it under the bushel basket, but on the lampstand, and it gives light to all in the house. In the same way, let your light shine before others, so that they may see your good works and give glory to your Father in heaven.'

- Jesus, the light of the world, came to shed light on a world in moral darkness. Each of us is called, as St Paul reminds us, to shine as lights in our world today. We can never overestimate the power of example for good or ill. Let us pray especially for parents and those with the responsibility of bringing up children.

Wednesday 11 June
St Barnabas, Apostle
Matthew 5:17–19

Jesus said, 'Do not think that I have come to abolish the law or the prophets; I have come not to abolish but to fulfil. For truly I tell you, until heaven and earth pass away, not one letter, not one stroke of a letter, will pass from the law until all is accomplished. Therefore, whoever breaks one of the least of these commandments, and teaches others to do the same, will be called least in the kingdom of heaven; but whoever does them and teaches them will be called great in the kingdom of heaven.'

• The law and the prophets were part of God's plan to save and guide us. But his Son Jesus, who came to fulfil the law, is now our Master and guide. Let us listen to him.

Thursday 12 June
Matthew 5:20–26

Jesus taught them, saying, 'For I tell you, unless your righteousness exceeds that of the scribes and Pharisees, you will never enter the kingdom of heaven.

'You have heard that it was said to those of ancient times, "You shall not murder"; and "whoever murders shall be liable to judgement." But I say to you that if you are angry with a brother or sister, you will be liable to judgement; and if you insult a brother or sister, you will be liable to the council; and if you say, "You fool", you will be liable to the hell of fire. So when you are offering your gift at the altar, if you remember that your brother or sister has something against you, leave your gift there before the altar and go; first be reconciled to your brother or sister, and then come and offer your gift. Come to terms quickly with your accuser while you are on the way to court with him, or your accuser may hand you over to the judge, and the judge to the guard, and you will be thrown into prison. Truly I tell you, you will never get out until you have paid the last penny.'

• Jesus came to reconcile us to God and to one another. His final word to us was that we were to love one another, and his great desire was that we be united. This involves forgiveness and being reconciled with each other, and then we can worship God as one people.

Friday 13 June
Matthew 5:27–32

Jesus said, 'You have heard that it was said, "You shall not commit adultery." But I say to you that everyone who looks at a woman with lust has already committed adultery with her in his heart. If your right eye causes you to sin, tear it out and throw it away; it is better for you to lose one of your members than for your whole body to be thrown into hell. And if your right hand causes you to sin, cut it off and throw it away; it is better for you to lose one of your members than for your whole body to go into hell.

'It was also said, "Whoever divorces his wife, let him give her a certificate of divorce." But I say to you that anyone who divorces his wife, except on the ground of unchastity, causes her to commit adultery; and whoever marries a divorced woman commits adultery.'

- Jesus came among us with a teaching that was new, the new wine of the kingdom of God, and he taught with authority, an authority from God the Father who sent him. He called us to honour and respect the dignity of every human person, for we are all the children of God. Our world would be a very different place if this were practised by all. What of our own attitudes to those who are different from us in gender, race or religion?

Saturday 14 June
Matthew 5:33–37

Jesus said to them, 'Again, you have heard that it was said to those of ancient times, "You shall not swear falsely, but carry out the vows you have made to the Lord." But I say to you, Do not swear at all, either by heaven, for it is the throne of God, or by the earth, for it is his footstool, or by Jerusalem, for it is the city of the great King. And do not swear by your head, for you cannot make one hair white or black. Let your word be "Yes, Yes" or "No, No"; anything more than this comes from the evil one.'

- In our present world the truth has had a difficult time. Pilate asked Jesus at his trial, 'What is truth?' and he did not bother to wait for a reply. Many of those in authority in our times show different meanings for the truth, and have even invented 'alternative facts'. So our 'yes' now often means 'no' and vice versa. Let us pray for our world and that our leaders become people of honesty and integrity.

Something to think and pray about each day this week:

Dachau was closer to the city of Munich than I realised. For some reason I thought I'd be lost in the countryside—out of sight and out of mind. On the tour I discovered that it was built in the early 1930s. It was built not to incarcerate any particular ethnic group, but anyone who disagreed publicly with Hitler's policies. This changed with time.

The tour was both sombre and intriguing. There was a lot to remember, but one part of the tour I'll never forget. At the end of the tour the guide described the days when the German soldiers left the camp, leaving the prisoners in their billets. Once the prisoners became aware that the soldiers were gone they wanted to leave the camp, but the Allied officers in charge of the prisoners insisted that they stayed where they were. Days later the Allied troops found their way into the camp and liberated those prisoners. The troops were shocked at what they found.

The Allied camp commanders were right. If the prisoners made their way on to open roads they might have died or might also have been attacked by the advancing troops, who would not have known from a distance who the approaching people were.

I stood in silence for a while as the tour was ending. A still small voice made its way into my soul and said 'it is often more difficult to manage freedom than captivity'. This still small voice and the image of that prison camp has come back to me on many occasions when I faced changes, with their accompanying fresh challenges and opportunities.

Alan Hilliard,
Dipping into Life: 40 Reflections for a Fragile Earth

The Presence of God
Dear Lord, as I come to you today, fill my heart, my whole being, with the wonder of your presence. Help me remain receptive to you as I put aside the cares of this world. Fill my mind with your peace.

Freedom
Lord, grant me the grace to be free from the excesses of this life. Let me not get caught up with the desire for wealth. Keep my heart and mind free to love and serve you.

Consciousness
I exist in a web of relationships: links to nature, people, God. I trace out these links, giving thanks for the life that flows through them. Some links are twisted or broken; I may feel regret, anger, disappointment. I pray for the gift of acceptance and forgiveness.

The Word
God speaks to each of us individually. I listen attentively to hear what he is saying to me. Read the text a few times, then listen. *(Please turn to the Scripture on the following pages. Inspiration points are there, should you need them. When you are ready, return here to continue.)*

Conversation
Jesus, you speak to me through the words of the Gospels. May I respond to your call today. Teach me to recognise your hand at work in my daily living.

Conclusion
I thank God for these moments we have spent together and for any insights I have been given concerning the text.

Sunday 15 June
The Most Holy Trinity
John 16:12–15

Jesus said to them, 'I still have many things to say to you, but you cannot bear them now. When the Spirit of truth comes, he will guide you into all the truth; for he will not speak on his own, but will speak whatever he hears, and he will declare to you the things that are to come. He will glorify me, because he will take what is mine and declare it to you. All that the Father has is mine. For this reason I said that he will take what is mine and declare it to you.'

- The Holy Spirit is the Spirit of Love between the Father and the Son. As the Spirit of Truth he continues the work of Jesus in teaching and enlightening us as Jesus promised us. Let us learn how to listen to him and ask him to lead our leaders and ourselves in the path of justice and truth.

Monday 16 June
Matthew 5:38–42

Jesus said, 'You have heard that it was said, "An eye for an eye and a tooth for a tooth." But I say to you, Do not resist an evildoer. But if anyone strikes you on the right cheek, turn the other also; and if anyone wants to sue you and take your coat, give your cloak as well; and if anyone forces you to go one mile, go also the second mile. Give to everyone who begs from you, and do not refuse anyone who wants to borrow from you.'

- The human race has made slow progress in its understanding of the ways of God. In the primitive understanding of God's people, it was okay for God to get angry and vengeful. But God, who never changes, did not do that. Here Jesus clearly reveals to us that our God is a God of mercy and love for all. And Jesus calls us to 'Be merciful, just as your Father is merciful' (Luke 6:36).

Tuesday 17 June
Matthew 5:43–48

Jesus said, 'You have heard that it was said, "You shall love your neighbour and hate your enemy." But I say to you, Love your enemies and pray for those who persecute you, so that you may be children of your Father in heaven; for he makes his sun rise on the evil and on the good, and sends rain on the righteous and on the unrighteous. For if you love those who love you, what reward do you have? Do not even the tax-collectors do the same? And if you greet only your brothers and sisters, what more are you doing than others? Do not even the Gentiles do the same? Be perfect, therefore, as your heavenly Father is perfect.'

• Our Christian religion was meant to bring to our world, love, joy, peace, forgiveness, kindness, courage, perseverance, all the gifts of the Holy Spirit. We are called to strive to 'Be perfect, therefore, as your Heavenly Father is perfect'. The demands of the kingdom are indeed high, but what a different world it would be if we could even aim at this standard. Let us pray to do our own little part in bringing about a new world, where hatred is dissolved in mercy and where kindness rules.

Wednesday 18 June
Matthew 6:1–6, 16–18

Jesus said to them, 'Beware of practising your piety before others in order to be seen by them; for then you have no reward from your Father in heaven.

'So whenever you give alms, do not sound a trumpet before you, as the hypocrites do in the synagogues and in the streets, so that they may be praised by others. Truly I tell you, they have received their reward. But when you give alms, do not let your left hand know what your right hand is doing, so that your alms may be done in secret; and your Father who sees in secret will reward you.

'And whenever you pray, do not be like the hypocrites; for they love to stand and pray in the synagogues and at the street corners, so that they may be seen by others. Truly I tell you, they have received their reward. But whenever you pray, go into your room and shut the door and pray to your Father who is in secret; and your Father who sees in secret will reward you. . . .

'And whenever you fast, do not look dismal, like the hypocrites, for they disfigure their faces so as to show others that they are fasting. Truly I tell you, they have received their reward. But when you fast, put oil on your head and wash your face, so that your fasting may be seen not by others but by your Father who is in secret; and your Father who sees in secret will reward you.'

- Our Lord likened the Pharisees to whitened tombs, as they prayed and fasted to be thought well of by others. We worship God and we pray to him because it is right and just, since we owe everything to him. It is a privilege to be allowed to meet and speak to our Creator, and every prayer from our hearts receives its reward.

Thursday 19 June
Matthew 6:7–15

Jesus taught them, 'When you are praying, do not heap up empty phrases as the Gentiles do; for they think that they will be heard because of their many words. Do not be like them, for your Father knows what you need before you ask him.

'Pray then in this way:
Our Father in heaven,
hallowed be your name.
Your kingdom come.
Your will be done,
    on earth as it is in heaven.
Give us this day our daily bread.
And forgive us our debts,
    as we also have forgiven our debtors.
And do not bring us to the time of trial,
    but rescue us from the evil one.

For if you forgive others their trespasses, your heavenly Father will also forgive you; but if you do not forgive others, neither will your Father forgive your trespasses.'

- Prayer is not a matter of using words but of meeting a Person. When we come to Jesus in prayer do we really value his company? Do we express this using words from our hearts or do we merely recite words we have learned off in childhood? Pope Francis has written, 'For each disciple it is essential to spend time with the Master, to listen to his words and to learn from him always . . . So let me ask you: Are there moments when you place yourself quietly in the Lord's presence, when you calmly spend time with him, when you bask in his gaze?'

Friday 20 June
Matthew 6:19–23

Jesus said, 'Do not store up for yourselves treasures on earth, where moth and rust consume and where thieves break in and steal; but store up for yourselves treasures in heaven, where neither moth nor rust consumes and where thieves do not break in and steal. For where your treasure is, there your heart will be also.

'The eye is the lamp of the body. So, if your eye is healthy, your whole body will be full of light; but if your eye is unhealthy, your whole body will be full of darkness. If then the light in you is darkness, how great is the darkness!'

- Where your treasure is, there your heart will be also. We can all ask ourselves if our hearts are set on acquiring the things of earth or the things of heaven. So often the Gospels challenge us to look beyond the visible and to seek out what endures. In our human frailty we become fixated by the visible and look for our security in amassing wealth. Without God we have nothing and can do nothing. We pray, 'Lord, let me see again.'

Saturday 21 June
Matthew 6:24–34

Jesus said to them, 'No one can serve two masters; for a slave will either hate the one and love the other, or be devoted to the one and despise the other. You cannot serve God and wealth.

'Therefore I tell you, do not worry about your life, what you will eat or what you will drink, or about your body, what you will wear. Is not life more than food, and the body more than clothing? Look at the birds of the air; they neither sow nor reap nor gather into barns, and yet your heavenly Father feeds them. Are you not of more value than they? And can any of you by worrying add a single hour to your span of life? And why do you worry about clothing? Consider the lilies of the field, how they grow; they neither toil nor spin, yet I tell you, even Solomon in all his glory was not clothed like one of these. But if God so clothes the grass of the field, which is alive today and tomorrow is thrown into the oven, will he not much more clothe you—you of little faith? Therefore do not worry, saying, "What will we eat?" or "What will we drink?" or "What will we wear?" For it is the Gentiles who strive for all these things; and indeed your heavenly Father knows that you need all these things. But strive first for the kingdom of God and his righteousness, and all these things will be given to you as well.

'So do not worry about tomorrow, for tomorrow will bring worries of its own. Today's trouble is enough for today.'

- We should pray often on this passage in St Matthew. 'If you worry you die, and if you don't worry you die. So why worry?' The birds of the air and the lilies of the field have not the faintest notion of what it is to worry. And look at them. They get on fine. Anthony de Mello once said, 'If you have made it to this day you have had all the love you need for your happiness.' We need to pray often for a greater trust in the providence of our God.

Something to think and pray about each day this week:

The popular image of a mystic is of someone who spends a lot of time alone in solitary prayer, cut off from the distracting world. The mysticism of nature, however, is a gift for everyone in the audience! You may not be a person who spends much time alone with God but as you contemplate nature are you growing in wonder, in awareness that every bit of creation is singing a song to you, and is inviting you to catch on to its melody? Do feelings of awe arise in you as you spend little moments now and then marvelling at what nature keeps coming up with? When you worry about the messiness of life can you envelop it in gratitude for the steadiness of nature's laws of growth? Can you hope that perhaps God hasn't abandoned this chaotic world of ours to its own destructive devices but is creatively at work to bring it to its intended beauty?

The Pope says:

To sense each creature singing the hymn of its existence is to live joyfully in God's love and hope. This contemplation of creation allows us to discover in each thing a teaching which God wishes to hand on to us, since for the believer, to contemplate creation is to hear a message, to listen to a paradoxical and silent voice. (*Laudato Si'*, 85)

To be a mystic, then, you don't have to be a person whose knees are wearing out—though God draws some hearts to that silent intimacy. All you have to do is look long and lovingly at creation, and let it speak to your heart.

Brian Grogan SJ,
Finding God in a Leaf: The Mysticism of Laudato Si'

The Presence of God

'I am standing at the door, knocking,' says the Lord. What a wonderful privilege that the Lord of all creation desires to come to me. I welcome his presence.

Freedom

I will ask God's help to be free from my own preoccupations, to come to know, love and serve God more.

Consciousness

In God's loving presence I unwind the past day, starting from now and looking back, moment by moment. I gather in all the goodness and light, in gratitude. I attend to the shadows and what they say to me, seeking healing, courage, forgiveness.

The Word

Now I turn to the Scripture set out for me this day. I read slowly over the words and see if any sentence or sentiment appeals to me. *(Please turn to the Scripture on the following pages. Inspiration points are there, should you need them. When you are ready, return here to continue.)*

Conversation

Sometimes I wonder what I might say if I were to meet you in person, Lord. I think I might say 'Thank you' because you are always there for me.

Conclusion

I thank God for these moments we have spent together and for any insights I have been given concerning the text.

Sunday 22 June
The Most Holy Body and Blood of Christ
Luke 9:11–17

When the crowds found out about it, they followed him; and he welcomed them, and spoke to them about the kingdom of God, and healed those who needed to be cured.

The day was drawing to a close, and the twelve came to him and said, 'Send the crowd away, so that they may go into the surrounding villages and countryside, to lodge and get provisions; for we are here in a deserted place.' But he said to them, 'You give them something to eat.' They said, 'We have no more than five loaves and two fish—unless we are to go and buy food for all these people.' For there were about five thousand men. And he said to his disciples, 'Make them sit down in groups of about fifty each.' They did so and made them all sit down. And taking the five loaves and the two fish, he looked up to heaven, and blessed and broke them, and gave them to the disciples to set before the crowd. And all ate and were filled. What was left over was gathered up, twelve baskets of broken pieces.

- When Jesus feeds the five thousand in this remote place we are reminded of how God fed his people with manna in the desert. On this feast of Corpus Christi it also speaks to us of the much greater miracle of Jesus giving us his own body and blood for more than two thousand years. St Ignatius urges us to 'always ponder with deep affection how the Lord wishes to give himself to us'.

- A gift that is not received and welcomed loses its power to bring us closer to the giver. At the holy sacrifice of the Mass do we receive our Lord with warmth and gratitude?

Monday 23 June
Matthew 7:1–5

Jesus said to them, 'Do not judge, so that you may not be judged. For with the judgement you make you will be judged, and the measure you give will be the measure you get. Why do you see the speck in your neighbour's eye, but do not notice the log in your own eye? Or how can you say to your neighbour, "Let me take the speck out of your eye", while the log is in your own eye? You hypocrite, first take the log out of your own eye, and then you will see clearly to take the speck out of your neighbour's eye.'

- In all our dealings with others one of the clearest commands of the Lord is that we must never, ever, judge our neighbour. We can judge their actions but never the person, because we simply cannot get inside someone else's head, or know the background to their actions. The Lord alone can see all of this. We pray to look to our own behaviour and to how we keep the Lord's command to love one another as he has loved us.

Tuesday 24 June
The Nativity of St John the Baptist
Luke 1:57–66, 80

Now the time came for Elizabeth to give birth, and she bore a son. Her neighbours and relatives heard that the Lord had shown his great mercy to her, and they rejoiced with her.

On the eighth day they came to circumcise the child, and they were going to name him Zechariah after his father. But his mother said, 'No; he is to be called John.' They said to her, 'None of your relatives has this name.' Then they began motioning to his father to find out what name he wanted to give him. He asked for a writing-tablet and wrote, 'His name is John.' And all of them were amazed. Immediately his mouth was opened and his tongue freed, and he began to speak, praising God. Fear came over all their neighbours, and all these things were talked about throughout the entire hill country of Judea. All who heard them pondered them and said, 'What then will this child become?' For, indeed, the hand of the Lord was with him. . . .

The child grew and became strong in spirit, and he was in the wilderness until the day he appeared publicly to Israel.

- The name 'John' is of Hebrew origin and means, 'God is gracious'. Both Elizabeth and Zechariah recognised that God had indeed been gracious to them. Our God is continuously gracious to each of us, loving us with an everlasting love.

- John the Baptist had a special mission from God and so we read 'the hand of the Lord was with him', which means that all the graces he needed for his mission were given to him. Each of us too has a mission from God that is unique to ourselves, and all the graces we need will be given to us also. Pope Francis reminds us that we are all missionaries.

Wednesday 25 June
Matthew 7:15–20

Jesus said to them, 'Beware of false prophets, who come to you in sheep's clothing but inwardly are ravenous wolves. You will know them by their fruits. Are grapes gathered from thorns, or figs from thistles? In the same way, every good tree bears good fruit, but the bad tree bears bad fruit. A good tree cannot bear bad fruit, nor can a bad tree bear good fruit. Every tree that does not bear good fruit is cut down and thrown into the fire. Thus you will know them by their fruits.'

- We are defined by what we do, and so our deeds are either good or bad. 'My disciples are those who *do* the will of my Father', Jesus said. Pope Francis says we should discern what is the will of God for us. Since God expects us to do his will each day then it cannot be too difficult to find it using our normal intelligence and the circumstances in which we find ourselves. Do I follow the call to love in every situation?

Thursday 26 June
Matthew 7:21–29

Jesus said to them, 'Not everyone who says to me, "Lord, Lord", will enter the kingdom of heaven, but only one who does the will of my Father in heaven. On that day many will say to me, "Lord, Lord, did we not prophesy in your name, and cast out demons in your name, and do many deeds of power in your name?" Then I will declare to them, "I never knew you; go away from me, you evildoers."

'Everyone then who hears these words of mine and acts on them will be like a wise man who built his house on rock. The rain fell, the floods came, and the winds blew and beat on that house, but it did not fall, because it had been founded on rock. And everyone who hears these words of mine and does not act on them will be like a foolish man who built his house on sand. The rain fell, and the floods came, and the winds blew and beat against that house, and it fell—and great was its fall!'

Now when Jesus had finished saying these things, the crowds were astounded at his teaching, for he taught them as one having authority, and not as their scribes.

- Unfortunately, far too many people build not only their houses but also their lives on very poor foundations. As Christians we are invited to build our lives on the rock that is Christ. St Paul reminds us that God has said, 'I will never leave you or forsake you' (Hebrews 13:5). If our lives are firmly placed on this foundation then no storms or difficulties can defeat us. Let us pray for this great grace.

Friday 27 June
The Most Sacred Heart of Jesus
Luke 15:3–7

So he told them this parable: 'Which one of you, having a hundred sheep and losing one of them, does not leave the ninety-nine in the wilderness and go after the one that is lost until he finds it? When he has found it, he lays it on his shoulders and rejoices. And when he comes home, he calls together his friends and neighbours, saying to them, "Rejoice with me, for I have found my sheep that was lost." Just so, I tell you, there will be more joy in heaven over one sinner who repents than over ninety-nine righteous people who need no repentance.'

- That the Good Shepherd would leave the rest of the flock and go in search of the lost one shows the immense love of the Lord for every soul. In the image of the Sacred Heart shown to St Margaret Mary the heart is on fire with love for all of us. St Margaret wrote that the Lord had said to her, 'Behold the heart that has so loved humankind and received in return only coldness and indifference.' Love always calls for a response. How can I now best respond to his love in my prayer?

Saturday 28 June
John 17:20–26

Jesus said to the Father, 'I ask not only on behalf of these, but also on behalf of those who will believe in me through their word, that they may all be one. As you, Father, are in me and I am in you, may they also be in us, so that the world may believe that you have sent me. The glory that you have given me I have given them, so that they may be one, as we are one, I in them and you in me, that they may become completely one, so that the world may know that you have sent me and have loved them even as you have loved me. Father, I desire that those also, whom you have given me, may be with me where I am, to see my glory, which you have given me because you loved me before the foundation of the world.

'Righteous Father, the world does not know you, but I know you; and these know that you have sent me. I made your name known to them, and I will make it known, so that the love with which you have loved me may be in them, and I in them.'

- Unity with one another and with the Father and the Son and the Holy Spirit was to be a sign to the world that Jesus was sent from God to teach us to love one another. The scandal of our disunity in the Christian family has done immense harm and it continues down to the present day. Let us pray for unity among us.

- To know God leads to loving him. Jesus reveals to us what he is like so that the love of God may be in us. Then the Trinity will come and make their home in us.

Something to think and pray about each day this week:

When you look at the priest in your parish, think about *who* you see rather than *what* you see. The *who* is the man that at some stage in his life felt that God wanted him to become a priest. The *who* is one that knows uncertainty, doubt and disappointment, but one who still finds faith rewarding and ministry his chosen way of life. The *who* is one that appreciates a kind word and absolutely needs the support of your prayers. If we see the priest as *what*, he becomes a function, a dispenser of services and something just to be contacted when a service is required. When Jesus sent out the twelve, he knew that the people needed them just as much as they needed the people. That truth remains unchanged.

Think now of the priests you know, the religious you know, and remember their interactions with you in life. Moments of sadness and grief, moments of uncertainty or fear, sickness or tension—moments too of celebration and joy, where was he or she? Chances are, very close to you and yours. Maybe when you hear criticism of priests or religious, when sincere, accept and understand it and empathise, but maybe when you feel it is not justified you could say, 'That hasn't been my experience'—in this, at least, you are acknowledging the path chosen in response to God's call because Jesus noticed people and felt they needed ministers in their midst. Maybe have a word after Mass; a smile, handshake and, 'Thanks for that, we're glad you are here among us. By the way, I said a prayer for you this weekend.'

Vincent Sherlock,
Let Advent Be Advent

The Presence of God
I pause for a moment and think of the love and the grace that God showers on me. I am created in the image and likeness of God; I am God's dwelling place.

Freedom
Lord, you granted me the great gift of freedom. In these times, O Lord, grant that I may be free from any form of racism or intolerance. Remind me that we are all equal in your loving eyes.

Consciousness
Knowing that God loves me unconditionally, I can afford to be honest about how I am. How has the day been, and how do I feel now? I share my feelings openly with the Lord.

The Word
I take my time to read the word of God slowly, a few times, allowing myself to dwell on anything that strikes me. *(Please turn to the Scripture on the following pages. Inspiration points are there, should you need them. When you are ready, return here to continue.)*

Conversation
Sometimes I wonder what I might say if I were to meet you in person, Lord. I think I might say 'Thank you' because you are always there for me.

Conclusion
I thank God for these moments we have spent together and for any insights I have been given concerning the text.

Sunday 29 June
Ss Peter and Paul, Apostles
Matthew 16:13–19

Now when Jesus came into the district of Caesarea Philippi, he asked his disciples, 'Who do people say that the Son of Man is?' And they said, 'Some say John the Baptist, but others Elijah, and still others Jeremiah or one of the prophets.' He said to them, 'But who do you say that I am?' Simon Peter answered, 'You are the Messiah, the Son of the living God.' And Jesus answered him, 'Blessed are you, Simon son of Jonah! For flesh and blood has not revealed this to you, but my Father in heaven. And I tell you, you are Peter, and on this rock I will build my church, and the gates of Hades will not prevail against it. I will give you the keys of the kingdom of heaven, and whatever you bind on earth will be bound in heaven, and whatever you loose on earth will be loosed in heaven.'

- Peter answers for the disciples that Jesus is 'the Messiah, the Son of the living God'. Only God can reveal God to us and so Jesus praises his Father for revealing this to Peter. The question that Jesus asks of his disciples, 'But who do you say that I am?' is one of the key questions that Jesus asks of all his followers. Who am I for you? What do I mean to you? Let us answer this question now in our prayer to the Lord.

- As we reflect and pray on this question, we can ask ourselves, 'Do I really like Jesus?' which is another way of asking, 'How well do I know him?' We can only love someone we know, and we are all called to love Jesus and to follow him. Although we can never understand God we can come to know and love him through his Son Jesus Christ.

Monday 30 June
Matthew 8:18–22

Now when Jesus saw great crowds around him, he gave orders to go over to the other side. A scribe then approached and said, 'Teacher, I will follow you wherever you go.' And Jesus said to him, 'Foxes have holes, and birds of the air have nests; but the Son of Man has nowhere to lay his head.' Another of his disciples said to him, 'Lord, first let me go and bury my father.' But Jesus said to him, 'Follow me, and let the dead bury their own dead.'

- There are sayings in the Gospels that are not intended to be taken literally, and 'let the dead bury their own dead' is one of them. Our Lord is really saying here that true discipleship costs and makes demands. God must always come first wherever there is a conflict of interest. Jesus always calls us to love in every situation in which we find ourselves. Let us pray for the gift of true discernment.

Tuesday 1 July
Matthew 8:23–27

And when he got into the boat, his disciples followed him. A gale arose on the lake, so great that the boat was being swamped by the waves; but he was asleep. And they went and woke him up, saying, 'Lord, save us! We are perishing!' And he said to them, 'Why are you afraid, you of little faith?' Then he got up and rebuked the winds and the sea; and there was a dead calm. They were amazed, saying, 'What sort of man is this, that even the winds and the sea obey him?'

- God is always with us, holding us in his hands and loving us. We have only to trust totally in him. Let us pray for a deeper trust.
- The question of who Jesus really is, is one that we can often bring to prayer and talk to Jesus about. To the disciples he looked like any other human being. 'What kind of man is this?' they asked. We pray to see beyond the visible to the hidden reality.

Wednesday 2 July
Matthew 8:28–34

When he came to the other side, to the country of the Gadarenes, two demoniacs coming out of the tombs met him. They were so fierce that no one could pass that way. Suddenly they shouted, 'What have you to do with us, Son of God? Have you come here to torment us before the time?' Now a large herd of swine was feeding at some distance from them. The demons begged him, 'If you cast us out, send us into the herd of swine.' And he said to them, 'Go!' So they came out and entered the swine; and suddenly, the whole herd rushed down the steep bank into the lake and perished in the water. The swineherds ran off, and on going into the town, they told the whole story about what had happened to the demoniacs. Then the whole town came out to meet Jesus; and when they saw him, they begged him to leave their neighbourhood.

- The evil spirits always recognised the authority of Jesus, and they ask his permission to enter the pigs. The townspeople ask Jesus to go away. They are closed to the gift he wishes to give them and are not willing to engage with him. How much do I value the Good News? Is it to me the pearl of great price, worth giving up everything for? Let us engage with Jesus about this.

Thursday 3 July
St Thomas, Apostle
John 20:24–29

But Thomas (who was called the Twin), one of the twelve, was not with them when Jesus came. So the other disciples told him, 'We have seen the Lord.' But he said to them, 'Unless I see the mark of the nails in his hands, and put my finger in the mark of the nails and my hand in his side, I will not believe.'

A week later his disciples were again in the house, and Thomas was with them. Although the doors were shut, Jesus came and stood among them and said, 'Peace be with you.' Then he said to Thomas, 'Put your finger here and see my hands. Reach out your hand and put it in my side. Do not doubt but believe.' Thomas answered him, 'My Lord and my God!' Jesus said to him, 'Have you believed because you have seen me? Blessed are those who have not seen and yet have come to believe.'

- How often over the centuries have people said to themselves, Oh, if only I could see God once or hear his voice. But God is Spirit and cannot be seen. The Jews saw a man and, given their background in the Old Testament, could have had no idea that this was God. St Paul reminds us in Philippians that although we once saw Jesus in the flesh that is not how we see him now. Now we see and hear him only through our faith. And we are blessed because we can now give Jesus joy through our faith in him. 'Lord, we believe, help our unbelief!'

Friday 4 July
Matthew 9:9–13

As Jesus was walking along, he saw a man called Matthew sitting at the tax booth; and he said to him, 'Follow me.' And he got up and followed him.

And as he sat at dinner in the house, many tax-collectors and sinners came and were sitting with him and his disciples. When the Pharisees saw this, they said to his disciples, 'Why does your teacher eat with tax-collectors and sinners?' But when he heard this, he said, 'Those who are well have no need of a physician, but those who are sick. Go and learn what this means, "I desire mercy, not sacrifice." For I have come to call not the righteous but sinners.'

- The tax collectors and sinners felt totally accepted in the company of Jesus. God has always loved the sinner and hated the sin. Jesus came to bring salvation to all of us. Do I, as the Pharisees did, judge others and condemn them?

- Here Jesus recalls the prophet Hosea: 'For I desire steadfast love and not sacrifices, the knowledge of God rather than burnt-offerings' (6:6). Jesus came to seek out the lost sheep. Our God is a God of mercy and love and we need to keep this before us constantly, for we are all sinners in need of his mercy. When Pope Francis called for the Year of Mercy he said that this was God's other name.

Saturday 5 July
Matthew 9:14–17

Then the disciples of John came to him, saying, 'Why do we and the Pharisees fast often, but your disciples do not fast?' And Jesus said to them, 'The wedding-guests cannot mourn as long as the bridegroom is with them, can they? The days will come when the bridegroom is taken away from them, and then they will fast. No one sews a piece of unshrunk cloth on an old cloak, for the patch pulls away from the cloak, and a worse tear is made. Neither is new wine put into old wineskins; otherwise, the skins burst, and the wine is spilled, and the skins are destroyed; but new wine is put into fresh wineskins, and so both are preserved.'

- New skins for the new wine of the kingdom of God. There is a time for everything under heaven, a time to be joyful, a time to mourn, a time to fast and a time to refrain from fasting. In the church's liturgical year there are times marked out for rejoicing, and times for doing penance.

- Fasting can not only be helpful to our bodies but it can train us to be more disciplined in how we live our Christian lives. A prayer life requires fidelity, perseverance and discipline. Unless we take up our cross daily we cannot be Christ's disciples.

6–12 July 2025

Something to think and pray about each day this week:

It is striking that widows tend to have a very positive profile in the gospels. In one of the parables that Jesus spoke, a widow keeps coming to a corrupt judge for the justice she is entitled to, until she finally gets him to take her seriously. Jesus told this parable as an encouragement to us to keep praying always and not lose heart. On another occasion, as Jesus was in the Temple in Jerusalem, he saw a widow put two copper coins, all she had to live on, into the Temple treasury. Jesus draws his disciples' attention to her as a model of complete self-giving to God. In one of the gospels we find a widow named Anna who never left the Temple, serving God night and day with fasting and prayer. Widows were vulnerable in the time of Jesus. If they didn't have children, they were especially vulnerable. It may have been their very vulnerable status which led them to entrust themselves to God. If they had no one to rely on, they could rely on God. Being somewhat alone in the world, there was a space in their lives which was filled with God. Anna was in constant prayerful communion with God. It was only fitting that she should happen to come by just at the time that Mary and Joseph brought their child into the Temple and Simeon was announcing who this child would become. Later on, the adult Jesus would say, 'Ask and it will be given to you; search and you will find.' Anna was someone who sought the Lord in prayer, and one day she found the one whom she sought. Having found him, she shared him with others. She spoke about the child to all who were looking forward to the deliverance of Jerusalem. We have much to learn from this widow. She reminds us that the Lord comes to those who prayerfully seek him and she encourages us to share with others the Lord who has come to us.

Martin Hogan,
The Word of God Is Living and Active

The Presence of God

God is with me, but even more astounding, God is within me. Let me dwell for a moment on God's life-giving presence in my body, in my mind, in my heart, as I sit here, right now.

Freedom

Lord, may I never take the gift of freedom for granted. You gave me the great blessing of freedom of spirit. Fill my spirit with your peace and joy.

Consciousness

I remind myself that I am in the presence of God, who is my strength in times of weakness and my comforter in times of sorrow.

The Word

I take my time to read the word of God slowly, a few times, allowing myself to dwell on anything that strikes me. *(Please turn to the Scripture on the following pages. Inspiration points are there, should you need them. When you are ready, return here to continue.)*

Conversation

Jesus, you always welcomed little children when you walked on this earth. Teach me to have a childlike trust in you. Teach me to live in the knowledge that you will never abandon me.

Conclusion

Glory be to the Father, and to the Son, and to the Holy Spirit,
As it was in the beginning, is now and ever shall be,
World without end. Amen.

Sunday 6 July
Fourteenth Sunday in Ordinary Time
Luke 10:1–12, 17–20

After this the Lord appointed seventy others and sent them on ahead of him in pairs to every town and place where he himself intended to go. He said to them, 'The harvest is plentiful, but the labourers are few; therefore ask the Lord of the harvest to send out labourers into his harvest. Go on your way. See, I am sending you out like lambs into the midst of wolves. Carry no purse, no bag, no sandals; and greet no one on the road. Whatever house you enter, first say, "Peace to this house!" And if anyone is there who shares in peace, your peace will rest on that person; but if not, it will return to you. Remain in the same house, eating and drinking whatever they provide, for the labourer deserves to be paid. Do not move about from house to house. Whenever you enter a town and its people welcome you, eat what is set before you; cure the sick who are there, and say to them, "The kingdom of God has come near to you." But whenever you enter a town and they do not welcome you, go out into its streets and say, "Even the dust of your town that clings to our feet, we wipe off in protest against you. Yet know this: the kingdom of God has come near." I tell you, on that day it will be more tolerable for Sodom than for that town. . . .

The seventy returned with joy, saying, 'Lord, in your name even the demons submit to us!' He said to them, 'I watched Satan fall from heaven like a flash of lightning. See, I have given you authority to tread on snakes and scorpions, and over all the power of the enemy; and nothing will hurt you. Nevertheless, do not rejoice at this, that the spirits submit to you, but rejoice that your names are written in heaven.'

- By instructing his disciples not to carry spare tunics or money or sandals he is telling them to focus not on themselves but rather on their mission to preach and to heal. God will provide all that they need through the people to whom they bring the message of the kingdom of God, 'for the labourer deserves to be paid'.

- Pope Francis has said we are all called to be missionaries. In whatever walk of life we choose we can witness to our faith by how we live, but there is also a need for those who are called to dedicate their lives to preaching the Good News of the kingdom of God. Let us pray for vocations to the priesthood and religious life.

Monday 7 July
Matthew 9:18–26

While he was saying these things to them, suddenly a leader of the synagogue came in and knelt before him, saying, 'My daughter has just died;
but come and lay your hand on her, and she will live.' And Jesus got up
and followed him, with his disciples. Then suddenly a woman who had
been suffering from haemorrhages for twelve years came up behind him
and touched the fringe of his cloak, for she said to herself, 'If I only touch
his cloak, I will be made well.' Jesus turned, and seeing her he said, 'Take
heart, daughter; your faith has made you well.' And instantly the woman
was made well. When Jesus came to the leader's house and saw the flute-
players and the crowd making a commotion, he said, 'Go away; for the
girl is not dead but sleeping.' And they laughed at him. But when the
crowd had been put outside, he went in and took her by the hand, and the
girl got up. And the report of this spread throughout that district.

- This synagogue official showed great faith in Jesus' power, even to
  restore life to the dead. His faith was rewarded when Jesus took the
  little girl by the hand and gave her back to her parents. In the Gospels,
  when Jesus takes people by the hand, a great healing follows. We ask
  our Lord to take us by the hand and lead us.

Tuesday 8 July
Matthew 9:32–37

After they had gone away, a demoniac who was mute was brought to
him. And when the demon had been cast out, the one who had been
mute spoke; and the crowds were amazed and said, 'Never has anything
like this been seen in Israel.' But the Pharisees said, 'By the ruler of the
demons he casts out the demons.'

Then Jesus went about all the cities and villages, teaching in their
synagogues, and proclaiming the good news of the kingdom, and curing every disease and every sickness. When he saw the crowds, he had
compassion for them, because they were harassed and helpless, like sheep
without a shepherd. Then he said to his disciples, 'The harvest is plentiful, but the labourers are few.'

- This is a picture of Jesus in the full flow of his ministry as he gave
  himself for others. In his compassion he could see their great need for

a shepherd. Our world, more than ever, needs shepherds who will give a witness to the unseen reality of God. Let us pray for vocations to the priesthood and religious life.

Wednesday 9 July
Matthew 10:1–7

Then Jesus summoned his twelve disciples and gave them authority over unclean spirits, to cast them out, and to cure every disease and every sickness. These are the names of the twelve apostles: first, Simon, also known as Peter, and his brother Andrew; James son of Zebedee, and his brother John; Philip and Bartholomew; Thomas and Matthew the tax-collector; James son of Alphaeus, and Thaddaeus; Simon the Cananaean, and Judas Iscariot, the one who betrayed him.

These twelve Jesus sent out with the following instructions: 'Go nowhere among the Gentiles, and enter no town of the Samaritans, but go rather to the lost sheep of the house of Israel. As you go, proclaim the good news, "The kingdom of heaven has come near."'

- In the presence of Jesus as he walked among us, the kingdom of God came near to us. He still walks with us and invites us to be his eyes, his hands, his voice and his feet, bringing to others the Good News of the kingdom. Let us pray the prayer of St Teresa of Ávila: 'Christ has no body but yours, no hands, no feet on earth but yours. Yours are the eyes with which he looks compassionately on this world. Yours are the feet with which he walks to do good. Yours are the hands with which he blesses all the world. You are his body. Christ has no body now but yours, no hands, no feet on earth but yours. Amen.'

Thursday 10 July
Matthew 10:7–15

Then he said to his disciples, 'As you go, proclaim the good news, "The kingdom of heaven has come near." Cure the sick, raise the dead, cleanse the lepers, cast out demons. You received without payment; give without payment. Take no gold, or silver, or copper in your belts, no bag for your journey, or two tunics, or sandals, or a staff; for labourers deserve their food. Whatever town or village you enter, find out who in it is worthy, and stay there until you leave. As you enter the house, greet it. If the house is worthy, let your peace come upon it; but if it is not worthy, let your peace return to you. If anyone will not welcome you or listen to your words, shake off the dust from your feet as you leave that house or town. Truly I tell you, it will be more tolerable for the land of Sodom and Gomorrah on the day of judgement than for that town.'

- Whatever success missionaries have comes only through the God who works through them. Their role is freely to offer the Good News, and it is up to the hearers to accept or reject the offer. God always leaves us free. Prayer is always an invitation to meet and spend time in the Lord's company. Every moment we spend doing this changes us and blesses us. We read, 'Now is the acceptable time.' Let us use our time in prayer well as this particular time will never come again.

Friday 11 July
St Benedict, Abbot
Matthew 10:16–23

He said to them, 'See, I am sending you out like sheep into the midst of wolves; so be wise as serpents and innocent as doves. Beware of them, for they will hand you over to councils and flog you in their synagogues; and you will be dragged before governors and kings because of me, as a testimony to them and the Gentiles. When they hand you over, do not worry about how you are to speak or what you are to say; for what you are to say will be given to you at that time; for it is not you who speak, but the Spirit of your Father speaking through you. Brother will betray brother to death, and a father his child, and children will rise against parents and have them put to death; and you will be hated by all because of my name. But the one who endures to the end will be saved. When they persecute you in one town, flee to the next; for truly I tell you, you will not have gone through all the towns of Israel before the Son of Man comes.'

- The followers of Christ have endured enormous persecutions down through the centuries, due mainly to an inexplicable hatred among those in authority for what is right and good. Of these the Book of Wisdom says, 'Thus they reasoned, but they were led astray, for their wickedness blinded them,' (2:21). We pray for the grace of perseverance and the courage to go on witnessing to the truth.

Saturday 12 July
Matthew 10:24–33

Jesus said to his disciples, 'A disciple is not above the teacher, nor a slave above the master; it is enough for the disciple to be like the teacher, and the slave like the master. If they have called the master of the house Beelzebul, how much more will they malign those of his household!

'So have no fear of them; for nothing is covered up that will not be uncovered, and nothing secret that will not become known. What I say to you in the dark, tell in the light; and what you hear whispered, proclaim from the housetops. Do not fear those who kill the body but cannot kill the soul; rather fear him who can destroy both soul and body in hell. Are not two sparrows sold for a penny? Yet not one of them will fall to the ground unperceived by your Father. And even the hairs of your head are all counted. So do not be afraid; you are of more value than many sparrows.

'Everyone therefore who acknowledges me before others, I also will acknowledge before my Father in heaven; but whoever denies me before others, I also will deny before my Father in heaven.'

- Every human being is precious in the eyes of God, with every hair on their head counted. Each of us has an immortal soul which no one outside ourselves can destroy, because we always have a choice. The martyrs have all been given a special grace of endurance that will be given to all. We give thanks to God for what St Paul calls 'this great cloud of witnesses', for their courage and inspiration to us.

- Jesus once said that he who is not against us is for us. Let us pray to acknowledge our allegiance to Christ before others.

Something to think and pray about each day this week:

Gardens offer endless scope for budding mystics! They are safe places, places of life, abounding in beauty. Where there is a garden, there will be water and living things with their varied beauty. Charles Darwin, although remembered as the great proponent of evolution, saw himself primarily as a beholder of the natural world. He spent much of his life contemplating the simplest things, and he ends his great work, *The Origin of Species*, by noting: 'It is interesting to contemplate an entangled bank . . . .' This humble bank he studied is clothed with many plants, with birds singing, insects flitting about and worms crawling through the damp earth. It leads him to reflect that 'these elaborately constructed forms, so different from each other and dependent on each other . . . have all been produced by laws acting around us.'

So, find your entangled bank, contemplate it, muse on its long history and reflect on what it is trying to say to you. Let this be your holy place where you fall in love with the natural world and with its maker. Let the tapestry of life come alive under your gaze. Perhaps you may exclaim, like Darwin, 'It has been for me a glorious day, like giving to a blind man eyes.'

Brian Grogan SJ,
Finding God in a Leaf: The Mysticism of Laudato Si'

The Presence of God
God is with me, but more, God is within me, giving me existence. Let me dwell for a moment on God's life-giving presence in my body, my mind, my heart, and in the whole of my life.

Freedom
Lord, you created me to live in freedom. May your Holy Spirit guide me to follow you freely. Instil in my heart a desire to know and love you more each day.

Consciousness
In God's loving presence I unwind the past day, starting from now and looking back, moment by moment. I gather in all the goodness and light, in gratitude. I attend to the shadows and what they say to me, seeking healing, courage, forgiveness.

The Word
God speaks to each of us individually. I listen attentively to hear what he is saying to me. Read the text a few times, then listen. *(Please turn to the Scripture on the following pages. Inspiration points are there, should you need them. When you are ready, return here to continue.)*

Conversation
Jesus, you always welcomed little children when you walked on this earth. Teach me to have a childlike trust in you. Teach me to live in the knowledge that you will never abandon me.

Conclusion
I thank God for these moments we have spent together and for any insights I have been given concerning the text.

Sunday 13 July
Fifteenth Sunday in Ordinary Time
Luke 10:25–37

Just then a lawyer stood up to test Jesus. 'Teacher,' he said, 'what must I do to inherit eternal life?' He said to him, 'What is written in the law? What do you read there?' He answered, 'You shall love the Lord your God with all your heart, and with all your soul, and with all your strength, and with all your mind; and your neighbour as yourself.' And he said to him, 'You have given the right answer; do this, and you will live.'

But wanting to justify himself, he asked Jesus, 'And who is my neighbour?' Jesus replied, 'A man was going down from Jerusalem to Jericho, and fell into the hands of robbers, who stripped him, beat him, and went away, leaving him half dead. Now by chance a priest was going down that road; and when he saw him, he passed by on the other side. So likewise a Levite, when he came to the place and saw him, passed by on the other side. But a Samaritan while travelling came near him; and when he saw him, he was moved with pity. He went to him and bandaged his wounds, having poured oil and wine on them. Then he put him on his own animal, brought him to an inn, and took care of him. The next day he took out two denarii, gave them to the innkeeper, and said, "Take care of him; and when I come back, I will repay you whatever more you spend." Which of these three, do you think, was a neighbour to the man who fell into the hands of the robbers?' He said, 'The one who showed him mercy.' Jesus said to him, 'Go and do likewise.'

- Our Lord reduced all the commandments to two, namely to love God with all our heart and our neighbour as ourselves. These two are really two parts of the one great commandment to love, which is the whole purpose for our being on this earth. When our Lord meets us in judgement upon our deaths, I believe the only question he will ask of us will be, 'How have you loved?' And if we have reached the full development of our individual capacity to love then we are ready to merge with God who is Love and so can enter heaven. It is out of the one loving heart that we love all.

Monday 14 July
Matthew 10:34—11:1

Jesus said to them, 'Do not think that I have come to bring peace to the earth; I have not come to bring peace, but a sword.

For I have come to set a man against his father,
and a daughter against her mother,
and a daughter-in-law against her mother-in-law;
and one's foes will be members of one's own household.

Whoever loves father or mother more than me is not worthy of me; and whoever loves son or daughter more than me is not worthy of me; and whoever does not take up the cross and follow me is not worthy of me. Those who find their life will lose it, and those who lose their life for my sake will find it.

'Whoever welcomes you welcomes me, and whoever welcomes me welcomes the one who sent me. Whoever welcomes a prophet in the name of a prophet will receive a prophet's reward; and whoever welcomes a righteous person in the name of a righteous person will receive the reward of the righteous; and whoever gives even a cup of cold water to one of these little ones in the name of a disciple—truly I tell you, none of these will lose their reward.'

Now when Jesus had finished instructing his twelve disciples, he went on from there to teach and proclaim his message in their cities.

- In the foundation principle of his Spiritual Exercises St Ignatius wrote, 'Mankind is created to praise, reverence and serve God our Lord, and in this way to save his soul.' Because God is God, he can never take second place in our lives. He must always take the first place, even if it means that we lose our physical lives. Pope Francis has asked that we reflect on what are the idols that we may be putting ahead of God in our lives. Let us pray for light and discernment about this.

Tuesday 15 July
Matthew 11:20–24

Then he began to reproach the cities in which most of his deeds of power had been done, because they did not repent. 'Woe to you, Chorazin! Woe to you, Bethsaida! For if the deeds of power done in you had been done in Tyre and Sidon, they would have repented long ago in sackcloth and ashes. But I tell you, on the day of judgement it will be more tolerable for Tyre and Sidon than for you. And you, Capernaum, will you be exalted to heaven?

No, you will be brought down to Hades.

For if the deeds of power done in you had been done in Sodom, it would have remained until this day. But I tell you that on the day of judgement it will be more tolerable for the land of Sodom than for you.'

- Chorazin and Bethsaida today are in ruins and barely recognisable as places of former human habitation. The great works of Jesus done in them called for a response and for a repentance that did not come. We have all been given opportunities in our lives to come closer to God. How have we responded to these?

Wednesday 16 July
Matthew 11:25–27

At that time Jesus said, 'I thank you, Father, Lord of heaven and earth, because you have hidden these things from the wise and the intelligent and have revealed them to infants; yes, Father, for such was your gracious will. All things have been handed over to me by my Father; and no one knows the Son except the Father, and no one knows the Father except the Son and anyone to whom the Son chooses to reveal him.'

- During our life on earth we have the opportunity to come to know and love our Saviour Jesus Christ through our daily encountering him in prayer. No one can come to the Father except through him. He will reveal the Father to us as he promised. Are we willing to take him at his word?

- Only God can reveal God to us. Let us pray to be open to his teaching and revealing himself to us.

Thursday 17 July
Matthew 11:28–30

At that time Jesus said, 'Come to me, all you that are weary and are carrying heavy burdens, and I will give you rest. Take my yoke upon you, and learn from me; for I am gentle and humble in heart, and you will find rest for your souls. For my yoke is easy, and my burden is light.'

- The Jesus who walked our earth is one who was 'gentle and humble in heart'. By reading the Gospels frequently and meditatively, we come to know *about* Jesus through his words and actions and how he interacted with all those he met. But we only come to *know* him through the encounter of personal prayer.

Friday 18 July
Matthew 12:1–8

At that time Jesus went through the cornfields on the sabbath; his disciples were hungry, and they began to pluck heads of grain and to eat. When the Pharisees saw it, they said to him, 'Look, your disciples are doing what is not lawful to do on the sabbath.' He said to them, 'Have you not read what David did when he and his companions were hungry? He entered the house of God and ate the bread of the Presence, which it was not lawful for him or his companions to eat, but only for the priests. Or have you not read in the law that on the sabbath the priests in the temple break the sabbath and yet are guiltless? I tell you, something greater than the temple is here. But if you had known what this means, "I desire mercy and not sacrifice", you would not have condemned the guiltless. For the Son of Man is lord of the sabbath.'

- The temple is not greater than the One who is present there and for whom it was adorned. The sabbath is not greater than the One who is worshipped on that day. Laws are meant to help lead us to God, not become an end in themselves or even an obstacle on our path to God. Jesus said, quoting Isaiah 29:13, 'This people honours me with their lips, but their hearts are far from me.' Do we recite the words of prayers endlessly without engaging in our heart with the Person who is there with us in our prayer?

Saturday 19 July
Matthew 12:14–21

But the Pharisees went out and conspired against him, how to destroy him.

When Jesus became aware of this, he departed. Many crowds followed him, and he cured all of them, and he ordered them not to make him known. This was to fulfil what had been spoken through the prophet Isaiah:

'Here is my servant, whom I have chosen,
  my beloved, with whom my soul is well pleased.
I will put my Spirit upon him,
  and he will proclaim justice to the Gentiles.
He will not wrangle or cry aloud,
  nor will anyone hear his voice in the streets.
He will not break a bruised reed
  or quench a smouldering wick
until he brings justice to victory.
  And in his name the Gentiles will hope.'

- The Jews became the chosen people of God. He made the covenants with them and his Son was to take his human body from their flesh and blood. It is their tragedy that they rejected the Messiah God sent to them and sought to destroy him. But God works through all things, including our mistakes, and their rejection opened up the message of the Good News about the kingdom of God to the Gentile world. No doubt it would have come anyhow, since God loves all, but perhaps it might not have come as quickly. We give thanks for the gift of faith and the gift of the Good News.

Something to think and pray about each day this week:

Our relationship with God involves our whole life, but it finds a particular expression in prayer. As changes take place in how we experience ourselves, there will be adjustments in how we relate to God too. An experience of God's love can lead to a changed relationship with God and, in turn, a change in our prayer and our sense of self.

If our image of ourselves changes, then our image of God will change, too, as will our prayer, and we will relate differently to others as well. All these elements are interconnected and influence each other. Noticing what is happening in us facilitates movement in response to the action of the Lord. Prayer that is 'real' and linked with life will help open the doors to change, or will help us to notice what gets in its way. It will take the main focus off ourselves and how we *have to be*, or how we *should be* in prayer and in life. Time is necessary if we are to break the notion that some day 'I will get it right.' We continue to acknowledge our need of God, so that we can let God lead.

Saying prayers is not the same as praying. Over time, God's desires can become more central in our prayer, with a diminishing focus on the self. Bringing the real issues of life to prayer involves an opening to change in all the relationships considered here—with self, God and others. By noting change in how we experience God, or in our sense of self as made in God's image, or in prayer itself, we are invited to make the link between them. This opens up the wider dimension of these relationships and the richness contained in them. The link between prayer and life becomes more obvious.

Michael Drennan SJ,
See God Act: The Ministry of Spiritual Direction

The Presence of God

I pause for a moment and think of the love and the grace that God showers on me. I am created in the image and likeness of God; I am God's dwelling place.

Freedom

I am free. When I look at these words in writing, they seem to create in me a feeling of awe. Yes, a wonderful feeling of freedom. Thank you, God.

Consciousness

In the presence of my loving Creator, I look honestly at my feelings over the past day: the highs, the lows and the level ground. Can I see where the Lord has been present?

The Word

I read the word of God slowly, a few times over, and I listen to what God is saying to me. *(Please turn to the Scripture on the following pages. Inspiration points are there, should you need them. When you are ready, return here to continue.)*

Conversation

Remembering that I am still in God's presence, I imagine Jesus standing or sitting beside me, and I say whatever is on my mind, whatever is in my heart, speaking as one friend to another.

Conclusion

Glory be to the Father, and to the Son, and to the Holy Spirit,
As it was in the beginning, is now and ever shall be,
World without end. Amen.

Sunday 20 July
Sixteenth Sunday in Ordinary Time
Luke 10:38–42

Now as they went on their way, he entered a certain village, where a woman named Martha welcomed him into her home. She had a sister named Mary, who sat at the Lord's feet and listened to what he was saying. But Martha was distracted by her many tasks; so she came to him and asked, 'Lord, do you not care that my sister has left me to do all the work by myself? Tell her then to help me.' But the Lord answered her, 'Martha, Martha, you are worried and distracted by many things; there is need of only one thing. Mary has chosen the better part, which will not be taken away from her.'

- In St John's Gospel we read that Jesus loved Martha and Mary and their brother Lazarus, and he was a familiar visitor to their home. Theirs was a home of faith, where they recognised Jesus as One sent by God, and they made him welcome. Martha helped with the material cup of tea, but Mary heard a different call as she sat at the Lord's feet and listened to him. In our own lives we can follow the example of both sisters by being contemplatives in action.

Monday 21 July
Matthew 12:38–42

Then some of the scribes and Pharisees said to him, 'Teacher, we wish to see a sign from you.' But he answered them, 'An evil and adulterous generation asks for a sign, but no sign will be given to it except the sign of the prophet Jonah. For just as Jonah was for three days and three nights in the belly of the sea monster, so for three days and three nights the Son of Man will be in the heart of the earth. The people of Nineveh will rise up at the judgement with this generation and condemn it, because they repented at the proclamation of Jonah, and see, something greater than Jonah is here! The queen of the South will rise up at the judgement with this generation and condemn it, because she came from the ends of the earth to listen to the wisdom of Solomon, and see, something greater than Solomon is here!'

- The true sign for all Christians is the sign of Christ on his cross and its reminder of his three days in the tomb and his resurrection. The motto for the Jesuit Wah Yan College in Hong Kong is *In hoc signo vinces*, written beneath a cross. 'In this sign you will conquer.' How well do I accept the crosses in my life?

Tuesday 22 July
St Mary Magdalene
John 20:1–2, 11–18

Early on the first day of the week, while it was still dark, Mary Magdalene came to the tomb and saw that the stone had been removed from the tomb. So she ran and went to Simon Peter and the other disciple, the one whom Jesus loved, and said to them, 'They have taken the Lord out of the tomb, and we do not know where they have laid him.' . . .

But Mary stood weeping outside the tomb. As she wept, she bent over to look into the tomb; and she saw two angels in white, sitting where the body of Jesus had been lying, one at the head and the other at the feet. They said to her, 'Woman, why are you weeping?' She said to them, 'They have taken away my Lord, and I do not know where they have laid him.' When she had said this, she turned round and saw Jesus standing there, but she did not know that it was Jesus. Jesus said to her, 'Woman, why are you weeping? For whom are you looking?' Supposing him to be the gardener, she said to him, 'Sir, if you have carried him away, tell me where you have laid him, and I will take him away.' Jesus said to her, 'Mary!' She turned and said to him in Hebrew, 'Rabbouni!' (which means Teacher). Jesus said to her, 'Do not hold on to me, because I have not yet ascended to the Father. But go to my brothers and say to them, "I am ascending to my Father and your Father, to my God and your God."' Mary Magdalene went and announced to the disciples, 'I have seen the Lord'; and she told them that he had said these things to her.

- Jesus calls Mary by her name and she instantly recognises his voice. He had said that his own sheep recognise the voice of the shepherd and follow him. Can I now have this same Lord call me by my name as he invites me to spend some precious time with him?

- Jesus says to Mary, 'Do not hold on to me, because I have not yet ascended to the Father.' There is an implication that when he does return to his Father, then we can cling to him in faith. In Psalm 63 we read, 'My soul clings to you; Your right hand upholds me.' The psalms are the ready-made heart prayers of the people of God. Let us make use of them in our prayer.

Wednesday 23 July
John 15:1–8

Jesus said to them, 'I am the true vine, and my Father is the vine-grower. He removes every branch in me that bears no fruit. Every branch that bears fruit he prunes to make it bear more fruit. You have already been cleansed by the word that I have spoken to you. Abide in me as I abide in you. Just as the branch cannot bear fruit by itself unless it abides in the vine, neither can you unless you abide in me. I am the vine, you are the branches. Those who abide in me and I in them bear much fruit, because apart from me you can do nothing. Whoever does not abide in me is thrown away like a branch and withers; such branches are gathered, thrown into the fire, and burned. If you abide in me, and my words abide in you, ask for whatever you wish, and it will be done for you. My Father is glorified by this, that you bear much fruit and become my disciples.'

- Jesus invites us to live in him as he has come to live in us. If he is the vine and we are the branches, then the sap is the love that flows between us, uniting us in the loving prayer of contemplation. 'But I have calmed and quieted my soul, like a weaned child with its mother; my soul is like the weaned child that is with me' (Psalm 131).

- Through the vicissitudes and difficulties in life we are pruned by a loving vine-dresser for better bearing of fruit. St Thérèse of Lisieux prayed, 'Lord, You are wonderful in all that You do in my life.' Let us echo her prayer, as we pray for a deeper trust in God's loving care and in everything that he is doing in us.

Thursday 24 July
Matthew 13:10–17

Then the disciples came and asked him, 'Why do you speak to them in parables?' He answered, 'To you it has been given to know the secrets of the kingdom of heaven, but to them it has not been given. For to those who have, more will be given, and they will have an abundance; but from those who have nothing, even what they have will be taken away. The reason I speak to them in parables is that "seeing they do not perceive, and hearing they do not listen, nor do they understand." With them indeed is fulfilled the prophecy of Isaiah that says:

"You will indeed listen, but never understand,
  and you will indeed look, but never perceive.
For this people's heart has grown dull,
  and their ears are hard of hearing,
    and they have shut their eyes;
      so that they might not look with their eyes,
  and listen with their ears,
and understand with their heart and turn –
  and I would heal them."

But blessed are your eyes, for they see, and your ears, for they hear. Truly I tell you, many prophets and righteous people longed to see what you see, but did not see it, and to hear what you hear, but did not hear it.'

- To those who are open to the message of Christ the parables will reveal God's word to them. To those who have closed their minds to Christ no light will remove their darkness. Let us pray for our world that has such need of the light of a Christ.

Friday 25 July
St James, Apostle
Matthew 20:20–28

Then the mother of the sons of Zebedee came to him with her sons, and kneeling before him, she asked a favour of him. And he said to her, 'What do you want?' She said to him, 'Declare that these two sons of mine will sit, one at your right hand and one at your left, in your kingdom.' But Jesus answered, 'You do not know what you are asking. Are you able to drink the cup that I am about to drink?' They said to him, 'We are able.' He said to them, 'You will indeed drink my cup, but to sit at my right hand and at my left, this is not mine to grant, but it is for those for whom it has been prepared by my Father.'

When the ten heard it, they were angry with the two brothers. But Jesus called them to him and said, 'You know that the rulers of the Gentiles lord it over them, and their great ones are tyrants over them. It will not be so among you; but whoever wishes to be great among you must be your servant, and whoever wishes to be first among you must be your slave; just as the Son of Man came not to be served but to serve, and to give his life a ransom for many.'

- Jesus uses the situations that come up to teach his disciples great truths. Here he shows them the path they are to take if they are to be his true followers and are willing to learn from his example. Jesus is also saying this to us. Let us pray to listen to him and for the grace to follow his example.

Saturday 26 July
Matthew 13:24–30

He put before them another parable: 'The kingdom of heaven may be compared to someone who sowed good seed in his field; but while everybody was asleep, an enemy came and sowed weeds among the wheat, and then went away. So when the plants came up and bore grain, then the weeds appeared as well. And the slaves of the householder came and said to him, "Master, did you not sow good seed in your field? Where, then, did these weeds come from?" He answered, "An enemy has done this." The slaves said to him, "Then do you want us to go and gather them?" But he replied, "No; for in gathering the weeds you would uproot the wheat along with them. Let both of them grow together until the harvest; and at harvest time I will tell the reapers, Collect the weeds first and bind them in bundles to be burned, but gather the wheat into my barn."'

- In Mark 7:21 Jesus said that it is from within, from the heart, that evil thoughts and wickedness come. We are all of us sinners and so we have a mixture of good and bad within our hearts. Since God who loves all can only love what is good, then we can take it that the good in us outweighs the bad. God in his loving patience is willing to wait for us to choose what is good so that it will outweigh the bad we do. Let us spend our time on earth well.

Something to think and pray about each day this week:

During the Covid-19 lockdown I remember visiting an elderly woman who lived alone. She was linked to the Mass on her granddaughter's laptop. She had two candles lit on each side of the screen and a few flowers in a vase 'to honour the Lord's presence in my home and heart', as she said to me. I was profoundly moved by her tangible faith.

This incident reminded me that the Lord's presence is at the heart of all our words, worship and witness. His presence is behind the veil of our anxieties, struggles and suspicions. The Lord is simply and profoundly there, for us and with us, as he promised to be, until the end of time. Nothing of value happens in the Church that does not start from seeing the Lord in our midst, suffering and transforming all our human dilemmas.

In essence, the Lord is saying to us: If you don't know why this matters, look for someone who does, the child, the poor, the forgotten. Learn from them. You will learn from me. You will find a life's mission. You will find rest for your soul. Sit and eat.

John Cullen,
The Sacred Heart Messenger,
September 2023

The Presence of God
I pause for a moment and reflect on God's life-giving presence in every part of my body, in everything around me, in the whole of my life.

Freedom
Many countries are at this moment suffering the agonies of war. I bow my head in thanksgiving for my freedom. I pray for all prisoners and captives.

Consciousness
Knowing that God loves me unconditionally, I look honestly over the past day, its events, and my feelings. Do I have something to be grateful for? Then I give thanks. Is there something I am sorry for? Then I ask forgiveness.

The Word
Now I turn to the Scripture set out for me this day. I read slowly over the words and see if any sentence or sentiment appeals to me. *(Please turn to the Scripture on the following pages. Inspiration points are there, should you need them. When you are ready, return here to continue.)*

Conversation
I know with certainty that there were times when you carried me, Lord. There were times when it was through your strength that I got through the dark times in my life.

Conclusion
Glory be to the Father, and to the Son, and to the Holy Spirit,
As it was in the beginning, is now and ever shall be,
World without end. Amen.

Sunday 27 July
Seventeenth Sunday in Ordinary Time
Luke 11:1–13

He was praying in a certain place, and after he had finished, one of his disciples said to him, 'Lord, teach us to pray, as John taught his disciples.' He said to them, 'When you pray, say:

Father, hallowed be your name.

Your kingdom come.

Give us each day our daily bread.

And forgive us our sins,

for we ourselves forgive everyone indebted to us.

And do not bring us to the time of trial.'

And he said to them, 'Suppose one of you has a friend, and you go to him at midnight and say to him, "Friend, lend me three loaves of bread; for a friend of mine has arrived, and I have nothing to set before him." And he answers from within, "Do not bother me; the door has already been locked, and my children are with me in bed; I cannot get up and give you anything." I tell you, even though he will not get up and give him anything because he is his friend, at least because of his persistence he will get up and give him whatever he needs.

'So I say to you, Ask, and it will be given to you; search, and you will find; knock, and the door will be opened for you. For everyone who asks receives, and everyone who searches finds, and for everyone who knocks, the door will be opened. Is there anyone among you who, if your child asks for a fish, will give a snake instead of a fish? Or if the child asks for an egg, will give a scorpion? If you then, who are evil, know how to give good gifts to your children, how much more will the heavenly Father give the Holy Spirit to those who ask him!'

- The Our Father can be seen as a guide to us for our prayer. In it the Father comes first in our petitions, and then we pray as the people of God when we say, 'Give us, forgive us, lead us.' In the prayer of petition we acknowledge that everything is from God and so we praise him.

- God hears every prayer but will answer in his own time as he sees best for us. Our part is to be patient with him and with our own poor efforts in prayer. We always need to persevere with prayer and remember that every encounter with God changes us and blesses us.

Monday 28 July
Matthew 13:31–35

He put before them another parable: 'The kingdom of heaven is like a mustard seed that someone took and sowed in his field; it is the smallest of all the seeds, but when it has grown it is the greatest of shrubs and becomes a tree, so that the birds of the air come and make nests in its branches.'

He told them another parable: 'The kingdom of heaven is like yeast that a woman took and mixed in with three measures of flour until all of it was leavened.'

Jesus told the crowds all these things in parables; without a parable he told them nothing. This was to fulfil what had been spoken through the prophet:

'I will open my mouth to speak in parables;
>   I will proclaim what has been hidden from the foundation of
>   the world.'

- It has been said that what grows slowly endures. At our baptism the life of grace began and the Holy Spirit came to dwell in our souls. Like the tiny mustard seed, this life of grace grows through faithful nurturing and nourishment from prayer and the sacraments. The kingdom of God is within us but it takes time and patience for God to reveal this to us on our spiritual journey through life. Let us ask the Holy Spirit to guide us, and ask that Jesus be our friend and life companion.

Tuesday 29 July
John 11:19–27

And many of the Jews had come to Martha and Mary to console them about their brother. When Martha heard that Jesus was coming, she went and met him, while Mary stayed at home. Martha said to Jesus, 'Lord, if you had been here, my brother would not have died. But even now I know that God will give you whatever you ask of him.' Jesus said to her, 'Your brother will rise again.' Martha said to him, 'I know that he will rise again in the resurrection on the last day.' Jesus said to her, 'I am the resurrection and the life. Those who believe in me, even though they die, will live, and everyone who lives and believes in me will never die. Do you believe this?'

She said to him, 'Yes, Lord, I believe that you are the Messiah, the Son of God, the one coming into the world.'

• Martha was no theologian. It was enough for her to know and believe that Jesus was the Messiah and that he had come from God. Our faith in the resurrection of Jesus is the bedrock of our spiritual lives. Daily in prayer and in our Christian lives we live this faith. Let us pray for the grace of perseverance and fidelity to our Christian calling.

Wednesday 30 July
Matthew 13:44–46

He put before them another parable: 'The kingdom of heaven is like treasure hidden in a field, which someone found and hid; then in his joy he goes and sells all that he has and buys that field.

'Again, the kingdom of heaven is like a merchant in search of fine pearls; on finding one pearl of great value, he went and sold all that he had and bought it.'

• To discover the treasure that Christ came to give us is a great joy and worth giving everything for. However, it can happen that after we have bought the field and hidden the treasure we forget exactly where we buried it, and so by neglect we lose out. Fr Gerard Hughes SJ wrote, 'Many sit guarding the treasure-box without ever opening it.'

• Prayer from our hearts is the key to discovering the treasure, and the immense joy that is at the heart of the gospels. St Teresa of Ávila wrote that we can even begin to experience heaven on earth and reminded us that the treasure is within us.

Thursday 31 July
St Ignatius Loyola
Matthew 13:47–53

He said to them, 'Again, the kingdom of heaven is like a net that was thrown into the sea and caught fish of every kind; when it was full, they drew it ashore, sat down, and put the good into baskets but threw out the bad. So it will be at the end of the age. The angels will come out and separate the evil from the righteous and throw them into the furnace of fire, where there will be weeping and gnashing of teeth.

'Have you understood all this?' They answered, 'Yes.' And he said to them, 'Therefore every scribe who has been trained for the kingdom of heaven is like the master of a household who brings out of his treasure what is new and what is old.' When Jesus had finished these parables, he left that place.

- God waits with infinite patience and love to the end of our lives before we have the first judgement which follows upon death. He allows the sun to shine and the rain to fall on the just and the unjust. We are all given the gift of choosing the good or the bad, but there will always be consequences. We pray for a true discernment of God's will for us and of what is the right way to live.

Friday 1 August
Matthew 13:54–58

He came to his home town and began to teach the people in their synagogue, so that they were astounded and said, 'Where did this man get this wisdom and these deeds of power? Is not this the carpenter's son? Is not his mother called Mary? And are not his brothers James and Joseph and Simon and Judas? And are not all his sisters with us? Where then did this man get all this?' And they took offence at him. But Jesus said to them, 'Prophets are not without honour except in their own country and in their own house.' And he did not do many deeds of power there, because of their unbelief.

- Jesus lived a fully human life and he was not spared the trials, disappointments and failures to which we are all subject. This would be his last time to visit his home village and it would be their loss. How well do I accept disappointments and my own failures? How well do I use the opportunities that are given to me to grow in trust and loving?

Saturday 2 August
Matthew 14:1–12

At that time Herod the ruler heard reports about Jesus; and he said to his servants, 'This is John the Baptist; he has been raised from the dead, and for this reason these powers are at work in him.' For Herod had arrested John, bound him, and put him in prison on account of Herodias, his brother Philip's wife, because John had been telling him, 'It is not lawful for you to have her.' Though Herod wanted to put him to death, he feared the crowd, because they regarded him as a prophet. But when Herod's birthday came, the daughter of Herodias danced before the company, and she pleased Herod so much that he promised on oath to grant her whatever she might ask. Prompted by her mother, she said, 'Give me the head of John the Baptist here on a platter.' The king was grieved, yet out of regard for his oaths and for the guests, he commanded it to be given; he sent and had John beheaded in the prison. The head was brought on a platter and given to the girl, who brought it to her mother. His disciples came and took the body and buried it; then they went and told Jesus.

• Herod had admired John the Baptist and he had listened to him. He would likely have regretted having killed him. By saying that he was now risen from the dead he may have been trying to ease his conscience. But no amount of wishful thinking can undo our actions. Let us pray for honesty and integrity in our lives.

Something to think and pray about each day this week:

I was once the proud owner of a moped, my economical transport to work at a Dublin hospital. One glorious day, I set off for work as usual. Then the heavens opened and a deluge of rain poured down on bone-dry tarmac, a treacherous combination. As I entered a major roundabout, the bike skidded, and I was thrown from it. As I lay prostrate on the ground and unable to move, a car approached. Two doctors got out of the car, examined me and called an ambulance. It was embarrassing to arrive in A&E in my workplace and to have to relate what had happened. However, I was treated with the utmost courtesy and care and witnessed the same compassion being extended to all around me. Fortunately I had not sustained any major injury and was discharged later that day, grateful to be alive.

Some years later I arrived at the scene of an accident in London. A young pizza delivery man had been knocked off his motorbike. He spoke no English and was clearly distressed. I attempted to comfort him as we awaited the ambulance. When the paramedics recommended hospital admission, he rose and stumbled away, leaving his bike by the roadside. I suspected that he may have been an undocumented worker and was afraid of either losing his job or being deported. My heart ached for him.

We meet many who are bruised and broken by harsh experiences. Some suffer great physical pain, others a dark cloud of sadness, the grief of loss robbing life of joy. Economic hardship and political turmoil ravage world peace. We place our hands into the glorified hands of Jesus, so that, fortified by his grace, we are more able to reach out a hand of friendship to all who suffer.

Sr Siobhán O'Keeffe,
The Sacred Heart Messenger,
January 2023

The Presence of God
I remind myself that I am in the presence of God, who is my strength in times of weakness and my comforter in times of sorrow.

Freedom
St Ignatius thought that a thick and shapeless tree trunk would never believe that it could become a statue, admired as a miracle of sculpture, and would never submit itself to the chisel of the sculptor, who sees by her genius what she can make of it. I ask for the grace to let myself be shaped by my loving Creator.

Consciousness
Dear Lord, help me to remember that you gave me life. Teach me to slow down, to be still and enjoy the pleasures created for me. To be aware of the beauty that surrounds me: the marvel of mountains, the calmness of lakes, the fragility of a flower petal. I need to remember that all these things come from you.

The Word
In this expectant state of mind, please turn to the text for the day with confidence. Believe that the Holy Spirit is present and may reveal whatever the passage has to say to you. Read reflectively, listening with a third ear to what may be going on in your heart. (Please turn to the Scripture on the following pages. Inspiration points are there, should you need them. When you are ready, return here to continue.)

Conversation
What feelings are rising in me as I pray and reflect on God's word? I imagine Jesus himself sitting or standing near me, and I open my heart to him.

Conclusion
I thank God for these moments we have spent together and for any insights I have been given concerning the text.

Sunday 3 August
Eighteenth Sunday in Ordinary Time
Luke 12:13–21

Someone in the crowd said to him, 'Teacher, tell my brother to divide the family inheritance with me.' But he said to him, 'Friend, who set me to be a judge or arbitrator over you?' And he said to them, 'Take care! Be on your guard against all kinds of greed; for one's life does not consist in the abundance of possessions.' Then he told them a parable: 'The land of a rich man produced abundantly. And he thought to himself, "What should I do, for I have no place to store my crops?" Then he said, "I will do this: I will pull down my barns and build larger ones, and there I will store all my grain and my goods. And I will say to my soul, Soul, you have ample goods laid up for many years; relax, eat, drink, be merry." But God said to him, "You fool! This very night your life is being demanded of you. And the things you have prepared, whose will they be?" So it is with those who store up treasures for themselves but are not rich towards God.'

- So many measure their worth by the amount of wealth they have accumulated. We have heard it said that there are no pockets in shrouds. In the end, we must let go of all our possessions. How often we put aside thoughts of eternity and the fact that we know not the day nor the hour of our leaving this earth.

- On the tombstone of a youth in County Armagh the following words were written: 'All you who come this grave to see, / As I am now so you shall be, / Prepare in time, make no delay, / For I in my bloom was called away.' Let us pray for the grace to be ready when our God calls us home.

Monday 4 August
Matthew 14:13–21

Now when Jesus heard this, he withdrew from there in a boat to a deserted place by himself. But when the crowds heard it, they followed him on foot from the towns. When he went ashore, he saw a great crowd; and he had compassion for them and cured their sick. When it was evening, the disciples came to him and said, 'This is a deserted place, and the hour is now late; send the crowds away so that they may go into the villages and buy food for themselves.' Jesus said to them, 'They need not go away; you give them something to eat.' They replied, 'We have nothing here but five loaves and two fish.' And he said, 'Bring them here to me.' Then he ordered the crowds to sit down on the grass. Taking the five loaves and the two fish, he looked up to heaven, and blessed and broke the loaves, and gave them to the disciples, and the disciples gave them to the crowds. And all ate and were filled; and they took up what was left over of the broken pieces, twelve baskets full. And those who ate were about five thousand men, besides women and children.

- The crowds flocked to him, giving him little time for rest. In his compassion Jesus teaches them and he understands their physical needs. They did not seem to notice their hunger because they were being fed on a spiritual level. When our souls are fed there is less need for material things. Do I give sufficient time to the needs of my soul?

- Jesus tells his apostles that it is for them to feed the people. Today he still calls on us to feed his people by giving them the word of God and the Eucharist. Let us pray for vocations to the priesthood and religious life and for the grace of perseverance for those in this way of life.

Tuesday 5 August
Matthew 14:22–36

Immediately he made the disciples get into the boat and go on ahead to the other side, while he dismissed the crowds. And after he had dismissed the crowds, he went up the mountain by himself to pray. When evening came, he was there alone, but by this time the boat, battered by the waves, was far from the land, for the wind was against them. And early in the morning he came walking towards them on the lake. But when the disciples saw him walking on the lake, they were terrified, saying, 'It is a ghost!' And they cried out in fear. But immediately Jesus spoke to them and said, 'Take heart, it is I; do not be afraid.'

Peter answered him, 'Lord, if it is you, command me to come to you on the water.' He said, 'Come.' So Peter got out of the boat, started walking on the water, and came towards Jesus. But when he noticed the strong wind, he became frightened, and beginning to sink, he cried out, 'Lord, save me!' Jesus immediately reached out his hand and caught him, saying to him, 'You of little faith, why did you doubt?' When they got into the boat, the wind ceased. And those in the boat worshipped him, saying, 'Truly you are the Son of God.'

When they had crossed over, they came to land at Gennesaret. After the people of that place recognised him, they sent word throughout the region and brought all who were sick to him, and begged him that they might touch even the fringe of his cloak; and all who touched it were healed.

- When Peter heard Jesus say to him, 'Come', he bravely got out of the boat and began to walk on the water towards Jesus. Jesus bids all of us to come to him through the ups and downs that we encounter in life. Have we the courage and faith to trust that he will support us in every circumstance?

- Peter pays too much attention to the wind and waves and so becomes fearful and loses his focus on the Lord. But Jesus takes him by the hand and rescues him. He will do this with us despite our fears and lack of faith. Let us pray to trust him more.

Wednesday 6 August
The Transfiguration of the Lord
Luke 9:28–36

Now about eight days after these sayings Jesus took with him Peter and John and James, and went up on the mountain to pray. And while he was praying, the appearance of his face changed, and his clothes became dazzling white. Suddenly they saw two men, Moses and Elijah, talking to him. They appeared in glory and were speaking of his departure, which he was about to accomplish at Jerusalem. Now Peter and his companions were weighed down with sleep; but since they had stayed awake, they saw his glory and the two men who stood with him. Just as they were leaving him, Peter said to Jesus, 'Master, it is good for us to be here; let us make three dwellings, one for you, one for Moses, and one for Elijah'—not knowing what he said. While he was saying this, a cloud came and over-shadowed them; and they were terrified as they entered the cloud. Then from the cloud came a voice that said, 'This is my Son, my Chosen; listen to him!' When the voice had spoken, Jesus was found alone. And they kept silent and in those days told no one any of the things they had seen.

- Again Luke tells us Jesus went away to pray accompanied by three of his disciples. It was while he was praying that his divinity appeared in his humanity, altering his appearance. When we meet Jesus in prayer, can we say with St Peter, 'Master, it is good for us to be here'?

- In the Old Testament, Moses and Elijah were privileged to meet and speak to the living God. Today all of us have this privilege through our faith. The Curé of Ars once said, 'We had deserved to have been incapable of praying, but God in his goodness has given us this privilege.' How well do we use it?

Thursday 7 August
Matthew 16:13–23

Now when Jesus came into the district of Caesarea Philippi, he asked his disciples, 'Who do people say that the Son of Man is?' And they said, 'Some say John the Baptist, but others Elijah, and still others Jeremiah or one of the prophets.' He said to them, 'But who do you say that I am?' Simon Peter answered, 'You are the Messiah, the Son of the living God.' And Jesus answered him, 'Blessed are you, Simon son of Jonah! For flesh and blood has not revealed this to you, but my Father in heaven. And I tell you, you are Peter, and on this rock I will build my church, and the gates of Hades will not prevail against it. I will give you the keys of the kingdom of heaven, and whatever you bind on earth will be bound in heaven, and whatever you loose on earth will be loosed in heaven.' Then he sternly ordered the disciples not to tell anyone that he was the Messiah.

From that time on, Jesus began to show his disciples that he must go to Jerusalem and undergo great suffering at the hands of the elders and chief priests and scribes, and be killed, and on the third day be raised. And Peter took him aside and began to rebuke him, saying, 'God forbid it, Lord! This must never happen to you.' But he turned and said to Peter, 'Get behind me, Satan! You are a stumbling-block to me; for you are setting your mind not on divine things but on human things.'

- When Jesus begins to tell his disciples about his own suffering and death, Peter is horrified. In the Jewish understanding to have a bad end like this would mean that God was opposed to them. This would destroy everything Jesus had tried to do. But Peter is seeing as humans see. Again and again we must remind ourselves that God's ways are not ours. We pray to trust in God's ways of doing things.

Friday 8 August
Matthew 16:24–28

Then Jesus told his disciples, 'If any want to become my followers, let them deny themselves and take up their cross and follow me. For those who want to save their life will lose it, and those who lose their life for my sake will find it. For what will it profit them if they gain the whole world but forfeit their life? Or what will they give in return for their life?

'For the Son of Man is to come with his angels in the glory of his Father, and then he will repay everyone for what has been done. Truly I tell you, there are some standing here who will not taste death before they see the Son of Man coming in his kingdom.'

- A servant cannot be above his master. Just like the martyrs we must be willing to give up even our earthly lives if fidelity in our following of Christ demands it. How often do we compare the material things of this world with the things of eternity?

Saturday 9 August
St Teresa Benedicta of the Cross (Edith Stein), Virgin and Martyr
Matthew 17:14–20

When they came to the crowd, a man came to him, knelt before him, and said, 'Lord, have mercy on my son, for he is an epileptic and he suffers terribly; he often falls into the fire and often into the water. And I brought him to your disciples, but they could not cure him.' Jesus answered, 'You faithless and perverse generation, how much longer must I be with you? How much longer must I put up with you? Bring him here to me.' And Jesus rebuked the demon, and it came out of him, and the boy was cured instantly. Then the disciples came to Jesus privately and said, 'Why could we not cast it out?' He said to them, 'Because of your little faith. For truly I tell you, if you have faith the size of a mustard seed, you will say to this mountain, 'Move from here to there', and it will move; and nothing will be impossible for you.'

- Cardinal Martini of Milan often answered questions by quoting Scripture. When he was asked about his fears for the future, he replied, 'Will the Son of man find faith anywhere on earth when he comes?' Our secular world encroaches on our lives, constantly challenging us in our faith. A living prayer life is more essential than ever.

- Pope St Paul VI said the great tragedy of our times was the separation of faith from the culture. But it is in the culture that we live and move and have our being. As Christians we are called to be the leaven in the lump. We pray for the grace of fidelity.

Nineteenth Week in Ordinary Time
10–16 August 2025

Something to think and pray about each day this week:

I am often struck by the way people greet each other before Mass begins. It is very obvious that people are glad to see one another and if some are missing, others ask about them and wonder how they are. The way we greet people, welcome them, can bring a blessing to them.

Upon arriving at Elizabeth's home in the hill country of Judah, Mary, we are told, greeted Elizabeth and, because of Mary's greeting, Elizabeth was filled with the Holy Spirit. It would be wonderful if we could greet others in ways that brought the Holy Spirit to life in them. Not only was Mary's greeting a source of blessing for Elizabeth, but Elizabeth's subsequent greeting of Mary was a source of blessing for Mary.

In greeting Mary, Elizabeth declares her the most blessed of all women, because of the special child she was carrying in her womb, and also because she believed the word of promise that the Lord had spoken to her through the Angel Gabriel.

Here was a meeting between two women that brought each of them closer to the Lord. There is a pattern here for all of us. Our calling is to be present to others, to greet others, in a way that brings them closer to the Lord and creates a space for the Lord to come alive more fully within them.

Martin Hogan,
The Word Is Near You, on Your Lips and in Your Heart

The Presence of God

I remind myself that, as I sit here now, God is gazing on me with love and holding me in being. I pause for a moment and think of this.

Freedom

'There are very few people who realise what God would make of them if they abandoned themselves into his hands, and let themselves be formed by his grace' (St Ignatius). I ask for the grace to trust myself totally to God's love.

Consciousness

Where do I sense hope, encouragement, and growth in my life? By looking back over the past few months, I may be able to see which activities and occasions have produced rich fruit. If I do notice such areas, I will determine to give those areas both time and space in the future.

The Word

Lord Jesus, you became human to communicate with me. You walked and worked on this earth. You endured the heat and struggled with the cold. All your time on this earth was spent in caring for humanity. You healed the sick, you raised the dead. Most important of all, you saved me from death. *(Please turn to the Scripture on the following pages. Inspiration points are there, should you need them. When you are ready, return here to continue.)*

Conversation

What is stirring in me as I pray? Am I consoled, troubled, left cold? I imagine Jesus standing or sitting at my side, and I share my feelings with him.

Conclusion

Glory be to the Father, and to the Son, and to the Holy Spirit,
As it was in the beginning, is now and ever shall be,
World without end. Amen.

Sunday 10 August
Nineteenth Sunday in Ordinary Time
Luke 12:32–48

He said to his disciples, 'Do not be afraid, little flock, for it is your Father's good pleasure to give you the kingdom. Sell your possessions, and give alms. Make purses for yourselves that do not wear out, an unfailing treasure in heaven, where no thief comes near and no moth destroys. For where your treasure is, there your heart will be also.

'Be dressed for action and have your lamps lit; be like those who are waiting for their master to return from the wedding banquet, so that they may open the door for him as soon as he comes and knocks. Blessed are those slaves whom the master finds alert when he comes; truly I tell you, he will fasten his belt and have them sit down to eat, and he will come and serve them. If he comes during the middle of the night, or near dawn, and finds them so, blessed are those slaves.

'But know this: if the owner of the house had known at what hour the thief was coming, he would not have let his house be broken into. You also must be ready, for the Son of Man is coming at an unexpected hour.'

Peter said, 'Lord, are you telling this parable for us or for everyone?' And the Lord said, 'Who then is the faithful and prudent manager whom his master will put in charge of his slaves, to give them their allowance of food at the proper time? Blessed is that slave whom his master will find at work when he arrives. Truly I tell you, he will put that one in charge of all his possessions. But if that slave says to himself, "My master is delayed in coming", and if he begins to beat the other slaves, men and women, and to eat and drink and get drunk, the master of that slave will come on a day when he does not expect him and at an hour that he does not know, and will cut him in pieces, and put him with the unfaithful. That slave who knew what his master wanted, but did not prepare himself or do what was wanted, will receive a severe beating. But one who did not know and did what deserved a beating will receive a light beating. From everyone to whom much has been given, much will be required; and from one to whom much has been entrusted, even more will be demanded.'

- God our Father wants all people to be saved and to possess the kingdom. If he wants it then only we can block it by the misuse of our free will. We should often take to prayer St Ignatius's advice to 'ponder with deep affection how the Lord wishes to give himself to us'.

- We live out of the desires in our hearts. What is it that I really want? What is my treasure that will not wither away or pour out like water? 'Come to me, all you that are weary and are carrying heavy burdens, and I will give you rest . . . For I am gentle and humble in heart, and you will find rest for your souls' (Matthew 11:28–29).

Monday 11 August
Matthew 17:22–27

As they were gathering in Galilee, Jesus said to them, 'The Son of Man is going to be betrayed into human hands, and they will kill him, and on the third day he will be raised.' And they were greatly distressed.

When they reached Capernaum, the collectors of the temple tax came to Peter and said, 'Does your teacher not pay the temple tax?' He said, 'Yes, he does.' And when he came home, Jesus spoke of it first, asking, 'What do you think, Simon? From whom do kings of the earth take toll or tribute? From their children or from others?' When Peter said, 'From others', Jesus said to him, 'Then the children are free. However, so that we do not give offence to them, go to the lake and cast a hook; take the first fish that comes up; and when you open its mouth, you will find a coin; take that and give it to them for you and me.'

- Peter is too embarrassed to tell the temple collectors that his Master does not give a fig about the temple tax and so he says that Jesus does pay it. Jesus, to get his friend off the hook for lying, tells him to go and hook a fish and get a coin and pay for them both. There is both a human and a humorous touch about this little story, but it also shows us that Jesus is both the Son of God and Lord of the whole natural world.

Tuesday 12 August
Matthew 18:1–5, 10, 12–14

At that time the disciples came to Jesus and asked, 'Who is the greatest in the kingdom of heaven?' He called a child, whom he put among them, and said, 'Truly I tell you, unless you change and become like children, you will never enter the kingdom of heaven. Whoever becomes humble like this child is the greatest in the kingdom of heaven. Whoever welcomes one such child in my name welcomes me. . . .

'Take care that you do not despise one of these little ones; for, I tell you, in heaven their angels continually see the face of my Father in heaven. . . . What do you think? If a shepherd has a hundred sheep, and one of them has gone astray, does he not leave the ninety-nine on the mountains and go in search of the one that went astray? And if he finds it, truly I tell you, he rejoices over it more than over the ninety-nine that never went astray. So it is not the will of your Father in heaven that one of these little ones should be lost.'

- In Palestine in Jesus' time the mortality rate among children was high, so they were not highly regarded.

- God loves everything that exists and he wants us all to be with him in heaven. But because we have free will we can refuse to go along with his plan for us. We pray in the Our Father that his will may be done.

Wednesday 13 August
Matthew 18:15–20

Jesus said to them, 'If another member of the church sins against you, go and point out the fault when the two of you are alone. If the member listens to you, you have regained that one. But if you are not listened to, take one or two others along with you, so that every word may be confirmed by the evidence of two or three witnesses. If the member refuses to listen to them, tell it to the church; and if the offender refuses to listen even to the church, let such a one be to you as a Gentile and a tax-collector. Truly I tell you, whatever you bind on earth will be bound in heaven, and whatever you loose on earth will be loosed in heaven. Again, truly I tell you, if two of you agree on earth about anything you ask, it will be done for you by my Father in heaven. For where two or three are gathered in my name, I am there among them.'

- Because we are all sinners it is easy for quarrels and disputes to arise between us. We must always have forgiveness and compassion in our hearts for those who offend us, and be eager to be reconciled with them. It takes courage to go to one who has offended us and to explain how their behaviour has affected us, but it is worth it if it leads to a reconciliation.

- People often ask where can we find God. Although God is with us always there is a special presence when even two or three meet to pray. There is a triple focus on God and it pleases him greatly when we pray together.

Thursday 14 August
Matthew 18:21—19:1

Then Peter came and said to him, 'Lord, if another member of the church sins against me, how often should I forgive? As many as seven times?' Jesus said to him, 'Not seven times, but, I tell you, seventy-seven times.

'For this reason the kingdom of heaven may be compared to a king who wished to settle accounts with his slaves. When he began the reckoning, one who owed him ten thousand talents was brought to him; and, as he could not pay, his lord ordered him to be sold, together with his wife and children and all his possessions, and payment to be made. So the slave fell on his knees before him, saying, "Have patience with me, and I will pay you everything." And out of pity for him, the lord of that slave released him and forgave him the debt. But that same slave, as he went out, came upon one of his fellow-slaves who owed him a hundred denarii; and seizing him by the throat, he said, "Pay what you owe." Then his fellow-slave fell down and pleaded with him, "Have patience with me, and I will pay you." But he refused; then he went and threw him into prison until he should pay the debt. When his fellow-slaves saw what had happened, they were greatly distressed, and they went and reported to their lord all that had taken place. Then his lord summoned him and said to him, "You wicked slave! I forgave you all that debt because you pleaded with me. Should you not have had mercy on your fellow-slave, as I had mercy on you?" And in anger his lord handed him over to be tortured until he should pay his entire debt. So my heavenly Father will also do to every one of you, if you do not forgive your brother or sister from your heart.'

When Jesus had finished saying these things, he left Galilee and went to the region of Judea beyond the Jordan.

- Jesus is saying here that there must be no limit to our forgiveness of others. In this we are to try in our own poor way to imitate our God who forgives endlessly. In this Gospel, as in the Our Father, we are told that the reason we should forgive is because we ourselves are constantly being forgiven by God. Let us pray for this grace.

- Our forgiveness is tied to the call never to judge others. We cannot judge others because we cannot get inside their minds to understand all that is going on in them. Only God can do this. So we have to make allowances for them and indeed for ourselves. Let us pray for generosity and greater understanding with this.

Friday 15 August
The Assumption of the BVM
Luke 1:39–56

In those days Mary set out and went with haste to a Judean town in the hill country, where she entered the house of Zechariah and greeted Elizabeth. When Elizabeth heard Mary's greeting, the child leapt in her womb. And Elizabeth was filled with the Holy Spirit and exclaimed with a loud cry, 'Blessed are you among women, and blessed is the fruit of your womb. And why has this happened to me, that the mother of my Lord comes to me? For as soon as I heard the sound of your greeting, the child in my womb leapt for joy. And blessed is she who believed that there would be a fulfilment of what was spoken to her by the Lord.'

MARY'S SONG OF PRAISE
    And Mary said,
    'My soul magnifies the Lord,
        and my spirit rejoices in God my Saviour,
    for he has looked with favour on the lowliness of his servant.
        Surely, from now on all generations will call me blessed;
    for the Mighty One has done great things for me,
        and holy is his name.
    His mercy is for those who fear him
        from generation to generation.
    He has shown strength with his arm;
        he has scattered the proud in the thoughts of their hearts.
    He has brought down the powerful from their thrones,
        and lifted up the lowly;
    he has filled the hungry with good things,
        and sent the rich away empty.

He has helped his servant Israel,
>   in remembrance of his mercy,
according to the promise he made to our ancestors,
>   to Abraham and to his descendants for ever.'

And Mary remained with her for about three months and then returned to her home.

- Elizabeth praises Mary for her faith in the fulfilment of God's promises to her. Mary is a great model of a Christian, a true follower of her Son Jesus Christ. She lived out her 'yes' to God through the events of her life and in all the joys and sorrows that came to her. At Cana she said to the servants, 'Do whatever he tells you.' We ask her to help us to be obedient to her Son.

- Mary is also a model in her humility. In her Magnificat she acknowledges her own littleness and gives praise to God for all the great things that he has done for her. Let us join with her in giving thanks to God for all he has done for us.

Saturday 16 August
Matthew 19:13–15

Then little children were being brought to him in order that he might lay his hands on them and pray. The disciples spoke sternly to those who brought them; but Jesus said, 'Let the little children come to me, and do not stop them; for it is to such as these that the kingdom of heaven belongs.' And he laid his hands on them and went on his way.

- People wanted Jesus to bless their children. Jesus has described himself as gentle and humble in heart. His kingdom is a kingdom for those who have a childlike attitude to the Heavenly Father and who can recognise their own littleness and dependence on God. Can we talk to Jesus now about this attitude?

- Jesus in his innocence felt at home with the innocence of the little children. He said, 'Unless you change and become like children, you will never enter the kingdom of heaven.'

Something to think and pray about each day this week:

The 'wise men' are also known as magi, from the Greek word *magos*, which can be translated as astronomer, sorcerer or visionary. The term *magi* referred to a group of Persian or Babylonian priests who studied the stars and planets to discern the meaning behind cosmic events. In recent years, many theories have been posited to account for the phenomenon of the star the magi followed to Bethlehem, from Halley's Comet (which was visible around 12 BC), to a new star, to an alignment between Jupiter and Saturn. Scientists are learning more about the universe all the time, about stars and planets and galaxies. If we were to hold up the smallest coin to a section of the night sky, the area it covers could contain the light from millions upon millions of stars, many of them no longer in existence. In 2003–4, the Hubble Telescope, which is in orbit around the Earth, took a picture of such a piece of sky. The Hubble Ultra-Deep Field is an image of a small region of space in the constellation Fornax, containing an estimated 10,000 galaxies, each one containing 100,000 million stars like our sun. The vastness of our universe can be just too much for us to take in.

We believe in a God who brought everything into being, from the moment of creation when our universe began. For the magi, the wondrous light in the sky led them to the light of the world, the hope of humankind. That is something to celebrate.

Tríona Doherty and Jane Mellett,
*The Deep End: A Journey with the Sunday Gospels
in the Year of Mark*

The Presence of God

Lord, help me to be fully alive to your holy presence. Enfold me in your love. Let my heart become one with yours. My soul longs for your presence, Lord. When I turn my thoughts to you, I find peace and contentment.

Freedom

Your death on the cross has set me free. I can live joyously and freely without fear of death. Your mercy knows no bounds.

Consciousness

At this moment, Lord, I turn my thoughts to you. I will leave aside my chores and preoccupations. I will take rest and refreshment in your presence.

The Word

The word of God comes down to us through the Scriptures. May the Holy Spirit enlighten my mind and my heart to respond to the Gospel teachings: to love my neighbour as myself, to care for my sisters and brothers in Christ. *(Please turn to the Scripture on the following pages. Inspiration points are there, should you need them. When you are ready, return here to continue.)*

Conversation

Begin to talk to Jesus about the Scripture you have just read. What part of it strikes a chord in you? Perhaps the words of a friend—or some story you have heard recently—will slowly rise to the surface of your consciousness. If so, does the story throw light on what the Scripture passage may be saying to you?

Conclusion

I thank God for these moments we have spent together and for any insights I have been given concerning the text.

Sunday 17 August
Twentieth Sunday in Ordinary Time
Luke 12:49–53

He said to his disciples, 'I came to bring fire to the earth, and how I wish it were already kindled! I have a baptism with which to be baptized, and what stress I am under until it is completed! Do you think that I have come to bring peace to the earth? No, I tell you, but rather division! From now on, five in one household will be divided, three against two and two against three; they will be divided:

father against son
    and son against father,
mother against daughter
    and daughter against mother,
mother-in-law against her daughter-in-law
    and daughter-in-law against mother-in-law.'

- There can be no compromise when it comes to putting God first in our lives, even if it means that those close to us will turn from us. Jesus came to bring the fire of love to the earth, a fire that makes huge demands upon us if we are to live as true followers of Jesus. He himself lived under the shadow of the cross and, being human, it was very stressful for him. We pray for the grace and courage to take up our own crosses and follow him.

Monday 18 August
Matthew 19:16–22

Then someone came to him and said, 'Teacher, what good deed must I do to have eternal life?' And he said to him, 'Why do you ask me about what is good? There is only one who is good. If you wish to enter into life, keep the commandments.' He said to him, 'Which ones?' And Jesus said, 'You shall not murder; You shall not commit adultery; You shall not steal; You shall not bear false witness; Honour your father and mother; also, You shall love your neighbour as yourself.' The young man said to him, 'I have kept all these; what do I still lack?' Jesus said to him, 'If you wish to be perfect, go, sell your possessions, and give the money to the poor, and you will have treasure in heaven; then come, follow me.' When the young man heard this word, he went away grieving, for he had many possessions.

- The young man's attachment to his wealth became an obstacle to him. He wanted eternal life but not at any price. It was not his priority. St Paul in Colossians 3:5 tells us that greed is a form of idolatry. The first of the Ten Commandments is, 'You shall have no other gods before me.' Pope Francis invites us to reflect on what are the idols that can become obstacles on our path to eternal life.

Tuesday 19 August
Matthew 19:23–30

Then Jesus said to his disciples, 'Truly I tell you, it will be hard for a rich person to enter the kingdom of heaven. Again I tell you, it is easier for a camel to go through the eye of a needle than for someone who is rich to en-ter the kingdom of God.' When the disciples heard this, they were greatly astounded and said, 'Then who can be saved?' But Jesus looked at them and said, 'For mortals it is impossible, but for God all things are possible.'

Then Peter said in reply, 'Look, we have left everything and followed you. What then will we have?' Jesus said to them, 'Truly I tell you, at the renewal of all things, when the Son of Man is seated on the throne of his glory, you who have followed me will also sit on twelve thrones, judging the twelve tribes of Israel. And everyone who has left houses or brothers or sisters or father or mother or children or fields, for my name's sake, will receive a hundredfold, and will inherit eternal life. But many who are first will be last, and the last will be first.'

- Jesus says it will be difficult for a rich man to enter the kingdom of heaven but not impossible, because for God everything is possible. We are told that the eye of a needle refers to a narrow gate into ancient Jerusalem. The camel has to have its baggage removed to enter by the gate. What is the baggage that we carry, especially from childhood? We pray for a true discernment.

Wednesday 20 August
Matthew 20:1–16

Then Jesus said to them, 'For the kingdom of heaven is like a landowner who went out early in the morning to hire labourers for his vineyard. After agreeing with the labourers for the usual daily wage, he sent them into his vineyard. When he went out about nine o'clock, he saw others standing idle in the market-place; and he said to them, "You also go into the vineyard, and I will pay you whatever is right." So they went. When he went out again about noon and about three o'clock, he did the same. And about five o'clock he went out and found others standing around; and he said to them, "Why are you standing here idle all day?" They said to him, "Because no one has hired us." He said to them, "You also go into the vineyard." When evening came, the owner of the vineyard said to his manager, "Call the labourers and give them their pay, beginning with the last and then going to the first." When those hired about five o'clock came, each of them received the usual daily wage. Now when the first came, they thought they would receive more; but each of them also received the usual daily wage. And when they received it, they grumbled against the landowner, saying, "These last worked only one hour, and you have made them equal to us who have borne the burden of the day and the scorching heat." But he replied to one of them, "Friend, I am doing you no wrong; did you not agree with me for the usual daily wage? Take what belongs to you and go; I choose to give to this last the same as I give to you. Am I not allowed to do what I choose with what belongs to me? Or are you envious because I am generous?" So the last will be first, and the first will be last.'

- Our God is a God of infinite generosity. Everything we have has come as a gift from him, including our lives. We have only to look at the extraordinary variety of things in our beautiful world and all the different fruits on our supermarket shelves. To God belongs everything that exists. In this gospel he says, 'I choose to give what belongs to me.' It is a joy to the Lover to give to the beloved. Let us be generous as our Heavenly Father is generous.

- You might like to pray the prayer for generosity in God's service attributed to St Ignatius: 'Lord teach me to be generous, to give and not to count the cost, to fight and not to heed the wounds, to toil and not to seek for rest, to labour and to look for no reward, save that of knowing that I do your will.'

Thursday 21 August
Matthew 22:1–14

Once more Jesus spoke to them in parables, saying: 'The kingdom of heaven may be compared to a king who gave a wedding banquet for his son. He sent his slaves to call those who had been invited to the wedding banquet, but they would not come. Again he sent other slaves, saying, "Tell those who have been invited: Look, I have prepared my dinner, my oxen and my fat calves have been slaughtered, and everything is ready; come to the wedding banquet." But they made light of it and went away, one to his farm, another to his business, while the rest seized his slaves, maltreated them, and killed them. The king was enraged. He sent his troops, destroyed those murderers, and burned their city. Then he said to his slaves, "The wedding is ready, but those invited were not worthy. Go therefore into the main streets, and invite everyone you find to the wedding banquet." Those slaves went out into the streets and gathered all whom they found, both good and bad; so the wedding hall was filled with guests.

'But when the king came in to see the guests, he noticed a man there who was not wearing a wedding robe, and he said to him, "Friend, how did you get in here without a wedding robe?" And he was speechless. Then the king said to the attendants, "Bind him hand and foot, and throw him into the outer darkness, where there will be weeping and gnashing of teeth." For many are called, but few are chosen.'

- We are all invited to the heavenly banquet, but some refuse and live as though they are not interested in it. We must watch and pray to be ready when we receive our invitation. 'Blessed are those slaves whom the master finds alert when he comes; truly I tell you, he will fasten his belt and have them sit down to eat, and he will come and serve them' (Luke 12:37).

- The wedding garment is the white robe of baptism which we must keep clean for our entry into heaven. We read in the Book of Revelation about those who have come through great persecution and have washed their robes and made them white in the blood of the Lamb (7:14).

Friday 22 August
Matthew 22:34–40

When the Pharisees heard that he had silenced the Sadducees, they gathered together, and one of them, a lawyer, asked him a question to test him. "Teacher, which commandment in the law is the greatest?" He said to him, "'You shall love the Lord your God with all your heart, and with all your soul, and with all your mind." This is the greatest and first commandment. And a second is like it: "You shall love your neighbour as yourself." On these two commandments hang all the law and the prophets.'

- All the commandments are summed up in these two commandments which are really one since it is out of the one heart that we live and love. St Augustine said, 'Love God and then do whatever you want.' Real love will guide all our actions.

- St John Vianney wrote, 'Humanity has a noble task, that of prayer and love. To pray and to love, that is our happiness on earth.' In fact, this is the whole purpose of our life on earth, namely to develop our own individual God-given capacity to love, so that in heaven we can merge with God who is Love.

Saturday 23 August
Matthew 23:1–12

Then Jesus said to the crowds and to his disciples, 'The scribes and the Pharisees sit on Moses' seat; therefore, do whatever they teach you and follow it; but do not do as they do, for they do not practise what they teach. They tie up heavy burdens, hard to bear, and lay them on the shoulders of others; but they themselves are unwilling to lift a finger to move them. They do all their deeds to be seen by others; for they make their phylacteries broad and their fringes long. They love to have the place of honour at banquets and the best seats in the synagogues, and to be greeted with respect in the market-places, and to have people call them rabbi. But you are not to be called rabbi, for you have one teacher, and you are all students. And call no one your father on earth, for you have one Father—the one in heaven. Nor are you to be called instructors, for you have one instructor, the Messiah. The greatest among you will be your

servant. All who exalt themselves will be humbled, and all who humble
themselves will be exalted.'

- Jesus points out the hypocrisy of the religious leaders of his day who
want to appear great in people's eyes. What matters is how we are in
God's eyes. Abraham Lincoln was once asked in relation to the Civil
War, 'Is God on our side? He replied, 'What matters is that we are on
God's side, for God is always right.'

- We have only one teacher, the Christ. 'This is my Beloved Son, listen
to him.' Do we take quiet time to listen to Jesus in our prayer?

Something to think and pray about each day this week:

Human beings desire happiness. We sometimes look for it in the wrong places and end up unhappier than when we went on our quest for happiness in the first place. It's sometimes this unreflective choice that spawns further personal and communal unhappiness. That recreational drug won't do me any harm. It's only a bit of fun. I'm okay, I'll drive. Human experience confirms that we're happiest when we're exercising compassion and generosity in the variety of ordinary circumstances of life, through all those 'little, nameless, unremembered, acts / Of kindness and of love' (William Wordsworth, 'Tintern Abbey') that usually fill most of our day. Attentiveness to others establishes a contentment and peace, which strengthens us to welcome joys and embrace the burdens of sorrow. Irresponsible stimuli sometimes pass for happiness. However, they are usually superficial and transitory, leaving a hollow afterglow. Happiness is the peace and contentment that helps us to stay the course responsibly. Superficial feelings of elation pass quickly. Developing a healthy spirituality will help us to find a lasting peace because the path to peace comes from reflective living and learning from experience what it really is to be an authentic person. If there is no pattern of at least some minimal reflection, we're living shallow lives.

Jim Maher SJ,
Reimagining Religion: A Jesuit Vision

The Presence of God
The more we call on God the more we can feel God's presence. Day by day we are drawn closer to the loving heart of God.

Freedom
I am free. When I look at these words in writing, they seem to create in me a feeling of awe. Yes, a wonderful feeling of freedom. Thank you, God.

Consciousness
Help me, Lord, become more conscious of your presence. Teach me to recognise your presence in others. Fill my heart with gratitude for the times your love has been shown to me through the care of others.

The Word
The word of God comes down to us through the Scriptures. May the Holy Spirit enlighten my mind and my heart to respond to the Gospel teachings. *(Please turn to the Scripture on the following pages. Inspiration points are there, should you need them. When you are ready, return here to continue.)*

Conversation
Conversation requires talking and listening. As I talk to Jesus, may I also learn to pause and listen. I picture the gentleness in his eyes and the love in his smile. I can be totally honest with Jesus as I tell him my worries and cares. I will open my heart to Jesus as I tell him my fears and doubts. I will ask him to help me place myself fully in his care, knowing that he always desires good for me.

Conclusion
Glory be to the Father, and to the Son, and to the Holy Spirit,
As it was in the beginning, is now and ever shall be,
World without end. Amen.

Sunday 24 August
Twenty-first Sunday in Ordinary Time
Luke 13:22–30

Jesus went through one town and village after another, teaching as he made his way to Jerusalem. Someone asked him, 'Lord, will only a few be saved?' He said to them, 'Strive to enter through the narrow door; for many, I tell you, will try to enter and will not be able. When once the owner of the house has got up and shut the door, and you begin to stand outside and to knock at the door, saying, "Lord, open to us", then in reply he will say to you, "I do not know where you come from." Then you will begin to say, "We ate and drank with you, and you taught in our streets." But he will say, "I do not know where you come from; go away from me, all you evildoers!" There will be weeping and gnashing of teeth when you see Abraham and Isaac and Jacob and all the prophets in the kingdom of God, and you yourselves thrown out. Then people will come from east and west, from north and south, and will eat in the kingdom of God. Indeed, some are last who will be first, and some are first who will be last.'

- All people are invited to the heavenly banquet, and to come to know the Lord, but we are free to refuse. In Hosea 6:6 we read, 'For I desire . . . the knowledge of God rather than burnt-offerings.' No one can ever force us to pray. We must want it ourselves and take the means to grow in it. 'Prayer is a gift given to those who pray' (St John Climacus).

Monday 25 August
Matthew 23:13–22

Then Jesus said to the crowds and to his disciples, 'But woe to you, scribes and Pharisees, hypocrites! For you lock people out of the kingdom of heaven. For you do not go in yourselves, and when others are going in, you stop them. Woe to you, scribes and Pharisees, hypocrites! For you cross sea and land to make a single convert, and you make the new convert twice as much a child of hell as yourselves.

'Woe to you, blind guides, who say, "Whoever swears by the sanctuary is bound by nothing, but whoever swears by the gold of the sanctuary is bound by the oath." You blind fools! For which is greater, the gold or the sanctuary that has made the gold sacred? And you say, "Whoever swears by the altar is bound by nothing, but whoever swears by the gift that is on the altar is bound by the oath." How blind you are! For which is greater, the gift or the altar that makes the gift sacred? So whoever swears by the altar, swears by it and by everything on it; and whoever swears by the sanctuary, swears by it and by the one who dwells in it; and whoever swears by heaven, swears by the throne of God and by the one who is seated upon it.'

- Over the centuries countless people have been led astray by false prophets and false doctrines. In our modern world we call it misinformation but in plain English it is simply lies. Jesus said he came to bear witness to the truth. Let us listen to him as the Father has bid us. We pray for the grace of discernment and to grow in our faith and to be faithful to whatever God asks of us.

Tuesday 26 August
Matthew 23:23–26

Then Jesus said to the crowds and to his disciples, 'Woe to you, scribes and Pharisees, hypocrites! For you tithe mint, dill, and cummin, and have neglected the weightier matters of the law: justice and mercy and faith. It is these you ought to have practised without neglecting the others. You blind guides! You strain out a gnat but swallow a camel!

'Woe to you, scribes and Pharisees, hypocrites! For you clean the outside of the cup and of the plate, but inside they are full of greed and self-indulgence. You blind Pharisee! First clean the inside of the cup, so that the outside also may become clean.'

- Shakespeare wrote, 'A goodly apple rotten at the heart. Oh, what a goodly outside falsehood.' we are all of us made to grow in our capacity to love and with God's grace to overcome the selfishness that is in us all. We pray for the gifts of the Holy Spirit, love, joy, peace, patience, kindness, fidelity and courage to seek and live the truth.

Wednesday 27 August
Matthew 23:27–32

Jesus said, 'Woe to you, scribes and Pharisees, hypocrites! For you are like whitewashed tombs, which on the outside look beautiful, but inside they are full of the bones of the dead and of all kinds of filth. So you also on the outside look righteous to others, but inside you are full of hypocrisy and lawlessness.

'Woe to you, scribes and Pharisees, hypocrites! For you build the tombs of the prophets and decorate the graves of the righteous, and you say, "If we had lived in the days of our ancestors, we would not have taken part with them in shedding the blood of the prophets." Thus you testify against yourselves that you are descendants of those who murdered the prophets. Fill up, then, the measure of your ancestors.'

- In his castigations of the scribes and Pharisees Jesus tries to jolt them out of their blindness to their own hypocrisy and sins. When we look at our world today we see that very little has changed over the centuries in terms of evil deeds and pride and self-seeking. We are all sinners and there is a darkness in the heart of humankind. Jesus told us that it is out of the human heart that evil deeds come. We pray for our world and for a change of heart and especially for our leaders, both political and religious. And we pray also for God's mercy on ourselves.

Thursday 28 August
Matthew 24:42–51

Jesus said to his disciples, 'Keep awake therefore, for you do not know on what day your Lord is coming. But understand this: if the owner of the house had known in what part of the night the thief was coming, he would have stayed awake and would not have let his house be broken into. Therefore you also must be ready, for the Son of Man is coming at an unexpected hour.

'Who then is the faithful and wise slave, whom his master has put in charge of his household, to give the other slaves their allowance of food at the proper time? Blessed is that slave whom his master will find at work when he arrives. Truly I tell you, he will put that one in charge of all his possessions. But if that wicked slave says to himself, "My master is delayed", and he begins to beat his fellow-slaves, and eats and drinks with drunkards, the master of that slave will come on a day when he does not expect him and at an hour that he does not know. He will cut him in pieces and put him with the hypocrites, where there will be weeping and gnashing of teeth.'

- All of us know with complete certainty that we will depart this life. A day or even a month is but the blink of an eye when compared to eternity. Jesus in this Gospel urges us to reflect on our own deaths, and to prepare by lives of prayer and watchfulness. Lord, help us to see the things that matter in the light of eternity.

Friday 29 August
Mark 6:17–29

For Herod himself had sent men who arrested John, bound him, and put him in prison on account of Herodias, his brother Philip's wife, because Herod had married her. For John had been telling Herod, 'It is not lawful for you to have your brother's wife.' And Herodias had a grudge against him, and wanted to kill him. But she could not, for Herod feared John, knowing that he was a righteous and holy man, and he protected him. When he heard him, he was greatly perplexed; and yet he liked to listen to him. But an opportunity came when Herod on his birthday gave a banquet for his courtiers and officers and for the leaders of Galilee. When his daughter Herodias came in and danced, she pleased Herod and his guests; and the king said to the girl, 'Ask me for whatever you wish, and I will give it.' And he solemnly swore to her, 'Whatever you ask me, I will give you, even half of my kingdom.' She went out and said to her mother, 'What should I ask for?' She replied, 'The head of John the baptizer.' Immediately she rushed back to the king and requested, 'I want you to give me at once the head of John the Baptist on a platter.' The king was deeply grieved; yet out of regard for his oaths and for the guests, he did not want to refuse her. Immediately the king sent a soldier of the guard with orders to bring John's head. He went and beheaded him in the prison, brought his head on a platter, and gave it to the girl. Then the girl gave it to her mother. When his disciples heard about it, they came and took his body, and laid it in a tomb.

- Although deeply grieved by what he was being asked to do, Herod thought it better to please his guests than to act by his conscience. How often we excuse our own bad actions and ignore what we know in our hearts we should do. How often we allow the opinion of others about us to guide our moral actions. Let us examine our consciences on our sinful actions and ask for forgiveness and the courage to do what we know to be right.

Saturday 30 August

Matthew 25:14–30

Jesus told them this parable, 'For it is as if a man, going on a journey, summoned his slaves and entrusted his property to them; to one he gave five talents, to another two, to another one, to each according to his ability. Then he went away. The one who had received the five talents went off at once and traded with them, and made five more talents. In the same way, the one who had the two talents made two more talents. But the one who had received the one talent went off and dug a hole in the ground and hid his master's money. After a long time the master of those slaves came and settled accounts with them. Then the one who had received the five talents came forward, bringing five more talents, saying, "Master, you handed over to me five talents; see, I have made five more talents." His master said to him, "Well done, good and trustworthy slave; you have been trustworthy in a few things, I will put you in charge of many things; enter into the joy of your master." And the one with the two talents also came forward, saying, "Master, you handed over to me two talents; see, I have made two more talents." His master said to him, "Well done, good and trustworthy slave; you have been trustworthy in a few things, I will put you in charge of many things; enter into the joy of your master." Then the one who had received the one talent also came forward, saying, "Master, I knew that you were a harsh man, reaping where you did not sow, and gathering where you did not scatter seed; so I was afraid, and I went and hid your talent in the ground. Here you have what is yours." But his master replied, "You wicked and lazy slave! You knew, did you, that I reap where I did not sow, and gather where I did not scatter? Then you ought to have invested my money with the bankers, and on my return I would have received what was my own with interest. So take the talent from him, and give it to the one with the ten talents. For to all those who have, more will be given, and they will have an abundance; but from those who have nothing, even what they have will be taken away. As for this worthless slave, throw him into the outer darkness, where there will be weeping and gnashing of teeth."'

- Each of us has been given our own unique talents to be used for the benefit of all. We will have to render an account on how well we have used them. No one is an island and our lives do make a difference to others, for better or for worse. Fear and laziness will prove very poor excuses on judgement day. How well do I use my gifts for the benefit of others?

- When we meet our Lord at death, may we hear the words, 'Well done, good and faithful servant! Enter into the joy of your Master.'

Something to think and pray about each day this week:

When we are grieving or in doubt, we know we can turn to the Bible in trust. When we turn to the Bible, to particular verses, we are in fact making our own personal map of the rooms where we feel at home with God and ourselves. These rooms become home to us. We can visit them as we begin the day or take a quiet break in them in the evening. These verses become places where we take root and from which we grow, like the fruitful tree in the first psalm, 'whose leaves never fade'.

The Bible and the gospels remind us that we never go home alone! God's word is an invitation to engage in conversation—whether verbal or silent. Often this conversation will bring us into the varied company of the people in the Bible stories.

Being at home in God's word allows us solitude when we need it. It also offers us the interesting company of people who can comfort us when we are disturbed, and disturb us when we are too comfortable.

Alan Hilliard,
The Sacred Heart Messenger,
July 2022

The Presence of God

'Be still, and know that I am God!' Lord, your words lead us to the calmness and greatness of your presence.

Freedom

'In these days, God taught me as a schoolteacher teaches a pupil' (St Ignatius). I remind myself that there are things God has to teach me yet, and I ask for the grace to hear them and let them change me.

Consciousness

How am I really feeling? Lighthearted? Heavyhearted? I may be very much at peace, happy to be here. Equally, I may be frustrated, worried or angry. I acknowledge how I really am. It is the real me whom the Lord loves.

The Word

God speaks to each of us individually. I listen attentively to hear what he is saying to me. Read the text a few times, then listen. *(Please turn to the Scripture on the following pages. Inspiration points are there, should you need them. When you are ready, return here to continue.)*

Conversation

Do I notice myself reacting as I pray with the word of God? Do I feel challenged, comforted, angry? Imagining Jesus sitting or standing by me, I speak out my feelings, as one trusted friend to another.

Conclusion

I thank God for these moments we have spent together and for any insights I have been given concerning the text.

Sunday 31 August
Twenty-second Sunday in Ordinary Time
Luke 14:1, 7–14

On one occasion when Jesus was going to the house of a leader of the Pharisees to eat a meal on the sabbath, they were watching him closely. . . .

When he noticed how the guests chose the places of honour, he told them a parable. 'When you are invited by someone to a wedding banquet, do not sit down at the place of honour, in case someone more distinguished than you has been invited by your host; and the host who invited both of you may come and say to you, "Give this person your place", and then in disgrace you would start to take the lowest place. But when you are invited, go and sit down at the lowest place, so that when your host comes, he may say to you, "Friend, move up higher"; then you will be honoured in the presence of all who sit at the table with you. For all who exalt themselves will be humbled, and those who humble themselves will be exalted.'

He said also to the one who had invited him, 'When you give a luncheon or a dinner, do not invite your friends or your brothers or your relatives or rich neighbours, in case they may invite you in return, and you would be repaid. But when you give a banquet, invite the poor, the crippled, the lame, and the blind. And you will be blessed, because they cannot repay you, for you will be repaid at the resurrection of the righteous.'

- The greatest among you must be the servant of all. 'The Son of Man came not to be served but to serve and to give his life a ransom for many.' Do I seek to be honoured by people instead of by God? The opinions of people about us will always be varied and, in the end, they simply don't matter.

- 'Lord, teach me to be generous, to give and not to count the cost, to fight and not to heed the wounds, to labour and not to look for any reward save that of knowing that I do your will' (St Ignatius).

Monday 1 September
Luke 4:16–30

When he came to Nazareth, where he had been brought up, he went to the synagogue on the sabbath day, as was his custom. He stood up to read, and the scroll of the prophet Isaiah was given to him. He unrolled the scroll and found the place where it was written:

'The Spirit of the Lord is upon me,
    because he has anointed me
        to bring good news to the poor.
He has sent me to proclaim release to the captives
    and recovery of sight to the blind,
        to let the oppressed go free,
    to proclaim the year of the Lord's favour.'

And he rolled up the scroll, gave it back to the attendant, and sat down. The eyes of all in the synagogue were fixed on him. Then he began to say to them, 'Today this scripture has been fulfilled in your hearing.' All spoke well of him and were amazed at the gracious words that came from his mouth. They said, 'Is not this Joseph's son?' He said to them, 'Doubtless you will quote to me this proverb, "Doctor, cure yourself!" And you will say, "Do here also in your home town the things that we have heard you did at Capernaum."' And he said, 'Truly I tell you, no prophet is accepted in the prophet's home town. But the truth is, there were many widows in Israel in the time of Elijah, when the heaven was shut up for three years and six months, and there was a severe famine over all the land; yet Elijah was sent to none of them except to a widow at Zarephath in Sidon. There were also many lepers in Israel in the time of the prophet Elisha, and none of them was cleansed except Naaman the Syrian.' When they heard this, all in the synagogue were filled with rage. They got up, drove him out of the town, and led him to the brow of the hill on which their town was built, so that they might hurl him off the cliff. But he passed through the midst of them and went on his way.

- Jesus lived a fully human life and he was not spared the trials, disappointments and failures to which we are all subject. How well do I accept disappointments and my own failures? And how well do I use the opportunities that are given to me to grow in trust and love?

- As I listen to the words of Jesus in the gospels do I receive them with faith and gratitude and humility? The same Jesus who spoke in that synagogue in Nazareth is with me now in prayer.

Tuesday 2 September
Luke 4:31–37

He went down to Capernaum, a city in Galilee, and was teaching them on the sabbath. They were astounded at his teaching, because he spoke with authority. In the synagogue there was a man who had the spirit of an unclean demon, and he cried out with a loud voice, 'Let us alone! What have you to do with us, Jesus of Nazareth? Have you come to destroy us? I know who you are, the Holy One of God.' But Jesus rebuked him, saying, 'Be silent, and come out of him!' When the demon had thrown him down before them, he came out of him without having done him any harm. They were all amazed and kept saying to one another, 'What kind of utterance is this? For with authority and power he commands the unclean spirits, and out they come!' And a report about him began to reach every place in the region.

- In the Gospels we read that the people were astounded and impressed by the authority with which Jesus spoke. Again and again he backs this authority up by works of power and of goodness. In our modern world, it is said that we have gone from the experience of authority to the authority of experience. How open am I to learning from my own experience of what gives life to me? And am I willing to accept the authority of the Gospels as to how I should live my life?

Wednesday 3 September
Luke 4:38–44

After leaving the synagogue he entered Simon's house. Now Simon's mother-in-law was suffering from a high fever, and they asked him about her. Then he stood over her and rebuked the fever, and it left her. Immediately she got up and began to serve them.

As the sun was setting, all those who had any who were sick with various kinds of diseases brought them to him; and he laid his hands on each of them and cured them. Demons also came out of many, shouting, 'You are the Son of God!' But he rebuked them and would not allow them to speak, because they knew that he was the Messiah.

At daybreak he departed and went into a deserted place. And the crowds were looking for him; and when they reached him, they wanted to prevent him from leaving them. But he said to them, 'I must proclaim the good news of the kingdom of God to the other cities also; for I was sent for this purpose.' So he continued proclaiming the message in the synagogues of Judea.

- People are always in need of healing but we tend to focus more on a physical healing than a spiritual one. Jesus came to call sinners to repentance and to live in a new way. Let us ask the Lord for the gift of true discernment.

- After that very busy day curing all those who were brought to him, Jesus rises early to go to a lonely place to pray. In our overly busy lives do we commit ourselves to spending time each day in a quiet place meeting our Lord in prayer? For some people this may mean getting up earlier in the morning.

Thursday 4 September
Luke 5:1–11

Once while Jesus was standing beside the lake of Gennesaret, and the crowd was pressing in on him to hear the word of God, he saw two boats there at the shore of the lake; the fishermen had gone out of them and were washing their nets. He got into one of the boats, the one belonging to Simon, and asked him to put out a little way from the shore. Then he sat down and taught the crowds from the boat. When he had finished speaking, he said to Simon, 'Put out into the deep water and let down your nets for a catch.' Simon answered, 'Master, we have worked all night long but have caught nothing. Yet if you say so, I will let down the nets.' When they had done this, they caught so many fish that their nets were beginning to break. So they signalled to their partners in the other boat to come and help them. And they came and filled both boats, so that they began to sink. But when Simon Peter saw it, he fell down at Jesus' knees, saying, 'Go away from me, Lord, for I am a sinful man!' For he and all who were with him were amazed at the catch of fish that they had taken; and so also were James and John, sons of Zebedee, who were partners with Simon. Then Jesus said to Simon, 'Do not be afraid; from now on you will be catching people.' When they had brought their boats to shore, they left everything and followed him.

- At this miracle Peter is awestruck in the presence of Jesus and becomes very aware of his own sinfulness. It is through becoming aware of our own weakness and sinfulness that we grow in humility and so become better instruments in the hands of God. Let us pray now for this greater awareness.

Friday 5 September
Luke 5:33–39

Then they said to him, 'John's disciples, like the disciples of the Pharisees, frequently fast and pray, but your disciples eat and drink.' Jesus said to them, 'You cannot make wedding-guests fast while the bridegroom is with them, can you? The days will come when the bridegroom will be taken away from them, and then they will fast in those days.' He also told them a parable: 'No one tears a piece from a new garment and sews it on an old garment; otherwise the new will be torn, and the piece from the new will not match the old. And no one puts new wine into old wineskins; otherwise the new wine will burst the skins and will be spilled, and the skins will be destroyed. But new wine must be put into fresh wineskins. And no one after drinking old wine desires new wine, but says, "The old is good."'

- The new wine of the kingdom of God brought to us by Jesus needs new wineskins. Jesus came to perfect the law and to usher in what St Paul calls a new creation. St John Henry Newman wrote, 'To live is to change, and to live well is to change often.'

Saturday 6 September
Luke 6:1–5

One sabbath while Jesus was going through the cornfields, his disciples plucked some heads of grain, rubbed them in their hands, and ate them. But some of the Pharisees said, 'Why are you doing what is not lawful on the sabbath?' Jesus answered, 'Have you not read what David did when he and his companions were hungry? He entered the house of God and took and ate the bread of the Presence, which it is not lawful for any but the priests to eat, and gave some to his companions.' Then he said to them, 'The Son of Man is lord of the sabbath.'

- If it was okay for David to break a manmade temple rule, how much more can the Son of Man do so? Jesus came to us with authority from heaven to show us how to live and how to love. At the washing of the feet in John's Gospel he said, 'You call me Teacher and Lord—and you are right, for that is what I am' (13:13). Jesus is always the guide and headline for our lives.

- To honour God on the sabbath and to pray is for our sake, not God's. It is we who need God, not vice versa. St Ignatius wrote in the First Principle of his Spiritual Exercises, 'Man is created to praise, reverence and serve God', but this is so that we will find happiness with God in heaven.

Something to think and pray about each day this week:

It is worthwhile to explore the riches of the Pope's chosen term for mother earth, our common home. The word 'home' stirs up in us a world of memories and emotions. If you have had a happy childhood, home is the place for which you feel the greatest affection; here, good relationships were blended with the particularities of the place where you began your life. As Elvis Presley has it, home is where the heart is. This resonates with the saying, 'It takes hands to build a house, but only hearts can build a home.'

The Pope says: 'Our common home is like a sister with whom we share our life and a beautiful mother who opens her arms to embrace us' (*Laudato Si'*, 1).

It is hard to imagine a more heart-stirring name for the world than 'our common home'. 'Our planet is a homeland and humanity is one people living in a common home' (*Laudato Si'*, 164).

We must rediscover what our ancestors enjoyed—a deep and loving sense of relationship with planet earth and all its inhabitants. As children we shared what was perhaps a small home; now we share a planet, and like St Francis of Assisi of old we in our time are charged with the task of protecting and repairing it.

Brian Grogan SJ,
Finding God in a Leaf: The Mysticism of Laudato Si'

The Presence of God

To be present is to arrive as one is and open up to the other. At this instant, as I arrive here, God is present waiting for me. God always arrives before me, desiring to connect with me even more than my most intimate friend. I take a moment and greet my loving God.

Freedom

Leave me here freely all alone. / In cell where never sunlight shone. / Should no one ever speak to me. / This golden silence makes me free!

—Part of a poem by Bl Titus Brandsma, written while he was a prisoner at Dachau concentration camp

Consciousness

Where am I with God? With others? Do I have something to be grateful for? Then I give thanks. Is there something I am sorry for? Then I ask forgiveness.

The Word

I take my time to read the word of God slowly, a few times, allowing myself to dwell on anything that strikes me. *(Please turn to the Scripture on the following pages. Inspiration points are there, should you need them. When you are ready, return here to continue.)*

Conversation

How has God's word moved me? Has it left me cold? Has it consoled me or moved me to act in a new way? I imagine Jesus standing or sitting beside me; I turn and share my feelings with him.

Conclusion

Glory be to the Father, and to the Son, and to the Holy Spirit,
As it was in the beginning, is now and ever shall be,
World without end. Amen.

Sunday 7 September
Twenty-third Sunday in Ordinary Time
Luke 14:25–33

Now large crowds were travelling with him; and he turned and said to them, 'Whoever comes to me and does not hate father and mother, wife and children, brothers and sisters, yes, and even life itself, cannot be my disciple. Whoever does not carry the cross and follow me cannot be my disciple. For which of you, intending to build a tower, does not first sit down and estimate the cost, to see whether he has enough to complete it? Otherwise, when he has laid a foundation and is not able to finish, all who see it will begin to ridicule him, saying, "This fellow began to build and was not able to finish." Or what king, going out to wage war against another king, will not sit down first and consider whether he is able with ten thousand to oppose the one who comes against him with twenty thousand? If he cannot, then, while the other is still far away, he sends a delegation and asks for the terms of peace. So therefore, none of you can become my disciple if you do not give up all your possessions.'

• Clearly the words 'hate father and mother etc. are not to be taken literally. It is a Semitic way of making a strong point. Discipleship does, of course, cost everything. 'The one who loses his life for my sake will find it.' God must always come first in our lives. This is our 'yes' to God in the commitment of faith. The reward is eternal life. We pray for the grace of perseverance.

Monday 8 September
The Nativity of the BVM
Matthew 1:1–16, 18–23

An account of the genealogy of Jesus the Messiah, the son of David, the son of Abraham.

Abraham was the father of Isaac, and Isaac the father of Jacob, and Jacob the father of Judah and his brothers, and Judah the father of Perez and Zerah by Tamar, and Perez the father of Hezron, and Hezron the father of Aram, and Aram the father of Aminadab, and Aminadab the father of Nahshon, and Nahshon the father of Salmon, and Salmon the father of Boaz by Rahab, and Boaz the father of Obed by Ruth, and Obed the father of Jesse, and Jesse the father of King David.

And David was the father of Solomon by the wife of Uriah, and Solomon the father of Rehoboam, and Rehoboam the father of Abijah, and Abijah the father of Asaph, and Asaph the father of Jehoshaphat, and Jehoshaphat the father of Joram, and Joram the father of Uzziah, and Uzziah the father of Jotham, and Jotham the father of Ahaz, and Ahaz the father of Hezekiah, and Hezekiah the father of Manasseh, and Manasseh the father of Amos, and Amos the father of Josiah, and Josiah the father of Jechoniah and his brothers, at the time of the deportation to Babylon.

And after the deportation to Babylon: Jechoniah was the father of Salathiel, and Salathiel the father of Zerubbabel, and Zerubbabel the father of Abiud, and Abiud the father of Eliakim, and Eliakim the father of Azor, and Azor the father of Zadok, and Zadok the father of Achim, and Achim the father of Eliud, and Eliud the father of Eleazar, and Eleazar the father of Matthan, and Matthan the father of Jacob, and Jacob the father of Joseph the husband of Mary, of whom Jesus was born, who is called the Messiah. . . .

Now the birth of Jesus the Messiah took place in this way. When his mother Mary had been engaged to Joseph, but before they lived together, she was found to be with child from the Holy Spirit. Her husband Joseph, being a righteous man and unwilling to expose her to public disgrace, planned to dismiss her quietly. But just when he had resolved to do this, an angel of the Lord appeared to him in a dream and said, 'Joseph, son of David, do not be afraid to take Mary as your wife, for the child conceived in her is from the Holy Spirit. She will bear a son, and you are to name him Jesus, for he will save his people from their sins.' All this took place to fulfil what had been spoken by the Lord through the prophet:

'Look, the virgin shall conceive and bear a son,
    and they shall name him Emmanuel',
which means, 'God is with us.'

• This must have been a very difficult time for both Mary and Joseph. It is clear that Joseph puzzled over what he should do and finally resolved on a particular course of action, before the angel intervened. We too are often left by God to puzzle over what we should do in difficult circumstances. Through prayer and careful discernment in the light of the Gospels we trust that God will show us the way.

- Jesus has promised to be with us always. Although he returned to his Father, he never left us and is within us through the Holy Spirit. Let us pray for a greater faith in the indwelling of the Most Holy Trinity in us.

Tuesday 9 September
Luke 6:12–19

Now during those days he went out to the mountain to pray; and he spent the night in prayer to God. And when day came, he called his disciples and chose twelve of them, whom he also named apostles: Simon, whom he named Peter, and his brother Andrew, and James, and John, and Philip, and Bartholomew, and Matthew, and Thomas, and James son of Alphaeus, and Simon, who was called the Zealot, and Judas son of James, and Judas Iscariot, who became a traitor.

He came down with them and stood on a level place, with a great crowd of his disciples and a great multitude of people from all Judea, Jerusalem, and the coast of Tyre and Sidon. They had come to hear him and to be healed of their diseases; and those who were troubled with unclean spirits were cured. And all in the crowd were trying to touch him, for power came out from him and healed all of them.

- The choices of God are always a mystery to us. To continue his mission on earth it was important that Jesus should choose well from among his many disciples, and so he spends the whole night in prayer. In our discernment for important decisions one of the means we use is to bring the matter up in prayer again and again. Let us pray for the grace to know whatever God is asking of us.

Wednesday 10 September
Luke 6:20–26

Then he looked up at his disciples and said:
    'Blessed are you who are poor,
        for yours is the kingdom of God.
    'Blessed are you who are hungry now,
        for you will be filled.
    'Blessed are you who weep now,
        for you will laugh.

'Blessed are you when people hate you, and when they exclude you, revile you, and defame you on account of the Son of Man. Rejoice on that day and leap for joy, for surely your reward is great in heaven; for that is what their ancestors did to the prophets.

'But woe to you who are rich,
    for you have received your consolation.
'Woe to you who are full now,
    for you will be hungry.
'Woe to you who are laughing now,
    for you will mourn and weep.
'Woe to you when all speak well of you, for that is what their ancestors did to the false prophets.'

- It is those who recognise their own poverty within themselves and their complete dependence on God who possess the kingdom of God. The values and ways of the world will always be different from those of the kingdom and so there will be opposition from a secular society. Let us pray for all who are persecuted for their faith and ask for the grace of perseverance in our fidelity to Christ.

- St Paul in his letters tells us to put on the mind of Christ. Let us pray to live by the values and teachings of Jesus.

Thursday 11 September
Luke 6:27–38

Jesus said to them, 'But I say to you that listen, Love your enemies, do good to those who hate you, bless those who curse you, pray for those who abuse you. If anyone strikes you on the cheek, offer the other also; and from anyone who takes away your coat do not withhold even your shirt. Give to everyone who begs from you; and if anyone takes away your goods, do not ask for them again. Do to others as you would have them do to you.

'If you love those who love you, what credit is that to you? For even sinners love those who love them. If you do good to those who do good to you, what credit is that to you? For even sinners do the same. If you lend to those from whom you hope to receive, what credit is that to you? Even sinners lend to sinners, to receive as much again. But love your enemies, do good, and lend, expecting nothing in return. Your reward will be great, and you will be children of the Most High; for he is kind to the ungrateful and the wicked. Be merciful, just as your Father is merciful.'

'Do not judge, and you will not be judged; do not condemn, and you will not be condemned. Forgive, and you will be forgiven; give, and it will be given to you. A good measure, pressed down, shaken together, running over, will be put into your lap; for the measure you give will be the measure you get back.'

- It is not easy to forgive those who have seriously hurt us but we have the example of Christ and the many martyrs. On the cross, Jesus prayed for his executioners, 'Father, forgive them; for they do not know what they are doing.' Let us pray for the grace to forgive others and to recognise our own need for forgiveness.

- Our Christian faith calls for us to live in a different way from that dictated by the secular culture. The gospels remind us of the golden rule to treat others as we would wish to be treated. Before Jesus departed from us he gave us a new commandment, to love one another. This was to be the distinguishing mark of his disciples. How well do we measure up to this?

Friday 12 September
Luke 6:39–42

He also told them a parable: 'Can a blind person guide a blind person? Will not both fall into a pit? A disciple is not above the teacher, but everyone who is fully qualified will be like the teacher. Why do you see the speck in your neighbour's eye, but do not notice the log in your own eye? Or how can you say to your neighbour, "Friend, let me take out the speck in your eye", when you yourself do not see the log in your own eye? You hypocrite, first take the log out of your own eye, and then you will see clearly to take the speck out of your neighbour's eye.'

- We are often slow to notice our own faults. If we want to change the world it is good to begin with ourselves. We pray for a greater awareness of how we live the gospel message, and we pray that we become better disciples of the Master.

Saturday 13 September
Luke 6:43–49

He said to them, 'No good tree bears bad fruit, nor again does a bad tree bear good fruit; for each tree is known by its own fruit. Figs are not gathered from thorns, nor are grapes picked from a bramble bush. The good person out of the good treasure of the heart produces good, and the evil person out of evil treasure produces evil; for it is out of the abundance of the heart that the mouth speaks.

'Why do you call me "Lord, Lord", and do not do what I tell you? I will show you what someone is like who comes to me, hears my words, and acts on them. That one is like a man building a house, who dug deeply and laid the foundation on rock; when a flood arose, the river burst against that house but could not shake it, because it had been well built. But the one who hears and does not act is like a man who built a house on the ground without a foundation. When the river burst against it, immediately it fell, and great was the ruin of that house.'

- We can spend too much time thinking about what to do and put off making a decision and putting it into practice. Jesus told us that his disciples are those who do the will of his Father.

- If we build our lives on the solid foundation of our faith we will be able to withstand the storms that come to every life. Jesus Christ, yesterday, today, the same forever, becomes the rock that anchors us, and leads us on the true path.

14–20 September 2025

Something to think and pray about each day this week:

We waste a lot of food.

   We buy too much.

   We are mesmerised by bargains like '3 for the price of 2'.

Pope Francis on waste of food: 'Our grandparents used to make a point of not throwing away leftover food. Consumerism has made us accustomed to wasting food daily, and we are unable to see its real value . . . throwing away food is like stealing from the table of those who are poor and hungry—around 1.3 billion metric tonnes (1.43 billion tons) of food, or one third of what is produced for human consumption, gets lost or wasted every year, according to the United Nation's food agency.'

Like Jesus, Pope Francis uses dramatic language to make a point. He reminds us of something we don't want to hear. When we waste food, we disrespect what the earth gives us. Caring for the earth is not only about environmentalism, it is about ensuring equal distribution of the earth's resources and being grateful to the earth for what it gives us.

Donal Neary SJ,
The Sacred Heart Messenger,
September 2022

The Presence of God

What is present to me is what has a hold on my becoming. I reflect on the presence of God always there in love, midst the many things that have a hold on me. I pause and pray that I may let God affect my becoming in this precise moment.

Freedom

By God's grace I was born to live in freedom. Free to enjoy the pleasures he created for me. Dear Lord, grant that I may live as you intended, with complete confidence in your loving care.

Consciousness

To be conscious about something is to be aware of it. Dear Lord, help me to remember that you gave me life. Thank you for the gift of life. Teach me to slow down, to be still and enjoy the pleasures created for me. To be aware of the beauty that surrounds me: the marvel of mountains, the calmness of lakes, the fragility of a flower petal. I need to remember that all these things come from you.

The Word

God speaks to each of us individually. I listen attentively to hear what he is saying to me. Read the text a few times, then listen. *(Please turn to the Scripture on the following pages. Inspiration points are there, should you need them. When you are ready, return here to continue.)*

Conversation

I begin to talk with Jesus about the Scripture I have just read. What part of it strikes a chord in me? Perhaps the words of a friend—or some story I have heard recently—will rise to the surface in my consciousness. If so, does the story throw light on what the Scripture passage may be saying to me?

Conclusion

Glory be to the Father, and to the Son, and to the Holy Spirit,
As it was in the beginning, is now and ever shall be,
World without end. Amen.

Sunday 14 September
The Exaltation of the Holy Cross
John 3:13–17

He said to them, 'No one has ascended into heaven except the one who descended from heaven, the Son of Man. And just as Moses lifted up the serpent in the wilderness, so must the Son of Man be lifted up, that whoever believes in him may have eternal life.

'For God so loved the world that he gave his only Son, so that everyone who believes in him may not perish but may have eternal life.

'Indeed, God did not send the Son into the world to condemn the world, but in order that the world might be saved through him.'

• God the Creator of everything loves all that he has made and he wants all of us to be saved. After we had thrown God's plan for our happiness into disarray the Trinity came up with a new plan, which was to save us through the life, death and resurrection of Jesus Christ. If God has given us his own Beloved Son then there is nothing he would ever refuse us that we need for our happiness. Let us turn to him with great trust and gratitude.

Monday 15 September
John 19:25–27

Meanwhile, standing near the cross of Jesus were his mother, and his mother's sister, Mary the wife of Clopas, and Mary Magdalene. When Jesus saw his mother and the disciple whom he loved standing beside her, he said to his mother, 'Woman, here is your son.' Then he said to the disciple, 'Here is your mother.' And from that hour the disciple took her into his own home.

• Even in his agony on the cross Jesus is mindful of others. Next to the gift of himself, his greatest gift to us must surely be his own Mother. Mary accepted her Son's dying wish and embraced her new role. As the apostles gathered in the Upper Room after the Ascension, she joined them as they prayed. This is the infant church, and Mary is the mother of the church. We pray for a greater devotion to her.

- Mary is truly the model of the perfect disciple. With extraordinary courage and love she is there at the foot of the cross as her Son gives his life for us. In heaven she continues to intercede for us with her Son.

Tuesday 16 September
Luke 7:11–17

Soon afterwards he went to a town called Nain, and his disciples and a large crowd went with him. As he approached the gate of the town, a man who had died was being carried out. He was his mother's only son, and she was a widow; and with her was a large crowd from the town. When the Lord saw her, he had compassion for her and said to her, 'Do not weep.' Then he came forward and touched the bier, and the bearers stood still. And he said, 'Young man, I say to you, rise!' The dead man sat up and began to speak, and Jesus gave him to his mother. Fear seized all of them; and they glorified God, saying, 'A great prophet has risen among us!' and 'God has looked favourably on his people!' This word about him spread throughout Judea and all the surrounding country.

- Without any request being made to him Jesus is filled with compassion for the grieving widow and says to her, 'Do not weep.' In one of his most astonishing miracles he then gives her back her son. This is he who is 'gentle and humble in heart'. Let us share with him our own troubles, trusting in his great compassion and love for us.

Wednesday 17 September
Luke 7:31–35

Jesus spoke to the crowds, saying, 'To what then will I compare the people of this generation, and what are they like? They are like children sitting in the market-place and calling to one another,

"We played the flute for you, and you did not dance;
     we wailed, and you did not weep."

For John the Baptist has come eating no bread and drinking no wine, and you say, "He has a demon"; the Son of Man has come eating and drinking, and you say, "Look, a glutton and a drunkard, a friend of tax-collectors and sinners!" Nevertheless, wisdom is vindicated by all her children.'

- The people in Judea and Galilee were given an extraordinary opportunity, as their God walked among them and worked great wonders. For centuries people had longed to see what they saw and never saw it, to hear what they heard and never heard it. But in the hardness of their hearts their leaders shut the eyes of their minds to it. There are none so blind as those who do not want to see.

- 'He has a demon, or he is a drunkard.' How easily we put up excuses for our own waywardness and excuse ourselves for not living up to our Christian calling. We pray, 'Lord, let me see again.'

Thursday 18 September
Luke 7:36–50

One of the Pharisees asked Jesus to eat with him, and he went into the Pharisee's house and took his place at the table. And a woman in the city, who was a sinner, having learned that he was eating in the Pharisee's house, brought an alabaster jar of ointment. She stood behind him at his feet, weeping, and began to bathe his feet with her tears and to dry them with her hair. Then she continued kissing his feet and anointing them with the ointment. Now when the Pharisee who had invited him saw it, he said to himself, 'If this man were a prophet, he would have known who and what kind of woman this is who is touching him—that she is a sinner.' Jesus spoke up and said to him, 'Simon, I have something to say to you.' 'Teacher,' he replied, 'speak.' 'A certain creditor had two debtors; one owed five hundred denarii, and the other fifty. When they could not pay, he cancelled the debts for both of them. Now which of them will love him more?' Simon answered, 'I suppose the one for whom he cancelled the greater debt.' And Jesus said to him, 'You have judged rightly.' Then turning towards the woman, he said to Simon, 'Do you see this woman? I entered your house; you gave me no water for my feet, but she has bathed my feet with her tears and dried them with her hair. You gave me no kiss, but from the time I came in she has not stopped kissing my feet. You did not anoint my head with oil, but she has anointed my feet with ointment. Therefore, I tell you, her sins, which were many, have been forgiven; hence she has shown great love. But the one to whom little is forgiven, loves little.' Then he said to her, 'Your sins are forgiven.' But those who were at the table with him began to say among themselves, 'Who is this who even forgives sins?' And he said to the woman, 'Your faith has saved you; go in peace.'

- This sinful woman already knew about the merciful Jesus from hearing him speak. Aware of his forgiveness she is now filled with love and gratitude. All of us have sinned and been forgiven. How often do we express our love and gratitude for this forgiveness?

- We forget so quickly how much we continue to receive from God. Let us give thanks for everything and especially for all the graces Jesus has won for us by his life, death and resurrection.

Friday 19 September
Luke 8:1–3

Soon afterwards he went on through cities and villages, proclaiming and bringing the good news of the kingdom of God. The twelve were with him, as well as some women who had been cured of evil spirits and infirmities: Mary, called Magdalene, from whom seven demons had gone out, and Joanna, the wife of Herod's steward Chuza, and Susanna, and many others, who provided for them out of their resources.

- These women were faithful followers of Jesus and some of them, including Mary Magdalene, stayed with him even to the foot of the cross. We can still support the ministry of Jesus in spreading his kingdom on earth by giving from our material goods. We pray to be faithful followers to the very end and especially through whatever crosses come our way.

Saturday 20 September
Luke 8:4–15

When a great crowd gathered and people from town after town came to him, he said in a parable: 'A sower went out to sow his seed; and as he sowed, some fell on the path and was trampled on, and the birds of the air ate it up. Some fell on the rock; and as it grew up, it withered for lack of moisture. Some fell among thorns, and the thorns grew with it and choked it. Some fell into good soil, and when it grew, it produced a hundredfold.' As he said this, he called out, 'Let anyone with ears to hear listen!'

Then his disciples asked him what this parable meant. He said, 'To you it has been given to know the secrets of the kingdom of God; but to others I speak in parables, so that

"looking they may not perceive,

and listening they may not understand."

'Now the parable is this: The seed is the word of God. The ones on the path are those who have heard; then the devil comes and takes away the word from their hearts, so that they may not believe and be saved. The ones on the rock are those who, when they hear the word, receive it with joy. But these have no root; they believe only for a while and in a time of testing fall away. As for what fell among the thorns, these are the ones who hear; but as they go on their way, they are choked by the cares and riches and pleasures of life, and their fruit does not mature. But as for that in the good soil, these are the ones who, when they hear the word, hold it fast in an honest and good heart, and bear fruit with patient endurance.'

- I recall reading about a little blind girl who said, 'You people who can see, what do you do with your gift of sight?' Do we admire the beautiful world we have been given and give God thanks for it? We are given so many opportunities to grow in grace, but it is so easy to be distracted by the 'things' of this world. We pray that we will nurture the seed that is the word of God and produce its fruit.

- What do we do with the gift of faith that we have been given?

Twenty-fifth Week in Ordinary Time
21–27 September 2025

Something to think and pray about each day this week:

There is a lot to be said for gratitude. Life is a precious gift, which we should appreciate and enjoy. I know a lovely lady who claims you should live with a grateful heart. Each morning and each evening, she thanks God. If only we could all live our lives like this every day. It is not only giving thanks to God for his precious gift to us. It is good for us to value things. It improves our outlook. We become more positive, and we see even more of the good things God has given us.

We take so much for granted, which can lead to a negative outlook. Living life with a grateful heart means knowing that God has given us everything and that he wants us to be happy. This is the day the Lord has made—rejoice and be glad.

Mary Hunt,
The Sacred Heart Messenger,
February 2022

The Presence of God
'Be still, and know that I am God!' Lord, your words lead us to the calmness and greatness of your presence.

Freedom
Everything has the potential to draw forth from me a fuller love and life. Yet my desires are often fixed, caught, on illusions of fulfilment. I ask that God, through my freedom, may orchestrate my desires in a vibrant, loving melody rich in harmony.

Consciousness
I exist in a web of relationships: links to nature, people, God. I trace out these links, giving thanks for the life that flows through them. Some links are twisted or broken; I may feel regret, anger, disappointment. I pray for the gift of acceptance and forgiveness.

The Word
I read the word of God slowly, a few times over, and I listen to what God is saying to me. *(Please turn to the Scripture on the following pages. Inspiration points are there, should you need them. When you are ready, return here to continue.)*

Conversation
Jesus, you speak to me through the words of the Gospels. May I respond to your call today. Teach me to recognise your hand at work in my daily living.

Conclusion
I thank God for these moments we have spent together and for any insights I have been given concerning the text.

Sunday 21 September
Twenty-fifth Sunday in Ordinary Time
Luke 16:1–13

Then Jesus said to the disciples, 'There was a rich man who had a manager, and charges were brought to him that this man was squandering
his property. So he summoned him and said to him, "What is this that I
hear about you? Give me an account of your management, because you
cannot be my manager any longer." Then the manager said to himself,
"What will I do, now that my master is taking the position away from
me? I am not strong enough to dig, and I am ashamed to beg. I have
decided what to do so that, when I am dismissed as manager, people
may welcome me into their homes." So, summoning his master's debtors
one by one, he asked the first, "How much do you owe my master?" He
answered, "A hundred jugs of olive oil." He said to him, "Take your bill,
sit down quickly, and make it fifty." Then he asked another, "And how
much do you owe?" He replied, "A hundred containers of wheat." He said
to him, "Take your bill and make it eighty." And his master commended
the dishonest manager because he had acted shrewdly; for the children of
this age are more shrewd in dealing with their own generation than are
the children of light. And I tell you, make friends for yourselves by means
of dishonest wealth so that when it is gone, they may welcome you into
the eternal homes.

'Whoever is faithful in a very little is faithful also in much; and whoever is dishonest in a very little is dishonest also in much. If then you
have not been faithful with the dishonest wealth, who will entrust to you
the true riches? And if you have not been faithful with what belongs to
another, who will give you what is your own? No slave can serve two masters; for a slave will either hate the one and love the other, or be devoted to
the one and despise the other. You cannot serve God and wealth.'

- It has been said that how you do anything is how you do everything.
  This is so true in how we do the little things and mirror this in our
  doing the big things. So many people became criminals because of the
  bad decisions they made while growing up. We pray to be faithful in
  the little things and then the bigger things will take care of themselves.

- If we are faced with a choice between God or wealth, God must always
  come first as he can never take second place.

Monday 22 September
Luke 8:16–18

He said in a parable, 'No one after lighting a lamp hides it under a jar, or puts it under a bed, but puts it on a lampstand, so that those who enter may see the light. For nothing is hidden that will not be disclosed, nor is anything secret that will not become known and come to light. Then pay attention to how you listen; for to those who have, more will be given; and from those who do not have, even what they seem to have will be taken away.'

- To state the obvious, a light is meant to be placed where it can light the way for all in a dark place. Christ is the Light of the World. We can light the way for others by how we live our Christian lives. Anthony de Mello said that God enriches with graces all those who seek to help others come to know Jesus Christ better.

Tuesday 23 September
Luke 8:19–21

Then his mother and his brothers came to him, but they could not reach him because of the crowd. And he was told, 'Your mother and your brothers are standing outside, wanting to see you.' But he said to them, 'My mother and my brothers are those who hear the word of God and do it.'

- There is a time to pray with others and a time to pray alone. Sometimes the clamour of a crowd can keep us from finding Jesus. In his own life on earth Jesus loved to go aside into a quiet place and be alone with his beloved Father.

- Because of the Incarnation and his coming amongst us as one of us and by his life, death and resurrection, Jesus has become our brother and made all who seek to follow him his new family. In having the one Spirit of Jesus within us we are united together and become brothers and sisters of each other. Let us join with Jesus in his prayer for unity among all Christians.

Wednesday 24 September
Luke 9:1–6

Then Jesus called the twelve together and gave them power and authority over all demons and to cure diseases, and he sent them out to proclaim the kingdom of God and to heal. He said to them, 'Take nothing for your journey, no staff, nor bag, nor bread, nor money—not even an extra tunic. Whatever house you enter, stay there, and leave from there. Wherever they do not welcome you, as you are leaving that town shake the dust off your feet as a testimony against them.' They departed and went through the villages, bringing the good news and curing diseases everywhere.

- All healing is from God, the creator of everything. Through his divine power Jesus gives his apostles authority to preach the Good News about the kingdom of God and to heal the sick. This same Jesus is at work in us today to carry on the message of the kingdom and to bring healing to a world still in great need of peace and healing. Let us pray to be open to his working through us with all whom we encounter.

- By instructing his disciples not to carry spare tunics or money or food, Jesus is telling them to focus not on themselves but rather on their mission to preach and heal the sick. God will provide all they need through the people they encounter, for 'the labourer deserves to be paid'. In Matthew we read, 'Strive first for the kingdom of God and his righteousness and all these things will be given you as well' (6:33).

Thursday 25 September
Luke 9:7–9

Now Herod the ruler heard about all that had taken place, and he was perplexed, because it was said by some that John had been raised from the dead, by some that Elijah had appeared, and by others that one of the ancient prophets had arisen. Herod said, 'John I beheaded; but who is this about whom I hear such things?' And he tried to see him.

- Herod had heard much about Jesus and he was both curious and puzzled about him, yet he did not go and hear Jesus speak. Zacchaeus was also curious about Jesus but he went to the trouble of climbing a tree to catch sight of him. How much do we want to come to know Jesus, and are we willing to give time and energy to reading the Gospels and to pray to him?

- In the Spiritual Exercises, the prayer St Ignatius asks to be repeated in every meditation of the Second Week is, 'Lord, help me to come to know you more, so that I may love you more, and follow you more closely in my life.'

Friday 26 September
Luke 9:18–22

Once when Jesus was praying alone, with only the disciples near him, he asked them, 'Who do the crowds say that I am?' They answered, 'John the Baptist; but others, Elijah; and still others, that one of the ancient prophets has arisen.' He said to them, 'But who do you say that I am?' Peter answered, 'The Messiah of God.'

He sternly ordered and commanded them not to tell anyone, saying, 'The Son of Man must undergo great suffering, and be rejected by the elders, chief priests, and scribes, and be killed, and on the third day be raised.'

- After Peter acknowledges that Jesus is the Son of God, Jesus foretells his own passion and death and resurrection. This would be next to impossible for his apostles to grasp and accept. But Jesus had to carry alone the burden of knowing about his coming suffering. In Luke's Gospel we read, 'I have a baptism with which to be baptized, and what stress I am under until it is completed!' (12:50). In our own lives many of us have to carry burdens within us that we cannot share with others. But there is one Friend with whom we can always share these burdens.

Saturday 27 September
Luke 9:43–45

While everyone was amazed at all that he was doing, he said to his disciples, 'Let these words sink into your ears: The Son of Man is going to be betrayed into human hands.' But they did not understand this saying; its meaning was concealed from them, so that they could not perceive it. And they were afraid to ask him about this saying.

- There are times when 'ignorance is bliss'. For his disciples to accept the end their beloved Master was to have was a bridge too far, and they were afraid even to ask him about it. While the people acclaimed him as a great wonder-worker, Jesus had to carry alone this burden of knowing about his coming suffering and death, but always with the help of his beloved Father. We can never really know all that is going on in another's mind and life. Let us pray never to judge them.

Twenty-sixth Week in Ordinary Time
28 September–4 October 2025

Something to think and pray about each day this week:

The feast of St Francis of Assisi is celebrated each year on 4 October. It marks the end of the Season of Creation and invites us to celebrate the patron saint of ecology. St Francis was a mystic who, 'faithful to Scripture, invites us to see nature as a magnificent book in which God speaks to us and grants us a glimpse of his infinite beauty and goodness' (*Laudato Si'*, 12).

Aware of just how deeply interconnected everything is, St Francis had a deep grasp of what we today call integral ecology. Just as Jesus spent much time in nature, contemplating the sparrows (Luke 12:6) and the tiniest of seeds (Luke 17:5–6), so St Francis also lived in full harmony with creation. He showed us that care for creation is inseparable from concern for each other, justice for the poor, and our own interior peace. Seeing that everything is connected, and living out this vision joyfully and with an open heart, St Francis was—and is—deeply loved. He takes us to the heart of what it is to be human and invites us to a profound interior conversion: 'Just as happens when we fall in love with someone, whenever Francis would gaze at the sun, the moon or the smallest of animals, he burst into song, drawing all other creatures into his praise' (*Laudato Si'*, 11).

We are called into this awareness so that we repair our broken relationship with the natural world and with each other. We are called to turn away from destruction and, feeling intimately connected to all that exists, to care more deeply for our common home.

Tríona Doherty and Jane Mellett,
The Sacred Heart Messenger,
October 2021

The Presence of God

'Come to me, all you that are weary and are carrying heavy burdens, and I will give you rest.' Here I am, Lord. I come to seek your presence. I long for your healing power.

Freedom

God is not foreign to my freedom. The Spirit breathes life into my most intimate desires, gently nudging me towards all that is good. I ask for the grace to let myself be enfolded by the Spirit.

Consciousness

I remind myself that I am in the presence of the Lord. I will take refuge in his loving heart. He is my strength in times of weakness. He is my comforter in times of sorrow.

The Word

I take my time to read the word of God slowly, a few times, allowing myself to dwell on anything that strikes me. *(Please turn to the Scripture on the following pages. Inspiration points are there, should you need them. When you are ready, return here to continue.)*

Conversation

Jesus, you always welcomed little children when you walked on this earth. Teach me to have a childlike trust in you. Teach me to live in the knowledge that you will never abandon me.

Conclusion

Glory be to the Father, and to the Son, and to the Holy Spirit,
As it was in the beginning, is now and ever shall be,
World without end. Amen.

Sunday 28 September
Twenty-sixth Sunday in Ordinary Time
Luke 16:19–31

Then Jesus said to his disciples, 'There was a rich man who was dressed in purple and fine linen and who feasted sumptuously every day. And at his gate lay a poor man named Lazarus, covered with sores, who longed to satisfy his hunger with what fell from the rich man's table; even the dogs would come and lick his sores. The poor man died and was carried away by the angels to be with Abraham. The rich man also died and was buried. In Hades, where he was being tormented, he looked up and saw Abraham far away with Lazarus by his side. He called out, "Father Abraham, have mercy on me, and send Lazarus to dip the tip of his finger in water and cool my tongue; for I am in agony in these flames." But Abraham said, "Child, remember that during your lifetime you received your good things, and Lazarus in like manner evil things; but now he is comforted here, and you are in agony. Besides all this, between you and us a great chasm has been fixed, so that those who might want to pass from here to you cannot do so, and no one can cross from there to us." He said, "Then, father, I beg you to send him to my father's house—for I have five brothers—that he may warn them, so that they will not also come into this place of torment." Abraham replied, "They have Moses and the prophets; they should listen to them." He said, "No, father Abraham; but if someone goes to them from the dead, they will repent." He said to him, "If they do not listen to Moses and the prophets, neither will they be convinced even if someone rises from the dead."'

- God respects our free choices and we have to take responsibility for them. St Paul reminds us in 2 Corinthians 6, 'Now is the acceptable time.' We pray to use our time on earth well and live our lives guided by the teaching and example of Jesus Christ, who is much greater than Moses and the prophets.

- Our faith is based on the fact, attested to by witnesses, that Jesus rose from the dead, but many people have still to be convinced. We thank God for the gift of faith and pray to grow in it.

Monday 29 September
Ss Michael, Gabriel and Raphael, Archangels
John 1:47–51

When Jesus saw Nathanael coming towards him, he said of him, 'Here is truly an Israelite in whom there is no deceit!' Nathanael asked him, 'Where did you come to know me?' Jesus answered, 'I saw you under the fig tree before Philip called you.' Nathanael replied, 'Rabbi, you are the Son of God! You are the King of Israel!' Jesus answered, 'Do you believe because I told you that I saw you under the fig tree? You will see greater things than these.' And he said to him, 'Very truly, I tell you, you will see heaven opened and the angels of God ascending and descending upon the Son of Man.'

- Nathaniel asks Jesus, 'Where did you come to know me?' All of us are totally known and understood and loved by God infinitely more than we can ever know ourselves. As Psalm 139:13 reminds us, 'For it was you who formed my inward parts; you knit me together in my mother's womb.' Let us speak now in prayer to this Person who knows and accepts us so totally.

- If we are faithful to our prayer time we will see great things, for 'What no eye has seen, nor ear heard, . . . God has prepared for those who love him'. This applies to our life on earth and also to the next life.

Tuesday 30 September
Luke 9:51–56

When the days drew near for him to be taken up, he set his face to go to Jerusalem. And he sent messengers ahead of him. On their way they entered a village of the Samaritans to make ready for him; but they did not receive him, because his face was set towards Jerusalem. When his disciples James and John saw it, they said, 'Lord, do you want us to command fire to come down from heaven and consume them?' But he turned and rebuked them. Then they went on to another village.

- The two disciples James and John, referred to in the Gospels as 'the sons of thunder', wanted to punish the villagers, but Jesus had told his disciples that when they were not accepted in one village they were to go on to the next village. Here he himself does this. God never forces anyone to pray because it is all about a relationship of love, which of its nature must always be free. Prayer is always a privileged invitation to meet and come to know and love God. Let us thank him for this as we recall the words of St John Climacus, 'Prayer is a gift given to those who pray.'

Wednesday 1 October
Luke 9:57–62

As they were going along the road, someone said to him, 'I will follow you wherever you go.' And Jesus said to him, 'Foxes have holes, and birds of the air have nests; but the Son of Man has nowhere to lay his head.' To another he said, 'Follow me.' But he said, 'Lord, first let me go and bury my father.' But Jesus said to him, 'Let the dead bury their own dead; but as for you, go and proclaim the kingdom of God.' Another said, 'I will follow you, Lord; but let me first say farewell to those at my home.' Jesus said to him, 'No one who puts a hand to the plough and looks back is fit for the kingdom of God.'

• Our faith is a personal decision and commitment we make to follow the Lord for all of our lives. When we live this with fidelity it becomes a part of who we are. The late Fr Michael Paul Gallagher SJ wrote, 'A faith that is not lived becomes lifeless.' We pray for the grace of perseverance.

Thursday 2 October
Matthew 18:1–5, 10

At that time the disciples came to Jesus and asked, 'Who is the greatest in the kingdom of heaven?' He called a child, whom he put among them, and said, 'Truly I tell you, unless you change and become like children, you will never enter the kingdom of heaven. Whoever becomes humble like this child is the greatest in the kingdom of heaven. Whoever welcomes one such child in my name welcomes me. . . .

'Take care that you do not despise one of these little ones; for, I tell you, in heaven their angels continually see the face of my Father in heaven.'

• Jesus sets the bar for entrance into the kingdom quite high: we must change and become like little children. Where do we need to change most? Ours is a world of narcissists, where so many are engrossed by themselves and their importance, so that being like a child is really counter-cultural. We ask for light and wisdom to see where and how we can become like little children.

- Jesus warns us to respect children. We let ourselves feel sorrow at the scandal of child abuse, within and without the church. We pray for the victims and the abusers, and for our leaders, humbly and compassionately. We consider how we look at the children present in our life.

Friday 3 October
Luke 10:13–16

He said to them, 'Woe to you, Chorazin! Woe to you, Bethsaida! For if the deeds of power done in you had been done in Tyre and Sidon, they would have repented long ago, sitting in sackcloth and ashes. But at the judgement it will be more tolerable for Tyre and Sidon than for you. And you, Capernaum,

> will you be exalted to heaven?
>> No, you will be brought down to Hades.

'Whoever listens to you listens to me, and whoever rejects you rejects me, and whoever rejects me rejects the one who sent me.'

- The Bible tells us that 'now is the acceptable time'. After death we cannot change ourselves, but instead, our souls need to be acted upon to change them. Let us choose to make good use of the time of our freedom.

Saturday 4 October
Luke 10:17–24

The seventy returned with joy, saying, 'Lord, in your name even the demons submit to us!' He said to them, 'I watched Satan fall from heaven like a flash of lightning. See, I have given you authority to tread on snakes and scorpions, and over all the power of the enemy; and nothing will hurt you. Nevertheless, do not rejoice at this, that the spirits submit to you, but rejoice that your names are written in heaven.'

At that same hour Jesus rejoiced in the Holy Spirit and said, 'I thank you, Father, Lord of heaven and earth, because you have hidden these things from the wise and the intelligent and have revealed them to infants; yes, Father, for such was your gracious will. All things have been handed over to me by my Father; and no one knows who the Son is except the Father, or who the Father is except the Son and anyone to whom the Son chooses to reveal him.'

Then turning to the disciples, Jesus said to them privately, 'Blessed are the eyes that see what you see! For I tell you that many prophets and kings desired to see what you see, but did not see it, and to hear what you hear, but did not hear it.'

- The disciples return from their missionary endeavours filled with joy at their success. Jesus too rejoices with them and in the Holy Spirit he gives thanks to his Father. Here we have an example of Jesus' own prayer as he speaks to his Father out of the situation in which he finds himself. Let us learn from his example.

- The choices of God are always mysterious to us. Only Jesus knows who the Father is and he came to reveal this to those who were open to his gift. 'I made your name known to them, and I will make it known' (John 17:26).

5–11 October 2025

Something to think and pray about each day this week:

In reading a piece about the last judgement a woman in her eighties wondered, 'If God has forgiven me, why is there a judgement?' I could understand her question. Taking some theological liberty, I said that the judgement after death was for God to say again to each of us that we are forgiven, and to remind us of the good we had done and had tried to do. Her reply was, 'Consoling for the once baptised who have fallen away'. Was she thinking not of herself, but of her children, most of whom were not churchgoers? I think so. Many people's religious questions often cloak a worry they have about others.

Many parents and grandparents worry about the lack of faith in their children and grandchildren. It is a deep sadness for a generation that did their best in handing on faith and practice. Some nuggets of wisdom can help: 'Let God look after them, he loves them even more than you do'; 'We all find our own way to God and in life'; 'Their faith will come at its own time'. It is consoling to think that much goodness—kindness, love for the poor, prayer, care and compassion—is passed on by parents, even if the faith of a younger generation might be expressed differently.

Mary and Joseph wondered what had got into Jesus to run off and leave them worried and anxious. His answer, 'I must be about my father's business', is relevant also for us. Many people are about their father's business in different ways than I am, or a parent is. The important thing is that somehow, somewhere, we are, in trying to live the good life, 'about our father's business'!

Donal Neary SJ,
The Sacred Heart Messenger,
January 2021

The Presence of God

'I am standing at the door, knocking,' says the Lord. What a wonderful privilege that the Lord of all creation desires to come to me. I welcome his presence.

Freedom

I will ask God's help to be free from my own preoccupations, to be open to God in this time of prayer, to come to know, love and serve God more.

Consciousness

In God's loving presence I unwind the past day, starting from now and looking back, moment by moment. I gather in all the goodness and light, in gratitude. I attend to the shadows and what they say to me, seeking healing, courage, forgiveness.

The Word

Now I turn to the Scripture set out for me this day. I read slowly over the words and see if any sentence or sentiment appeals to me. *(Please turn to the Scripture on the following pages. Inspiration points are there, should you need them. When you are ready, return here to continue.)*

Conversation

Sometimes I wonder what I might say if I were to meet you in person, Lord. I think I might say, 'Thank you', because you are always there for me.

Conclusion

I thank God for these moments we have spent together and for any insights I have been given concerning the text.

Sunday 5 October
Twenty-seventh Sunday in Ordinary Time
Luke 17:5–10

The apostles said to the Lord, 'Increase our faith!' The Lord replied, 'If you had faith the size of a mustard seed, you could say to this mulberry tree, 'Be uprooted and planted in the sea', and it would obey you.

'Who among you would say to your slave who has just come in from ploughing or tending sheep in the field, "Come here at once and take your place at the table"? Would you not rather say to him, "Prepare supper for me, put on your apron and serve me while I eat and drink; later you may eat and drink"? Do you thank the slave for doing what was commanded? So you also, when you have done all that you were ordered to do, say, "We are worthless slaves; we have done only what we ought to have done!"'

- Mary the Mother of God said, 'Here am I, the servant of the Lord; let it be with me according to your word.' We are all the servants of God who does not need us for his happiness. It is we who, in the truth of our existence, need to worship our God. St Ignatius of Loyola wrote in the Foundation Principle of his Spiritual Exercises, 'Man is created to praise, reverence, and serve God our Lord, and by this means to save his soul.' It is right and fitting that we should do this as we owe everything to God.

Monday 6 October
Luke 10:25–37

Just then a lawyer stood up to test Jesus. 'Teacher,' he said, 'what must I do to inherit eternal life?' He said to him, 'What is written in the law? What do you read there?' He answered, 'You shall love the Lord your God with all your heart, and with all your soul, and with all your strength, and with all your mind; and your neighbour as yourself.' And he said to him, 'You have given the right answer; do this, and you will live.'

But wanting to justify himself, he asked Jesus, 'And who is my neighbour?' Jesus replied, 'A man was going down from Jerusalem to Jericho, and fell into the hands of robbers, who stripped him, beat him, and went away, leaving him half dead. Now by chance a priest was going down that road; and when he saw him, he passed by on the other side. So likewise a Levite, when he came to the place and saw him, passed by on the other side. But a Samaritan while travelling came near him; and when he saw him, he was moved with pity. He went to him and bandaged his wounds, having poured oil and wine on them. Then he put him on his own animal, brought him to an inn, and took care of him. The next day he took out two denarii, gave them to the innkeeper, and said, "Take care of him; and when I come back, I will repay you whatever more you spend.' Which of these three, do you think, was a neighbour to the man who fell into the hands of the robbers?" He said, 'The one who showed him mercy.' Jesus said to him, 'Go and do likewise.'

- The whole purpose of our life on this earth is to love and develop with God's grace our own individual capacity to love. It is on this that we will be judged. St John of the Cross wrote, 'In the evening of life we will be tested by love.' If at the time of our death we are fully loving according to our ability, then we are ready to merge with God who is Love Itself, and so to enter heaven.

- Without other people we will never know if we are truly loving. Jesus said, 'you always have the poor with you.' Every day we need to exercise charity, tolerance, forgiveness and humility, for we are all sinners in need of God's mercy.

Tuesday 7 October
Luke 10:38–42

Now as they went on their way, he entered a certain village, where a woman named Martha welcomed him into her home. She had a sister named Mary, who sat at the Lord's feet and listened to what he was saying. But Martha was distracted by her many tasks; so she came to him and asked, 'Lord, do you not care that my sister has left me to do all the work by myself? Tell her then to help me.' But the Lord answered her, 'Martha, Martha, you are worried and distracted by many things; there is need of only one thing. Mary has chosen the better part, which will not be taken away from her.'

- All of us have the gift of free will, for without it we cannot love. Even in the Nazi prison camps it was the one thing that could never be taken away. But our choices have consequences that we must live with. Mary in Bethany, as a model of the contemplative, chose to sit at the Lord's feet and listen to him.

Wednesday 8 October
Luke 11:1–4

He was praying in a certain place, and after he had finished, one of his disciples said to him, 'Lord, teach us to pray, as John taught his disciples.' He said to them, 'When you pray, say:

Father, hallowed be your name.

Your kingdom come.

Give us each day our daily bread.

And forgive us our sins,

for we ourselves forgive everyone indebted to us.

And do not bring us to the time of trial.'

- St Luke, more than any of the other evangelists, writes of Our Lord at prayer. We should often ask God to teach us to grow in prayer. Dom John Chapman OSB said that we should pray as we can, not as we cannot. We learn prayer by doing it, and the more frequently, the better.

- In the Our Father, Jesus teaches us the right attitude to have in prayer, that God must have the first place in our lives. We also learn that we must have forgiveness in our hearts for others. In our petitions we should pray not only for ourselves but for all people.

Thursday 9 October
Luke 11:5–13

And he said to them, 'Suppose one of you has a friend, and you go to him at midnight and say to him, "Friend, lend me three loaves of bread; for a friend of mine has arrived, and I have nothing to set before him." And he answers from within, "Do not bother me; the door has already been locked, and my children are with me in bed; I cannot get up and give you anything." I tell you, even though he will not get up and give him anything because he is his friend, at least because of his persistence he will get up and give him whatever he needs.

'So I say to you, Ask, and it will be given to you; search, and you will find; knock, and the door will be opened for you. For everyone who asks receives, and everyone who searches finds, and for everyone who knocks, the door will be opened. Is there anyone among you who, if your child asks for a fish, will give a snake instead of a fish? Or if the child asks for an egg, will give a scorpion? If you then, who are evil, know how to give good gifts to your children, how much more will the heavenly Father give the Holy Spirit to those who ask him!'

• Every prayer is heard by God and those who persevere in searching for him will find him. God wants to be found by us, so this should not be too difficult for those who have faith. God knows we need this gift and he will never refuse it to those who ask for it. So, as Sr Wendy Beckett wrote, 'Simply ask for it and then go and live it.' We pray for the grace of perseverance and for a greater trust.

Friday 10 October
Luke 11:15–26

But some of them said, 'He casts out demons by Beelzebul, the ruler of the demons.' Others, to test him, kept demanding from him a sign from heaven. But he knew what they were thinking and said to them, 'Every kingdom divided against itself becomes a desert, and house falls on house. If Satan also is divided against himself, how will his kingdom stand?—for you say that I cast out the demons by Beelzebul. Now if I cast out the demons by Beelzebul, by whom do your exorcists cast them out? Therefore they will be your judges. But if it is by the finger of God that I cast out the demons, then the kingdom of God has come to you. When a strong man, fully armed, guards his castle, his property is safe. But when one stronger than he attacks him and overpowers him, he takes away his armour in which he trusted and divides his plunder. Whoever is not with me is against me, and whoever does not gather with me scatters.

'When the unclean spirit has gone out of a person, it wanders through waterless regions looking for a resting-place, but not finding any, it says, "I will return to my house from which I came." When it comes, it finds it swept and put in order. Then it goes and brings seven other spirits more evil than itself, and they enter and live there; and the last state of that person is worse than the first.'

- Satan, the evil one, constantly seeks a congenial dwelling place. We are urged to be on our guard and to recognise his subtle approaches. We read in the Breviary, 'Do not give the devil his opportunity.' St Ignatius advises that we shut the door at the first sign of his temptations. Let us pray for discernment.

- Remember that Satan is powerless against those who are striving to live a genuine prayer life. Jesus said that no one can steal or snatch out of the Father's hand, those whom the Father has given him (John 10:29).

Saturday 11 October
Luke 11:27–28

While he was saying this, a woman in the crowd raised her voice and said to him, 'Blessed is the womb that bore you and the breasts that nursed you!' But he said, 'Blessed rather are those who hear the word of God and obey it!'

- Yes, blessed is Mary among women, and more blessed is the fruit of her womb, Jesus. Jesus said his mother and brothers and sisters are those who do the will of his Father. Holy Mary, Mother of God, pray for us sinners now and at the hour of our death. Amen.

Something to think and pray about each day this week:

A friend, facing a terminal diagnosis, remarked that he was now going to be engaged in the serious business of dying, letting go of all that was still holding him and attending to unfinished business in his life and relationships. Getting older is not about settling down with pipe, slippers and rocking chair. It involves some serious work for which we were not equipped in earlier years.

The butterfly has much to teach us here. As she flies over the forest where she first hatched and experienced her metamorphosis, she gazes down on her descendants, still crawling along the branches as caterpillars, with no idea of what lies ahead. It's all about feeding and self-defence. The butterfly sees the bigger picture. She knows caterpillar life is not the end of the story. She knows that just when you feel you are helplessly disintegrating, something amazing may be about to emerge.

When you can see the bigger picture, everything changes. You know that everything passes and the human spirit survives. You see life from a different perspective. You are looking through the lens of the mystic. Your ability to see the bigger picture can help the younger people in your life deal better with and perhaps see beyond the passing struggles of their own lives.

As he looks upon the infant Jesus, Simeon declares that he is now ready to depart, for he has seen the fulfilment of God's dream. Like Simeon, you have climbed your life's mountain. You can see the broad horizon, with its beauty and its dangers. You have seen the power of God at work in your own life. And even as you approach the point of departure from everything you know and love, you, like the emerging butterfly, are standing on the threshold of transformation.

Margaret Silf,
The Sacred Heart Messenger,
December 2023

The Presence of God
'Be still, and know that I am God!' Lord, your words lead us to the calmness and greatness of your presence.

Freedom
If God were trying to tell me something, would I know? If God were reassuring me or challenging me, would I notice? I ask for the grace to be free of my own preoccupations and open to what God may be saying to me.

Consciousness
In the presence of my loving Creator, I look honestly at my feelings over the past day: the highs, the lows, and the level ground. Can I see where the Lord has been present?

The Word
In this expectant state of mind, please turn to the text for the day with confidence. Believe that the Holy Spirit is present and may reveal whatever the passage has to say to you. Read reflectively, listening with a third ear to what may be going on in your heart. (Please turn to the Scripture on the following pages. Inspiration points are there, should you need them. When you are ready, return here to continue.)

Conversation
Remembering that I am still in God's presence, I imagine Jesus standing or sitting beside me, and I say whatever is on my mind, whatever is in my heart, speaking as one friend to another.

Conclusion
Glory be to the Father, and to the Son, and to the Holy Spirit,
As it was in the beginning, is now and ever shall be,
World without end. Amen.

Sunday 12 October
Twenty-eighth Sunday in Ordinary Time
Luke 17:11–19

On the way to Jerusalem Jesus was going through the region between Samaria and Galilee. As he entered a village, ten lepers approached him. Keeping their distance, they called out, saying, 'Jesus, Master, have mercy on us!' When he saw them, he said to them, 'Go and show yourselves to the priests.' And as they went, they were made clean. Then one of them, when he saw that he was healed, turned back, praising God with a loud voice. He prostrated himself at Jesus' feet and thanked him. And he was a Samaritan. Then Jesus asked, 'Were not ten made clean? But the other nine, where are they? Was none of them found to return and give praise to God except this foreigner?' Then he said to him, 'Get up and go on your way; your faith has made you well.'

- Our Lord might well ask, where are the other nine? Do we ever find ourselves among the nine who forgot to thank the Lord? St Ignatius stresses that gratitude is a very important attitude to develop on our spiritual journey. It is a most helpful way to get into prayer, because the more aware we become of the gift, the more aware we can become of the Giver. Everything we have is a gift from God. St Paul wrote, 'Always be thankful.'

Monday 13 October
Luke 11:29–32

When the crowds were increasing, he began to say, 'This generation is an evil generation; it asks for a sign, but no sign will be given to it except the sign of Jonah. For just as Jonah became a sign to the people of Nineveh, so the Son of Man will be to this generation. The queen of the South will rise at the judgement with the people of this generation and condemn them, because she came from the ends of the earth to listen to the wisdom of Solomon, and see, something greater than Solomon is here! The people of Nineveh will rise up at the judgement with this generation and condemn it, because they repented at the proclamation of Jonah, and see, something greater than Jonah is here!'

- The figure of Jesus the Son of God on the cross will always be a sign of God's immense love for us. Christ's victory belongs to all of us. Let us give thanks to him.

- Let us recognise who is on that cross. Jesus promised that he would be with us always. This is the gift of God and Jesus is with us now in our prayer.

Tuesday 14 October
Luke 11:37–41

While he was speaking, a Pharisee invited him to dine with him; so he went in and took his place at the table. The Pharisee was amazed to see that he did not first wash before dinner. Then the Lord said to him, 'Now you Pharisees clean the outside of the cup and of the dish, but inside you are full of greed and wickedness. You fools! Did not the one who made the outside make the inside also? So give for alms those things that are within; and see, everything will be clean for you.'

- Jesus denounces the Pharisees and scholars of the law for their blindness in judging goodness by the external observance of the law. He accuses them of being full of greed and wickedness. Human pride leads to an inner blindness much deeper than any loss of sight. Let us ask the Lord to show us how we may be blocking the light of the gospel in our own lives.

Wednesday 15 October
Luke 11:42–46

The Lord said, 'But woe to you Pharisees! For you tithe mint and rue and herbs of all kinds, and neglect justice and the love of God; it is these you ought to have practised, without neglecting the others. Woe to you Pharisees! For you love to have the seat of honour in the synagogues and to be greeted with respect in the market-places. Woe to you! For you are like unmarked graves, and people walk over them without realising it.'

One of the lawyers answered him, 'Teacher, when you say these things, you insult us too.' And he said, 'Woe also to you lawyers! For you load people with burdens hard to bear, and you yourselves do not lift a finger to ease them.'

- Jesus castigates the Pharisees for their neglect of justice and for their lack of love for God. They are zealous in policing the keeping of their own manmade regulations but refuse to help others in their difficulties. Charity covers a multitude of sins; we ask that the Lord keep us mindful of his commandment to love one another.

Thursday 16 October
Luke 11:47–54

And he said to the Pharisees, 'Woe to you! For you build the tombs of the prophets whom your ancestors killed. So you are witnesses and approve of the deeds of your ancestors; for they killed them, and you build their tombs. Therefore also the Wisdom of God said, "I will send them prophets and apostles, some of whom they will kill and persecute", so that this generation may be charged with the blood of all the prophets shed since the foundation of the world, from the blood of Abel to the blood of Zechariah, who perished between the altar and the sanctuary. Yes, I tell you, it will be charged against this generation. Woe to you lawyers! For you have taken away the key of knowledge; you did not enter yourselves, and you hindered those who were entering.'

When he went outside, the scribes and the Pharisees began to be very hostile towards him and to cross-examine him about many things, lying in wait for him, to catch him in something he might say.

• The scribes are those who have studied the law and the prophets, and they should have passed on this knowledge to the people. Jesus warns that they are shutting themselves out from God's kingdom. Do I look for opportunities to grow in my understanding of my faith? How well do I try to pass this on to my children? How well do I support my parish in its efforts to spread the Good News of the gospel? May I never hinder others from entering the kingdom of God by my bad example.

Friday 17 October
Luke 12:1–7

Meanwhile, when the crowd gathered in thousands, so that they trampled on one another, he began to speak first to his disciples, 'Beware of the yeast of the Pharisees, that is, their hypocrisy. Nothing is covered up that will not be uncovered, and nothing secret that will not become known. Therefore whatever you have said in the dark will be heard in the light, and what you have whispered behind closed doors will be proclaimed from the housetops.

'I tell you, my friends, do not fear those who kill the body, and after that can do nothing more. But I will warn you whom to fear: fear him who, after he has killed, has authority to cast into hell. Yes, I tell you, fear him! Are not five sparrows sold for two pennies? Yet not one of them is forgotten in God's sight. But even the hairs of your head are all counted. Do not be afraid; you are of more value than many sparrows.'

- Yet again Jesus calls us not to be afraid, for our God who loves us holds us in his hands at every instant. Those who persecute others for their beliefs can never take away our freedom to choose, even if they kill the body. Every human being is precious in God's eyes, including those who injure us or differ from us in religion. God alone sees the heart and God alone can judge rightly. Let us pray to see people as God sees them, and for tolerance in our broken world.

Saturday 18 October
St Luke, Evangelist
Luke 10:1–9

After this the Lord appointed seventy others and sent them on ahead of him in pairs to every town and place where he himself intended to go. He said to them, 'The harvest is plentiful, but the labourers are few; therefore ask the Lord of the harvest to send out labourers into his harvest. Go on your way. See, I am sending you out like lambs into the midst of wolves. Carry no purse, no bag, no sandals; and greet no one on the road. Whatever house you enter, first say, "Peace to this house!" And if anyone is there who shares in peace, your peace will rest on that person; but if not, it will return to you. Remain in the same house, eating and drinking whatever they provide, for the labourer deserves to be paid. Do not move about from house to house. Whenever you enter a town and its people welcome you, eat what is set before you; cure the sick who are there, and say to them, "The kingdom of God has come near to you."'

- By instructing his disciples not to carry spare tunics or money or sandals he is telling them to focus not on themselves but rather on their mission to preach and heal the sick. God will provide all that they need through the people they encounter.
- Our world has great need of spiritual guides and shepherds. Let us pray for vocations to the priesthood and religious life.

Something to think and pray about each day this week:

The debate about refugees who are illegally trafficked, as to whether they deserve or are entitled to any resources, is one that dominates discussions and can lead to suspicious and censorious comments that exploit divisions between people and promote fear and hatred. This is where populism and extremism thrive.

The story about the Good Samaritan leaves us with questions about who we are, where we put ourselves in the story, and it leaves us with an uneasy sense that we could be any or all of the characters in the story. We are people who find easy and at times religious excuses for not doing what is required of us. We are people who are left helpless at the side of the road by a violent and meaningless world. We are people who, like the despised Samaritan, can offer to a stranger a service of compassion, friendship and hospitality.

We are invited to be surprising strangers of welcome to one another! This implies that we will receive unexpected hospitality from surprising strangers—who are our neighbours.

Giving sanctuary was a service that hallmarked the Church. It needs to be revived. No one should feel excluded from our Church. Giving sanctuary is a faithful witness of the message and mission of the Church. Giving sanctuary is the synodal way of being faithful, hopeful and loving. This means rendering ourselves vulnerable to others whom we don't understand and probably don't like and may even find scandalous or threatening.

John Cullen,
The Sacred Heart Messenger,
July 2023

The Presence of God
'Be still, and know that I am God!' Lord, your words lead us to the calmness and greatness of your presence.

Freedom
If God were trying to tell me something, would I know? If God were reassuring me or challenging me, would I notice? I ask for the grace to be free of my own preoccupations and open to what God may be saying to me.

Consciousness
In the presence of my loving Creator, I look honestly at my feelings over the past day: the highs, the lows and the level ground. Can I see where the Lord has been present?

The Word
In this expectant state of mind, please turn to the text for the day with confidence. Believe that the Holy Spirit is present and may reveal whatever the passage has to say to you. Read reflectively, listening with a third ear to what may be going on in your heart. *(Please turn to the Scripture on the following pages. Inspiration points are there, should you need them. When you are ready, return here to continue.)*

Conversation
Remembering that I am still in God's presence, I imagine Jesus standing or sitting beside me, and I say whatever is on my mind, whatever is in my heart, speaking as one friend to another.

Conclusion
Glory be to the Father, and to the Son, and to the Holy Spirit,
As it was in the beginning, is now and ever shall be,
World without end. Amen.

Sunday 19 October
Twenty-ninth Sunday in Ordinary Time
Luke 18:1–8

Then Jesus told them a parable about their need to pray always and not to lose heart. He said, 'In a certain city there was a judge who neither feared God nor had respect for people. In that city there was a widow who kept coming to him and saying, "Grant me justice against my opponent." For a while he refused; but later he said to himself, "Though I have no fear of God and no respect for anyone, yet because this widow keeps bothering me, I will grant her justice, so that she may not wear me out by continually coming."' And the Lord said, "Listen to what the unjust judge says. And will not God grant justice to his chosen ones who cry to him day and night? Will he delay long in helping them? I tell you, he will quickly grant justice to them. And yet, when the Son of Man comes, will he find faith on earth?"'

- Fr Henri Nouwen wrote, 'Unless prayer is seen as essential, it is meaningless.' We must never give up prayer, which is as necessary for our souls as air is for our bodies. Every prayer we make from the heart blesses us and changes us. It brings us closer to God who hears every prayer and will answer in his own way.

- The history of God's people in the Old Testament tells us of how they again and again turned away from God and how God in his mercy brought them back through a faithful remnant. Let us pray to be among the faithful remnant through whom God will renew his church and our world.

Monday 20 October
Luke 12:13–21

Someone in the crowd said to him, 'Teacher, tell my brother to divide the family inheritance with me.' But he said to him, 'Friend, who set me to be a judge or arbitrator over you?' And he said to them, 'Take care! Be on your guard against all kinds of greed; for one's life does not consist in the abundance of possessions.' Then he told them a parable: 'The land of a rich man produced abundantly. And he thought to himself, "What should I do, for I have no place to store my crops?" Then he said, "I will do this: I will pull down my barns and build larger ones, and there I will store all my grain and my goods. And I will say to my soul, Soul, you have ample goods laid up for many years; relax, eat, drink, be merry." But God said to him, "You fool! This very night your life is being demanded of you. And the things you have prepared, whose will they be?" So it is with those who store up treasures for themselves but are not rich towards God.'

- God in his infinite mercy and kindness gives us time to repent and convert to living a good life. But the day of our death will inevitably come around. Our life on earth is a precious gift when we can come to know and love our God because after death we cannot choose to change. Instead our souls are mysteriously acted upon. So now is the acceptable time. Let us pray to use it well.

- All of us know with complete certainty that at some time we will depart this life. We pray to be ready when God calls us.

Tuesday 21 October
Luke 12:35–38

He said to his disciples, 'Be dressed for action and have your lamps lit; be like those who are waiting for their master to return from the wedding banquet, so that they may open the door for him as soon as he comes and knocks. Blessed are those slaves whom the master finds alert when he comes; truly I tell you, he will fasten his belt and have them sit down to eat, and he will come and serve them. If he comes during the middle of the night, or near dawn, and finds them so, blessed are those slaves.'

- In Matthew's Gospel it is the Master who refuses to open the door to the bridesmaids who are not ready for his coming. The Lord will invite those servants who are alert and ready to sit down at the heavenly banquet, and he will serve them. Let us pray for the grace to be ready when the Lord bids us come home to him.

Wednesday 22 October
Luke 12:39–48

He said to them, 'But know this: if the owner of the house had known at what hour the thief was coming, he would not have let his house be broken into. You also must be ready, for the Son of Man is coming at an unexpected hour.'

Peter said, 'Lord, are you telling this parable for us or for everyone?' And the Lord said, 'Who then is the faithful and prudent manager whom his master will put in charge of his slaves, to give them their allowance of food at the proper time? Blessed is that slave whom his master will find at work when he arrives. Truly I tell you, he will put that one in charge of all his possessions. But if that slave says to himself, 'My master is delayed in coming', and if he begins to beat the other slaves, men and women, and to eat and drink and get drunk, the master of that slave will come on a day when he does not expect him and at an hour that he does not know, and will cut him in pieces, and put him with the unfaithful. That slave who knew what his master wanted, but did not prepare himself or do what was wanted, will receive a severe beating. But one who did not know and did what deserved a beating will receive a light beating. From everyone to whom much has been given, much will be required; and from one to whom much has been entrusted, even more will be demanded.'

- St Ignatius of Loyola said that God deals directly with each soul, and no two people go the same way to God. Because prayer is all about a relationship it is for each of us to learn, by practice and perseverance, our own best way to pray. God gives different graces to each person and he expects different returns on his investment. Let us pray to be faithful to our own calling from God and to use well the gifts and graces we have been given.

Thursday 23 October
Luke 12:49–53

Jesus said, 'I came to bring fire to the earth, and how I wish it were already kindled! I have a baptism with which to be baptized, and what stress I am under until it is completed! Do you think that I have come to bring peace to the earth? No, I tell you, but rather division! From now on, five in one household will be divided, three against two and two against three; they will be divided:

father against son
    and son against father,
mother against daughter
    and daughter against mother,
mother-in-law against her daughter-in-law
    and daughter-in-law against mother-in-law.'

- Jesus came on earth to shatter our complacency with his call to love everyone, including our enemies.

- Pope Francis wrote in *Rejoice and be Glad*, 'So let me ask you: Are there moments when you place yourself quietly in the Lord's presence, when you calmly spend time with him, when you bask in his gaze? Do you let his fire inflame your heart? Unless you let him warm your heart more and more with his love and tenderness, you will not catch fire.'

Friday 24 October
Luke 12:54–59

He also said to the crowds, 'When you see a cloud rising in the west, you immediately say, "It is going to rain"; and so it happens. And when you see the south wind blowing, you say, "There will be scorching heat"; and it happens. You hypocrites! You know how to interpret the appearance of earth and sky, but why do you not know how to interpret the present time?

'And why do you not judge for yourselves what is right? Thus, when you go with your accuser before a magistrate, on the way make an effort to settle the case, or you may be dragged before the judge, and the judge hand you over to the officer, and the officer throw you in prison. I tell you, you will never get out until you have paid the very last penny.'

- Pope Francis frequently stresses the importance of discerning the will of God for us. We need to read the signs of the times. With the abundance of information from our modern media we know much about what is going on in our world. We see a world where there is little peace and many lives are torn apart by wars and strife. In the light of the gospel how do I interpret the signs of the times and how do I judge what is the right thing for me to do? We pray for wisdom and perseverance.

Saturday 25 October
Luke 13:1–9

At that very time there were some present who told him about the Galileans whose blood Pilate had mingled with their sacrifices. He asked them, 'Do you think that because these Galileans suffered in this way they were worse sinners than all other Galileans? No, I tell you; but unless you repent, you will all perish as they did. Or those eighteen who were killed when the tower of Siloam fell on them—do you think that they were worse offenders than all the others living in Jerusalem? No, I tell you; but unless you repent, you will all perish just as they did.'

Then he told this parable: 'A man had a fig tree planted in his vineyard; and he came looking for fruit on it and found none. So he said to the gardener, "See here! For three years I have come looking for fruit on this fig tree, and still I find none. Cut it down! Why should it be wasting the soil?" He replied, "Sir, let it alone for one more year, until I dig round it and put manure on it. If it bears fruit next year, well and good; but if not, you can cut it down."'

- In the past many people thought that physical suffering was a punishment from God for our sins. Jesus does away with that idea but he points out that if we do not change and convert to living a good life then we can lose our souls. A conversion means a greater turning to God, and we should pray often for the grace of many conversions.

26 October –1 November 2025

Something to think and pray about each day this week:

Give us eyes to see the deepest needs in people's lives.

Give us hearts full of love for our neighbours as well as for the strangers we meet.

Help us to understand what it means to love others as we love ourselves.

Teach us care in a way that strengthens those who are sick.

Fill us with generosity as we feed the hungry and give drink to the thirsty.

Let us be the healing presence for those who are weak and weary, by offering our welcome and kindness to them.

May we remember to listen and to offer a helping hand and heart, when the opportunity presents itself to us.

Give us hearts of understanding when we disagree, but let us never be disagreeable to one another.

Inspire us to go out of our way to include those who are unknown and unnoticed.

Help us to be inclusive to all who come to our door.

John Cullen,
The Sacred Heart Messenger,
August 2023

The Presence of God

As I sit here, the beating of my heart, the ebb and flow of my breathing, the movements of my mind are all signs of God's ongoing creation of me. I pause for a moment and become aware of this presence of God within me.

Freedom

It is so easy to get caught up with the trappings of wealth in this life. Grant, O Lord, that I may be free from greed and selfishness. Remind me that the best things in life are free: love, laughter, caring and sharing.

Consciousness

Knowing that God loves me unconditionally, I can afford to be honest about how I am. How has the day been, and how do I feel now? I share my feelings openly with the Lord.

The Word

Lord Jesus, you became human to communicate with me. You walked and worked on this earth. You endured the heat and struggled with the cold. All your time on this earth was spent in caring for humanity. You healed the sick, you raised the dead. Most important of all, you saved me from death. *(Please turn to the Scripture on the following pages. Inspiration points are there, should you need them. When you are ready, return here to continue.)*

Conversation

Sometimes I wonder what I might say if I were to meet you in person, Lord. I think I might say, 'Thank you', because you are always there for me.

Conclusion

I thank God for these moments we have spent together and for any insights I have been given concerning the text.

Sunday 26 October
Thirtieth Sunday in Ordinary Time
Luke 18:9–14

He also told this parable to some who trusted in themselves that they were righteous and regarded others with contempt: 'Two men went up to the temple to pray, one a Pharisee and the other a tax-collector. The Pharisee, standing by himself, was praying thus, "God, I thank you that I am not like other people: thieves, rogues, adulterers, or even like this tax-collector. I fast twice a week; I give a tenth of all my income." But the tax-collector, standing far off, would not even look up to heaven, but was beating his breast and saying, "God, be merciful to me, a sinner!" I tell you, this man went down to his home justified rather than the other; for all who exalt themselves will be humbled, but all who humble themselves will be exalted.'

- In his prayer the Pharisee focused on himself and all he had done. The tax collector focused on God and his great mercy. St Teresa of Ávila taught that real prayer is more about loving than thinking. There is a lot of truth in the statement that when we are thinking in prayer we are with ourselves and when we are loving in prayer we are with God. Prayer is all about a special friendship. Do we go to prayer just to ask for things for ourselves and others, or do we spend most of our time staying with the Lord and sharing with him and listening to him?

Monday 27 October
Luke 13:10–17

Now he was teaching in one of the synagogues on the sabbath. And just then there appeared a woman with a spirit that had crippled her for eighteen years. She was bent over and was quite unable to stand up straight. When Jesus saw her, he called her over and said, 'Woman, you are set free from your ailment.' When he laid his hands on her, immediately she stood up straight and began praising God. But the leader of the synagogue, indignant because Jesus had cured on the sabbath, kept saying to the crowd, 'There are six days on which work ought to be done; come on those days and be cured, and not on the sabbath day.' But the Lord answered him and said, 'You hypocrites! Does not each of you on the sabbath untie his ox or his donkey from the manger, and lead it away to give it water? And ought not this woman, a daughter of Abraham whom Satan bound for eighteen long years, be set free from this bondage on the sabbath day?' When he said this, all his opponents were put to shame; and the entire crowd was rejoicing at all the wonderful things that he was doing.

- In his compassion for this afflicted woman Jesus calls her over and cures her without her even asking him. In contrast we see the unfeeling harshness of the synagogue leader, who is more concerned with the keeping of his human rules than about the suffering of this woman. Jesus said, 'Be merciful, just as your heavenly Father is merciful.' Let us pray to become more like Jesus in his attitude towards others.

Tuesday 28 October
Ss Simon and Jude, Apostles
Luke 6:12–19

Now during those days he went out to the mountain to pray; and he spent the night in prayer to God. And when day came, he called his disciples and chose twelve of them, whom he also named apostles: Simon, whom he named Peter, and his brother Andrew, and James, and John, and Philip, and Bartholomew, and Matthew, and Thomas, and James son of Alphaeus, and Simon, who was called the Zealot, and Judas son of James, and Judas Iscariot, who became a traitor.

He came down with them and stood on a level place, with a great crowd of his disciples and a great multitude of people from all Judea, Jerusalem, and the coast of Tyre and Sidon. They had come to hear him and to be healed of their diseases; and those who were troubled with unclean spirits were cured. And all in the crowd were trying to touch him, for power came out from him and healed all of them.

- The choices of God are always a mystery to us. To continue his mission on earth it was important that Jesus should choose well from among his many disciples, and so he spends the whole night in prayer. In our discernment for important decisions one of the means we use must be to bring the matter up in prayer again and again. Let us pray for the grace to know whatever God is asking of us.

- Jesus is always the example for how we should live. That he would spend a whole night in prayer shows us how vital prayer is in our lives. If we are faithful to our prayer life then our eyes will be opened.

Wednesday 29 October
Luke 13:22–30

Jesus went through one town and village after another, teaching as he made his way to Jerusalem. Someone asked him, 'Lord, will only a few be saved?' He said to them, 'Strive to enter through the narrow door; for many, I tell you, will try to enter and will not be able. When once the owner of the house has got up and shut the door, and you begin to stand outside and to knock at the door, saying, "Lord, open to us", then in reply he will say to you, "I do not know where you come from." Then you will begin to say, "We ate and drank with you, and you taught in our streets." But he will say, "I do not know where you come from; go away from me, all you evildoers!" There will be weeping and gnashing of teeth when you see Abraham and Isaac and Jacob and all the prophets in the kingdom of God, and you yourselves thrown out. Then people will come from east and west, from north and south, and will eat in the kingdom of God. Indeed, some are last who will be first, and some are first who will be last.'

- Our Lord invites us to come to know him personally and to become his friend. St Margaret Mary Alacoque said that the Lord once described St Claude de la Colombière as 'his perfect friend'. How terrible it would be if, when we meet the Lord, as we all do at death, that he should say to us, 'I do not know where you come from; go away from me.'

Thursday 30 October
Luke 13:31–35

At that very hour some Pharisees came and said to him, 'Get away from here, for Herod wants to kill you.' He said to them, 'Go and tell that fox for me, "Listen, I am casting out demons and performing cures today and tomorrow, and on the third day I finish my work. Yet today, tomorrow, and the next day I must be on my way, because it is impossible for a prophet to be killed away from Jerusalem." Jerusalem, Jerusalem, the city that kills the prophets and stones those who are sent to it! How often have I desired to gather your children together as a hen gathers her brood under her wings, and you were not willing! See, your house is left to you. And I tell you, you will not see me until the time comes when you say, "Blessed is the one who comes in the name of the Lord."'

- Jesus shows great tenderness and compassion in his use of the image of the brooding hen gathering her chicks under her wing. I am reminded of a line in G. M. Hopkins's poem 'God's Grandeur'—'Because the Holy Ghost over the bent / world broods with warm breast and with ah! bright wings.' Our God still longs to gather each of us to himself with great mercy and tenderness.

Friday 31 October
Luke 14:1–6

On one occasion when Jesus was going to the house of a leader of the Pharisees to eat a meal on the sabbath, they were watching him closely. Just then, in front of him, there was a man who had dropsy. And Jesus asked the lawyers and Pharisees, 'Is it lawful to cure people on the sabbath, or not?' But they were silent. So Jesus took him and healed him, and sent him away. Then he said to them, 'If one of you has a child or an ox that has fallen into a well, will you not immediately pull it out on a sabbath day?' And they could not reply to this.

- When Jesus put these direct questions to his accusers, they were silent and would not answer because in their hearts they could glimpse their own hypocrisy and their lack of compassion for the sick. In our own lives we can be tempted to brush under the carpet our own un-Christian attitudes to the poor, the deprived, the sick, migrants, and others. Jesus cures this sick man regardless of how it might antagonise the Pharisees further against him. We pray for the courage to be true to ourselves and do the right thing regardless of the opinion of other people.

Saturday 1 November
All Saints
Matthew 5:1–12

When Jesus saw the crowds, he went up the mountain; and after he sat down, his disciples came to him. Then he began to speak, and taught them, saying:

'Blessed are the poor in spirit, for theirs is the kingdom of heaven.

'Blessed are those who mourn, for they will be comforted.

'Blessed are the meek, for they will inherit the earth.

'Blessed are those who hunger and thirst for righteousness, for they will be filled.

'Blessed are the merciful, for they will receive mercy.

'Blessed are the pure in heart, for they will see God.

'Blessed are the peacemakers, for they will be called children of God.

'Blessed are those who are persecuted for righteousness' sake, for theirs is the kingdom of heaven.

'Blessed are you when people revile you and persecute you and utter all kinds of evil against you falsely on my account. Rejoice and be glad, for your reward is great in heaven, for in the same way they persecuted the prophets who were before you.'

- This is Jesus' first major sermon in the gospels. In it he lays out many of the values of the kingdom of God. They run counter to so many of the world's values. They also reflect the values by which Jesus himself lived. Let us pray to imitate him and to strive as best we can to 'be perfect as our Heavenly Father is perfect.'

Thirty-first Week in Ordinary Time
2–8 November 2025

Something to think and pray about each day this week:

November is a month to pray for our dead and to celebrate their lives. We have memories of those who have gone before us. We have a treasure trove of good memories of loving family members and maybe some painful memories of separation and reconciliation; there are memories of school, the neighbourhood and countless small kindnesses.

At a time of death, we can look back and see that many unexpected things in life were well worthwhile and brought us happiness, even if they were difficult at the time. Our faith helps with those painful memories of others, whether we miss them or regret some part of our relationship with them. They are now with God and the fullness of love, with maybe repentance for faults, sins and failings. With God we will be at our best in eternity.

A popular funeral reading is the 'time for everything' reading from Ecclesiastes. Our time of death is not of our choosing. It's not that God had the date of death planned, rather it is that the body has its own 'clock' and can last only so long. At that time God is close, very near, near to welcome us home.

The funeral liturgy remembers with thanks a person's life but also faces the question—where is he/she now? All we can say is that we will see God face to face and, in some mysterious way, be united with all those we knew and loved on earth.

At every funeral each of us can bring away something we got from knowing the dead person—help from them, their prayers, their love. Even in sadness we can go from our funeral rituals and answer the question, 'How did this person enhance my life?'

Donal Neary SJ,
The Sacred Heart Messenger,
November 2023

The Presence of God

At any time of the day or night we can call on Jesus. He is always waiting, listening for our call. What a wonderful blessing. No phone needed, no e-mails, just a whisper.

Freedom

Lord, grant me the grace to have freedom of the spirit. Cleanse my heart and soul so that I may live joyously in your love.

Consciousness

Knowing that God loves me unconditionally, I look honestly over the past day, its events, and my feelings. Do I have something to be grateful for? Then I give thanks. Is there something I am sorry for? Then I ask forgiveness.

The Word

The word of God comes down to us through the Scriptures. May the Holy Spirit enlighten my mind and my heart to respond to the Gospel teachings: to love my neighbour as myself, to care for my sisters and brothers in Christ. *(Please turn to the Scripture on the following pages. Inspiration points are there, should you need them. When you are ready, return here to continue.)*

Conversation

I know with certainty that there were times when you carried me, Lord. There were times when it was through your strength that I got through the dark times in my life.

Conclusion

Glory be to the Father, and to the Son, and to the Holy Spirit,
As it was in the beginning, is now and ever shall be,
World without end. Amen.

Sunday 2 November
The Commemoration of All the Faithful Departed
Luke 7:11–17

Soon afterwards he went to a town called Nain, and his disciples and a large crowd went with him. As he approached the gate of the town, a man who had died was being carried out. He was his mother's only son, and she was a widow; and with her was a large crowd from the town. When the Lord saw her, he had compassion for her and said to her, 'Do not weep.' Then he came forward and touched the bier, and the bearers stood still. And he said, 'Young man, I say to you, rise!' The dead man sat up and began to speak, and Jesus gave him to his mother. Fear seized all of them; and they glorified God, saying, 'A great prophet has risen among us!' and 'God has looked favourably on his people!' This word about him spread throughout Judea and all the surrounding country.

- Without any request being made to him, Jesus is filled with compassion for the grieving widow and says to her, 'Do not weep.' He then gives her back her son. This is he who is 'gentle and humble of heart'. Jesus Christ knows intimately all the circumstances of our lives and he is at work in them for our good. Let us share with him about our own troubles, trusting in his great compassion and love for us.

Monday 3 November
Luke 14:12–14

He said also to the one who had invited him, 'When you give a luncheon or a dinner, do not invite your friends or your brothers or your relatives or rich neighbours, in case they may invite you in return, and you would be repaid. But when you give a banquet, invite the poor, the crippled, the lame, and the blind. And you will be blessed, because they cannot repay you, for you will be repaid at the resurrection of the righteous.'

- God in his infinite generosity invites everyone to the eternal banquet in heaven. St Paul reminds us that there is nothing we have that has not been given to us freely by God. Our gifts and talents are to be put at the service of others. Let us be generous to the needy and share the good things of this world.

Tuesday 4 November
Luke 14:15–24

One of the dinner guests, on hearing this, said to him, 'Blessed is anyone who will eat bread in the kingdom of God!' Then Jesus said to him, 'Someone gave a great dinner and invited many. At the time for the dinner he sent his slave to say to those who had been invited, "Come; for everything is ready now." But they all alike began to make excuses. The first said to him, "I have bought a piece of land, and I must go out and see it; please accept my apologies." Another said, "I have bought five yoke of oxen, and I am going to try them out; please accept my apologies." Another said, "I have just been married, and therefore I cannot come." So the slave returned and reported this to his master. Then the owner of the house became angry and said to his slave, "Go out at once into the streets and lanes of the town and bring in the poor, the crippled, the blind, and the lame." And the slave said, "Sir, what you ordered has been done, and there is still room." Then the master said to the slave, "Go out into the roads and lanes, and compel people to come in, so that my house may be filled. For I tell you, none of those who were invited will taste my dinner."'

- This gospel is all about an invitation. We are called to a holiness of life, which means to the banquet feast in heaven. It is the whole purpose of our being on this earth. As the poet Paddy Kavanagh wrote, 'Those who have not flown home to God, have not flown at all.'

- This is the challenge to every Christian, no matter our vocation in life, that we have to choose to respond to or reject this invitation to a real lived relationship with God. We can make excuses like the people in this Gospel did—that we have farms to manage and businesses to run and families to rear—but in the end we must decide and then live that decision. Pope Francis wrote, 'I do not believe in a holiness without prayer.'

Wednesday 5 November
Luke 14:25–33

Now large crowds were travelling with him; and he turned and said to them, 'Whoever comes to me and does not hate father and mother, wife and children, brothers and sisters, yes, and even life itself, cannot be my disciple. Whoever does not carry the cross and follow me cannot be my disciple. For which of you, intending to build a tower, does not first sit down and estimate the cost, to see whether he has enough to complete it? Otherwise, when he has laid a foundation and is not able to finish, all who see it will begin to ridicule him, saying, "This fellow began to build and was not able to finish." Or what king, going out to wage war against another king, will not sit down first and consider whether he is able with ten thousand to oppose the one who comes against him with twenty thousand? If he cannot, then, while the other is still far away, he sends a delegation and asks for the terms of peace. So therefore, none of you can become my disciple if you do not give up all your possessions.'

- At first sight this might seem a very harsh gospel passage but these passages are not to be taken in isolation from the rest of the Gospel, and certainly not to be taken literally. Jesus has told us to love others, not to hate them. It was part of the Jewish pedagogy to exaggerate for emphasis. God and the kingdom of God must always come first in our lives, and attachment to material things can come between us and God. We pray for right judgement and a proper detachment from things.

Thursday 6 November
Luke 15:1–10

Now all the tax-collectors and sinners were coming near to listen to him. And the Pharisees and the scribes were grumbling and saying, 'This fellow welcomes sinners and eats with them.'

So he told them this parable: 'Which one of you, having a hundred sheep and losing one of them, does not leave the ninety-nine in the wilderness and go after the one that is lost until he finds it? When he has found it, he lays it on his shoulders and rejoices. And when he comes home, he calls together his friends and neighbours, saying to them, "Rejoice with me, for I have found my sheep that was lost." Just so, I tell you, there will be more joy in heaven over one sinner who repents than over ninety-nine righteous people who need no repentance.

'Or what woman having ten silver coins, if she loses one of them, does not light a lamp, sweep the house, and search carefully until she finds it? When she has found it, she calls together her friends and neighbours, saying, "Rejoice with me, for I have found the coin that I had lost." Just so, I tell you, there is joy in the presence of the angels of God over one sinner who repents.'

- For Jesus in the gospels it is clear that every individual is special and important. He touches lepers and lays his hands upon the sick. At Bethsaida he leads a blind man by the hand and restores his sight. God wants everyone to be saved. Let us pray for all who do not yet know the immense love of God for each one. And let us pray that we might have a great trust in his love for us.

Friday 7 November
Luke 16:1–8

Then Jesus said to the disciples, 'There was a rich man who had a manager, and charges were brought to him that this man was squandering his property. So he summoned him and said to him, "What is this that I hear about you? Give me an account of your management, because you cannot be my manager any longer." Then the manager said to himself, "What will I do, now that my master is taking the position away from me? I am not strong enough to dig, and I am ashamed to beg. I have decided what to do so that, when I am dismissed as manager, people may welcome me into their homes." So, summoning his master's debtors one by one, he asked the first, "How much do you owe my master?" He answered, "A hundred jugs of olive oil." He said to him, "Take your bill, sit down quickly, and make it fifty." Then he asked another, "And how much do you owe?' He replied, 'A hundred containers of wheat.' He said to him, 'Take your bill and make it eighty." And his master commended the dishonest manager because he had acted shrewdly; for the children of this age are more shrewd in dealing with their own generation than are the children of light.'

- On a first reading of this Gospel we might think that Our Lord is commending the actions of the unjust steward, but in the last line we see that he is being contrasted with the children of light. We are those who have been given the light of the truth and we are challenged by how we are using this gift. How are we preparing ourselves for the world of eternity? Do I take the means to grow in my faith and in my knowledge and love of Jesus Christ through reading and prayer and the sacraments? Let us pray to live in a more enlightened way.

- St Augustine wrote, 'As a Christian I will have to give an account of my life to God, and as a leader I will have to give an account of my stewardship.'

Saturday 8 November
Luke 16:9–15

And I tell you, make friends for yourselves by means of dishonest wealth so that when it is gone, they may welcome you into the eternal homes.

'Whoever is faithful in a very little is faithful also in much; and whoever is dishonest in a very little is dishonest also in much. If then you have not been faithful with the dishonest wealth, who will entrust to you the true riches? And if you have not been faithful with what belongs to another, who will give you what is your own? No slave can serve two masters; for a slave will either hate the one and love the other, or be devoted to the one and despise the other. You cannot serve God and wealth.'

The Pharisees, who were lovers of money, heard all this, and they ridiculed him. So he said to them, 'You are those who justify yourselves in the sight of others; but God knows your hearts; for what is prized by human beings is an abomination in the sight of God.'

- The opposing ways and values of the world and those of God are being contrasted. We need to pray for a detachment from everything that hinders God's working in us. Pope Francis urges us to discern the false gods we cling to in this life. We pray for the grace to do this and to let go of our attachments.

Thirty-second Week in Ordinary Time
9–15 November 2025

Something to think and pray about each day this week:

All of us will eventually come to the end of our journey here on earth. For Christians the belief is that life is changed but not ended. We are all on a journey, and many of us will experience loss. We have hope in Christ, but that is not to deny that we will indeed grieve for our lost loved one and experience broken hearts.

You never replace a person who has died as we are all unique. We will discover new loves, but we will not and should not forget. Perhaps God's plan is to create a unity among people—'May they be one as you and I, Father, are one.' When we lose someone dear we can comfort each other as Jesus taught, but I don't think he ever meant that one person could replace another.

Your loved one will leave behind many treasured memories. Perhaps they had their own ritual, and we can celebrate their life by repeating this. We can also do something in their memory, such as planting a tree or dedicating a book. This piece is dedicated to my much-loved mother who passed away recently. I am lucky to have the support of friends and family, but I miss her a lot. No one will replace your lost loved one. But love can't go nowhere and love cannot die.

Mary Hunt,
The Sacred Heart Messenger,
November 2023

The Presence of God

Dear Jesus, as I call on you today, I realise that often I come asking for favours. Today I'd like just to be in your presence. Draw my heart in response to your love.

Freedom

God my creator, you gave me life and the gift of freedom. Through your love I exist in this world. May I never take the gift of life for granted. May I always respect others' right to life.

Consciousness

Dear Lord, help me to remember that you gave me life. Teach me to slow down, to be still and enjoy the pleasures created for me. To be aware of the beauty that surrounds me: the marvel of mountains, the calmness of lakes, the fragility of a flower petal. I need to remember that all these things come from you.

The Word

The word of God comes down to us through the Scriptures. May the Holy Spirit enlighten my mind and my heart to respond to the Gospel teachings. *(Please turn to the Scripture on the following pages. Inspiration points are there, should you need them. When you are ready, return here to continue.)*

Conversation

What feelings are rising in me as I pray and reflect on God's word? I imagine Jesus himself sitting or standing near me, and I open my heart to him.

Conclusion

I thank God for these moments we have spent together and for any insights I have been given concerning the text.

Sunday 9 November
The Dedication of the Lateran Basilica
John 2:13–22

The Passover of the Jews was near, and Jesus went up to Jerusalem. In the temple he found people selling cattle, sheep, and doves, and the money-changers seated at their tables. Making a whip of cords, he drove all of them out of the temple, both the sheep and the cattle. He also poured out the coins of the money-changers and overturned their tables. He told those who were selling the doves, 'Take these things out of here! Stop making my Father's house a market-place!' His disciples remembered that it was written, 'Zeal for your house will consume me.' The Jews then said to him, 'What sign can you show us for doing this?' Jesus answered them, 'Destroy this temple, and in three days I will raise it up.' The Jews then said, 'This temple has been under construction for forty-six years, and will you raise it up in three days?' But he was speaking of the temple of his body. After he was raised from the dead, his disciples remembered that he had said this; and they believed the scripture and the word that Jesus had spoken.

- There are two kinds of anger. One is a righteous anger at encountering injustice that we see being done to people. The other is a vengeful anger that wants to punish those who have hurt us, and this can lead us to fail to love all. Let us pray for discernment in this.

- In this passage, notice that Jesus uses a whip of cords to drive out the sellers of animals and the money-changers but he simply speaks to the less well-off sellers of doves and tells them to remove them from the temple.

Monday 10 November
Luke 17:1–6

Jesus said to his disciples, 'Occasions for stumbling are bound to come, but woe to anyone by whom they come! It would be better for you if a millstone were hung around your neck and you were thrown into the sea than for you to cause one of these little ones to stumble. Be on your guard! If another disciple sins, you must rebuke the offender, and if there is repentance, you must forgive. And if the same person sins against you seven times a day, and turns back to you seven times and says, "I repent", you must forgive.'

The apostles said to the Lord, 'Increase our faith!' The Lord replied, 'If you had faith the size of a mustard seed, you could say to this mulberry tree, "Be uprooted and planted in the sea", and it would obey you.'

- In Matthew 18:21–22, when Peter asked Jesus how many times he should forgive a brother who has sinned against him and would seven times be enough, Jesus replied, 'I do not say to you seven times but seventy times seven.' This injunction is so strong that it is included in the Our Father, where we ask God to forgive us in the way we forgive others. Do I strive to forgive others with my will and mind and heart as best I can? Do I pray for those who have hurt me?

Tuesday 11 November
Luke 17:7–10

Jesus said to his disciples, 'Who among you would say to your slave who has just come in from ploughing or tending sheep in the field, "Come here at once and take your place at the table"? Would you not rather say to him, "Prepare supper for me, put on your apron and serve me while I eat and drink; later you may eat and drink"? Do you thank the slave for doing what was commanded? So you also, when you have done all that you were ordered to do, say, "We are worthless slaves; we have done only what we ought to have done!"'

- We are all the servants of God, who does not need us for his happiness. It is we who, in the truth of our existence, have a duty to worship God. We owe everything to God. What do we have that we have not received?

Wednesday 12 November
Luke 17:11–19

On the way to Jerusalem Jesus was going through the region between Samaria and Galilee. As he entered a village, ten lepers approached him. Keeping their distance, they called out, saying, 'Jesus, Master, have mercy on us!' When he saw them, he said to them, 'Go and show yourselves to the priests.' And as they went, they were made clean. Then one of them, when he saw that he was healed, turned back, praising God with a loud voice. He prostrated himself at Jesus' feet and thanked him. And he was a Samaritan. Then Jesus asked, 'Were not ten made clean? But the other nine, where are they? Was none of them found to return and give praise to God except this foreigner?' Then he said to him, 'Get up and go on your way; your faith has made you well.'

- Everything we have is a gift from God. St Paul wrote, 'Always be thankful.' As we begin our prayer gratitude is the most helpful way to recall the gifts and the love of our God. The more aware we become of the gift, the more aware we become of the Giver.

Thursday 13 November
Luke 17:20–25

Once Jesus was asked by the Pharisees when the kingdom of God was coming, and he answered, 'The kingdom of God is not coming with things that can be observed; nor will they say, "Look, here it is!" or "There it is!" For, in fact, the kingdom of God is among you.'

Then he said to the disciples, 'The days are coming when you will long to see one of the days of the Son of Man, and you will not see it. They will say to you, "Look there!" or "Look here!" Do not go, do not set off in pursuit. For as the lightning flashes and lights up the sky from one side to the other, so will the Son of Man be in his day. But first he must endure much suffering and be rejected by this generation.'

- The kingdom of God is a spiritual kingdom where God reigns in our hearts. Jesus said to the woman at the well, 'God is spirit, and those who worship him must worship in spirit and truth.' Our God is within us, nearer than our own skin. To worship in spirit is to engage our spirit with God's Spirit (heart speaks to heart). We pray to him in the truth of our own nothingness and our complete dependence upon him.

Friday 14 November
Luke 17:26–37

He said to the disciples, 'Just as it was in the days of Noah, so too it will be in the days of the Son of Man. They were eating and drinking, and marrying and being given in marriage, until the day Noah entered the ark, and the flood came and destroyed all of them. Likewise, just as it was in the days of Lot: they were eating and drinking, buying and selling, planting and building, but on the day that Lot left Sodom, it rained fire and sulphur from heaven and destroyed all of them—it will be like that on the day that the Son of Man is revealed. On that day, anyone on the housetop who has belongings in the house must not come down to take them away; and likewise anyone in the field must not turn back. Remember Lot's wife. Those who try to make their life secure will lose it, but those who lose their life will keep it. I tell you, on that night there will be two in one bed; one will be taken and the other left. There will be two women grinding meal together; one will be taken and the other left.' Then they asked him, 'Where, Lord?' He said to them, 'Where the corpse is, there the vultures will gather.'

- All human life is fragile. Every day we read of disasters and tragic loss of life. This gospel reminds us that we know not the day nor the hour of our own departure from this life. Let us pray to be ready when our own time comes to go home to the Father.

Saturday 15 November
Luke 18:1–8

Then Jesus told them a parable about their need to pray always and not to lose heart. He said, 'In a certain city there was a judge who neither feared God nor had respect for people. In that city there was a widow who kept coming to him and saying, "Grant me justice against my opponent." For a while he refused; but later he said to himself, "Though I have no fear of God and no respect for anyone, yet because this widow keeps bothering me, I will grant her justice, so that she may not wear me out by continually coming."' And the Lord said, 'Listen to what the unjust judge says. And will not God grant justice to his chosen ones who cry to him day and night? Will he delay long in helping them? I tell you, he will quickly grant justice to them. And yet, when the Son of Man comes, will he find faith on earth?'

- Some people who have made their requests to God again and again and yet have not received them begin to doubt that God is listening. But God hears every prayer and will answer in the way that is best for each person. Since prayer is all about a relationship, then every prayer from our hearts changes us and brings us nearer to God. In a real sense prayer is its own reward and an extraordinary privilege. Let us pray for a deeper trust.

Something to think and pray about each day this week:

Christ is risen in us. Sometimes we're too busy to see this truth. But when we do, when we realise that God truly is in all things and is embracing each of us, then we change our posture and disposition. We desire to make ourselves available to this God of love and compassion. We desire to manifest God's will.

And so, our hands stop doing for the sake of doing and we are put at the disposal of God's dream. We allow God's spirit to work through our hands—our very bodies—humbly and patiently, as we discern our unique place in God's dream. Our hands learn to do the Lord's work as we enter more deeply into the mystery of God's very self.

Eric Clayton,
The Sacred Heart Messenger,
September 2023

The Presence of God
Dear Jesus, I come to you today longing for your presence. I desire to love you as you love me. May nothing ever separate me from you.

Freedom
Lord, grant me the grace to be free from the excesses of this life. Let me not get caught up with the desire for wealth. Keep my heart and mind free to love and serve you.

Consciousness
Where do I sense hope, encouragement and growth in my life? By looking back over the past few months, I may be able to see which activities and occasions have produced rich fruit. If I do notice such areas, I will determine to give those areas both time and space in the future.

The Word
God speaks to each of us individually. I listen attentively, to hear what he is saying to me. Read the text a few times, then listen. *(Please turn to the Scripture on the following pages. Inspiration points are there should you need them. When you are ready, return here to continue.)*

Conversation
What is stirring in me as I pray? Am I consoled, troubled, left cold? I imagine Jesus standing or sitting at my side, and I share my feelings with him.

Conclusion
Glory be to the Father, and to the Son, and to the Holy Spirit,
As it was in the beginning, is now and ever shall be,
World without end. Amen.

Sunday 16 November
Thirty-third Sunday in Ordinary Time
Luke 21:5–19

When some were speaking about the temple, how it was adorned with beautiful stones and gifts dedicated to God, he said, 'As for these things that you see, the days will come when not one stone will be left upon another; all will be thrown down.'

They asked him, 'Teacher, when will this be, and what will be the sign that this is about to take place?' And he said, 'Beware that you are not led astray; for many will come in my name and say, "I am he!" and, "The time is near!" Do not go after them.

'When you hear of wars and insurrections, do not be terrified; for these things must take place first, but the end will not follow immediately.' Then he said to them, 'Nation will rise against nation, and kingdom against kingdom; there will be great earthquakes, and in various places famines and plagues; and there will be dreadful portents and great signs from heaven.

'But before all this occurs, they will arrest you and persecute you; they will hand you over to synagogues and prisons, and you will be brought before kings and governors because of my name. This will give you an opportunity to testify. So make up your minds not to prepare your defence in advance; for I will give you words and a wisdom that none of your opponents will be able to withstand or contradict. You will be betrayed even by parents and brothers, by relatives and friends; and they will put some of you to death. You will be hated by all because of my name. But not a hair of your head will perish. By your endurance you will gain your souls.'

- On reading the lives of the martyrs one is struck by the extraordinary courage with which they endure their sufferings. They receive a special grace from God for this. Let us pray for the grace to endure persecution if it comes and for the grace of perseverance in our Christian lives.

- In the Lord's sight a thousand years are but a day. God is outside of time, which is a human construct. Every moment consists of a series of instants. This instant with God in prayer has never been before and it will never be again. Can I stay in this special 'now' with God, even for a short while?

Monday 17 November
Luke 18:35–43

As he approached Jericho, a blind man was sitting by the roadside begging. When he heard a crowd going by, he asked what was happening. They told him, 'Jesus of Nazareth is passing by.' Then he shouted, 'Jesus, Son of David, have mercy on me!' Those who were in front sternly ordered him to be quiet; but he shouted even more loudly, 'Son of David, have mercy on me!' Jesus stood still and ordered the man to be brought to him; and when he came near, he asked him, 'What do you want me to do for you?' He said, 'Lord, let me see again.' Jesus said to him, 'Receive your sight; your faith has saved you.' Immediately he regained his sight and followed him, glorifying God; and all the people, when they saw it, praised God.

- Every day in our daily lives Jesus of Nazareth is passing by. He has promised to be with us always. In how many of our churches does he wait each day for his brothers and sisters to come and keep him company? Pope St Paul VI once said, 'The faithful should not omit visiting the Blessed Sacrament each day.'

- God will never turn a deaf ear to a cry for mercy from the human heart. We are always in need of his mercy and love.

Tuesday 18 November
Luke 19:1–10

He entered Jericho and was passing through it. A man was there named Zacchaeus; he was a chief tax-collector and was rich. He was trying to see who Jesus was, but on account of the crowd he could not, because he was short in stature. So he ran ahead and climbed a sycamore tree to see him, because he was going to pass that way. When Jesus came to the place, he looked up and said to him, 'Zacchaeus, hurry and come down; for I must stay at your house today.' So he hurried down and was happy to welcome him. All who saw it began to grumble and said, 'He has gone to be the guest of one who is a sinner.' Zacchaeus stood there and said to the Lord, 'Look, half of my possessions, Lord, I will give to the poor; and if I have defrauded anyone of anything, I will pay back four times as much.' Then Jesus said to him, 'Today salvation has come to this house, because he too

is a son of Abraham. For the Son of Man came to seek out and to save
the lost.'

- Zacchaeus showed a great desire to see Jesus. He ran and climbed a tree.
  In John 1:38 we read of the two disciples who asked Jesus, 'Where are
  you staying?' And they spent the rest of the day with him. St Ignatius
  stresses the importance of our desire for God. To pray Psalm 62 slowly
  is a wonderful help in this.

- Jesus looked up at Zacchaeus in the tree and said, 'Zacchaeus, hurry
  and come down; for I must stay at your house today.' In the moment
  that their eyes met Zacchaeus recognised the love and compassion that
  was inviting him to a conversion of heart. We can now encounter in
  prayer this same Lord who looks lovingly upon us and is inviting us to
  come now and meet him.

Wednesday 19 November
Luke 19:11–28

As they were listening to this, he went on to tell a parable, because he
was near Jerusalem, and because they supposed that the kingdom of God
was to appear immediately. So he said, 'A nobleman went to a distant
country to get royal power for himself and then return. He summoned
ten of his slaves, and gave them ten pounds, and said to them, "Do business with these until I come back. But the citizens of his country hated
him and sent a delegation after him, saying, "We do not want this man to
rule over us." When he returned, having received royal power, he ordered
these slaves, to whom he had given the money, to be summoned so that
he might find out what they had gained by trading. The first came forward and said, "Lord, your pound has made ten more pounds." He said
to him, "Well done, good slave! Because you have been trustworthy in a
very small thing, take charge of ten cities." Then the second came, saying,
"Lord, your pound has made five pounds." He said to him, "And you,
rule over five cities." Then the other came, saying, "Lord, here is your
pound. I wrapped it up in a piece of cloth, for I was afraid of you, because
you are a harsh man; you take what you did not deposit, and reap what
you did not sow." He said to him, "I will judge you by your own words,
you wicked slave! You knew, did you, that I was a harsh man, taking what
I did not deposit and reaping what I did not sow? Why then did you not

put my money into the bank? Then when I returned, I could have collected it with interest." He said to the bystanders, "Take the pound from him and give it to the one who has ten pounds." (And they said to him, "Lord, he has ten pounds!") "I tell you, to all those who have, more will be given; but from those who have nothing, even what they have will be taken away. But as for these enemies of mine who did not want me to be king over them—bring them here and slaughter them in my presence."' After he had said this, he went on ahead, going up to Jerusalem.

• We have all been entrusted with something very precious, namely a human life and an immortal soul. We get only one chance, one lifetime, short or long, to look after them properly. Our human gifts and talents are freely given for the good of ourselves and of all those whom we encounter. Let us pray in gratitude for these gifts and then for the grace to use them well for ourselves and for others.

Thursday 20 November
Luke 19:41–44

As he came near and saw the city, he wept over it, saying, 'If you, even you, had only recognised on this day the things that make for peace! But now they are hidden from your eyes. Indeed, the days will come upon you, when your enemies will set up ramparts around you and surround you, and hem you in on every side. They will crush you to the ground, you and your children within you, and they will not leave within you one stone upon another; because you did not recognise the time of your visitation from God.'

• 'O that today you would listen to his voice! Do not harden your hearts' (Psalm 95). In this month of November we pray especially for our dead and we reflect upon our own end. I often think that our prisons have many people in them who regret past acts and decisions and would give anything to reverse them. As we look back are there times when we did not recognise the visitation of God in our lives and times, even when we heard but did not heed his voice? Let us pray to use well the time and the opportunities that are still left to us.

Friday 21 November
Luke 19:45–48

Then he entered the temple and began to drive out those who were selling things there; and he said, 'It is written,

'My house shall be a house of prayer';
but you have made it a den of robbers.'

Every day he was teaching in the temple. The chief priests, the scribes, and the leaders of the people kept looking for a way to kill him; but they did not find anything they could do, for all the people were spellbound by what they heard.

* In our churches every day the Lord waits for our company with great longing. In the Book of Genesis we read that Jacob had a dream in which God spoke to him. When he awoke, he said, 'Surely the Lord is in this place—and I did not know it! . . . How awesome is this place! This is none other than the house of God, and this is the gate of heaven' (Genesis 28:16–17). Sometimes we see people behave in our churches as though they were in a secular meeting hall. Do I always value it as a house of prayer? Do I recognise in faith who is present there?

Saturday 22 November
Luke 20:27–40

Some Sadducees, those who say there is no resurrection, came to him and asked him a question, 'Teacher, Moses wrote for us that if a man's brother dies, leaving a wife but no children, the man shall marry the widow and raise up children for his brother. Now there were seven brothers; the first married, and died childless; then the second and the third married her, and so in the same way all seven died childless. Finally the woman also died. In the resurrection, therefore, whose wife will the woman be? For the seven had married her.'

Jesus said to them, 'Those who belong to this age marry and are given in marriage; but those who are considered worthy of a place in that age and in the resurrection from the dead neither marry nor are given in marriage. Indeed they cannot die any more, because they are like angels and are children of God, being children of the resurrection. And the fact that the dead are raised Moses himself showed, in the story about the bush, where he speaks of the Lord as the God of Abraham, the God of Isaac, and the God of Jacob. Now he is God not of the dead, but of the living; for to him all of them are alive.' Then some of the scribes answered, 'Teacher, you have spoken well.' For they no longer dared to ask him another question.

- Marriage and the begetting of children are clearly designed to continue the human race on earth. People die. Not so in heaven. The children of the resurrection will enjoy an eternity of joy and happiness. We give thanks to the Lord for all that he has won for us by his life, death and resurrection.

23–29 November 2025

Something to think and pray about each day this week:

In an individualist culture, perhaps more than ever, we need to learn from the lesson placed before us by Christ the King. We are our brother's and our sister's keeper. 'We live in each other's shadow', as one Irish saying puts it. While independence is all fine and well, inter-dependence—a kindly heart and open hand—is the greater good. The plight of war refugees has been well documented, but there were and are disquieting voices raising opposition. The Irish Rune on hospitality says:

> We saw a stranger yesterday
> We put food in the eating place,
> Drink in the drinking place,
> Music in the listening place.
> And with the sacred name of the triune God
> We were blessed, and our house,
> Our cattle and our dear ones.
> As the lark says in her song:
> Often, often, often goes the Christ
> In the stranger's guise.

Welcoming the stranger blesses ourselves as well as it aids the recipient of our hospitality. In God's family there are no strangers, only kin or clan, as we might say. Kinship is God's dream come true. It's about imagining a circle of compassion and then imagining no one standing outside that circle. For whatever you do with love has eternal value.

Today Christ the King says to us, 'What you do for others, you do for me'.

Tom Cox,
The Sacred Heart Messenger,
November 2023

The Presence of God

'Be still, and know that I am God!' Lord, may your spirit guide me to seek your loving presence more and more for it is there I find rest and refreshment from this busy world.

Freedom

By God's grace I was born to live in freedom. Free to enjoy the pleasures he created for me. Dear Lord, grant that I may live as you intended, with complete confidence in your loving care.

Consciousness

How am I today? Where am I with God? With others? Do I have something to be grateful for? Then I give thanks. Is there something I am sorry for? Then I ask forgiveness.

The Word

God speaks to each of us individually. I need to listen, to hear what he is saying to me. Read the text a few times, then listen. *(Please turn to the Scripture on the following pages. Inspiration points are there, should you need them. When you are ready, return here to continue.)*

Conversation

How has God's word moved me? Has it left me cold? Has it consoled me or moved me to act in a new way? I imagine Jesus standing or sitting beside me. I turn and share my feelings with him.

Conclusion

I thank God for these moments we have spent together and for any insights I have been given concerning the text.

Sunday 23 November
Our Lord Jesus Christ, King of the Universe
Luke 23:35–43

And the people stood by, watching; but the leaders scoffed at him, saying, 'He saved others; let him save himself if he is the Messiah of God, his chosen one!' The soldiers also mocked him, coming up and offering him sour wine, and saying, 'If you are the King of the Jews, save yourself!' There was also an inscription over him, 'This is the King of the Jews.'

One of the criminals who were hanged there kept deriding him and saying, 'Are you not the Messiah? Save yourself and us!' But the other rebuked him, saying, 'Do you not fear God, since you are under the same sentence of condemnation? And we indeed have been condemned justly, for we are getting what we deserve for our deeds, but this man has done nothing wrong.' Then he said, 'Jesus, remember me when you come into your kingdom.' He replied, 'Truly I tell you, today you will be with me in Paradise.'

- It may seem somewhat cruel to say of the good criminal that he was in the right place at the right time, but his acknowledgment of Jesus' innocence and his heartfelt prayer to Jesus for mercy found an immediate answer. In these extraordinary circumstances it brings out yet again the infinite love and mercy of our God. Let us, too, ask Jesus to remember us.

- The people were silent but the soldiers and one of the criminals mocked him. As we read in the Book of Wisdom, 'Let us test him with insult and torture, so that we may find out how gentle he is, and make trial of his forbearance. . . . Thus they reasoned, but they were led astray, for their wickedness blinded them.' Let us pray for the courage to put up with whatever insults and derision come from the living of our faith.

Monday 24 November
Luke 21:1–4

He looked up and saw rich people putting their gifts into the treasury; he also saw a poor widow put in two small copper coins. He said, 'Truly I tell you, this poor widow has put in more than all of them; for all of them have contributed out of their abundance, but she out of her poverty has put in all she had to live on.'

- It is one thing to give out of your abundance, but quite another thing to give away the little you have to live on. But God is the One who gives us every moment of life and the Scriptures and the lives of the saints contain many stories of his endless providence and generosity. You may wish to recall any of these stories or simply to take Matthew 6:25–36 and pray on it.

Tuesday 25 November
Luke 21:5–11

When some were speaking about the temple, how it was adorned with beautiful stones and gifts dedicated to God, he said, 'As for these things that you see, the days will come when not one stone will be left upon another; all will be thrown down.'

They asked him, 'Teacher, when will this be, and what will be the sign that this is about to take place?' And he said, 'Beware that you are not led astray; for many will come in my name and say, 'I am he!' and, 'The time is near!' Do not go after them.

'When you hear of wars and insurrections, do not be terrified; for these things must take place first, but the end will not follow immediately.' Then he said to them, 'Nation will rise against nation, and kingdom against kingdom; there will be great earthquakes, and in various places famines and plagues; and there will be dreadful portents and great signs from heaven.'

- Jesus foretells the destruction of Jerusalem in 70 AD. As we approach the end of the liturgical year we focus on the end-time of the world. For each of us the end-time will be when we die and meet with Jesus to whom all judgement has been given by the Father. Let us pray for the grace to be ready for our own death-day, and that it will be a joyful meeting with the One who has become, as G. M. Hopkins put it in his poem 'The Lantern out of Doors', 'our first, fast, last Friend'.

Wednesday 26 November
Luke 21:12–19

He said, 'But before all this occurs, they will arrest you and persecute you; they will hand you over to synagogues and prisons, and you will be brought before kings and governors because of my name. This will give you an opportunity to testify. So make up your minds not to prepare your defence in advance; for I will give you words and a wisdom that none of your opponents will be able to withstand or contradict. You will be betrayed even by parents and brothers, by relatives and friends; and they will put some of you to death. You will be hated by all because of my name. But not a hair of your head will perish. By your endurance you will gain your souls.'

- Jesus foretells the coming persecutions for his followers but he promises salvation to those who endure to the end. Lord, you have told us that you will never forsake us or fail us. Help us to have the courage to place our complete trust in you, knowing that your Holy Spirit is within us.

- In his passion and death on the cross Jesus gave us the example of perseverance to the very end, despite the mocking and jeering of his persecutors. We pray for the grace of fidelity to the God who loves us with an everlasting love.

Thursday 27 November
Luke 21:20–28

Jesus said to them, 'When you see Jerusalem surrounded by armies, then know that its desolation has come near. Then those in Judea must flee to the mountains, and those inside the city must leave it, and those out in the country must not enter it; for these are days of vengeance, as a fulfilment of all that is written. Woe to those who are pregnant and to those who are nursing infants in those days! For there will be great distress on the earth and wrath against this people; they will fall by the edge of the sword and be taken away as captives among all nations; and Jerusalem will be trampled on by the Gentiles, until the times of the Gentiles are fulfilled.'

There will be signs in the sun, the moon, and the stars, and on the earth distress among nations confused by the roaring of the sea and the waves. People will faint from fear and foreboding of what is coming upon the world, for the powers of the heavens will be shaken. Then they will see "the Son of Man coming in a cloud" with power and great glory. Now when these things begin to take place, stand up and raise your heads, because your redemption is drawing near.'

- The prophecies in the Scriptures must be fulfilled and in the fullness of time all will come about. In just forty short years what Jesus foretold here came about. God, who is the Supreme Being and all-powerful, will bring about all that he has decided. Let us take the first half of the Our Father and, using St Ignatius's second method of prayer, go through it phrase by phrase.

Friday 28 November
Luke 21:29–33

Then he told them a parable: 'Look at the fig tree and all the trees; as soon as they sprout leaves you can see for yourselves and know that summer is already near. So also, when you see these things taking place, you know that the kingdom of God is near. Truly I tell you, this generation will not pass away until all things have taken place. Heaven and earth will pass away, but my words will not pass away.'

- The springtime comes around year after year, bringing the new leaves to the trees so that we might think that this will go on for ever. But it is all temporal and in the meantime even the trees will outlive us. As we age we begin to experience the difficulties that come with old age and we recognise our own end-time approaching. Let us pray to accept our growing weakness graciously and to surrender more and more to God.

Saturday 29 November
Luke 21:34–36

And he said to them, 'Be on guard so that your hearts are not weighed down with dissipation and drunkenness and the worries of this life, and that day does not catch you unexpectedly, like a trap. For it will come upon all who live on the face of the whole earth. Be alert at all times, praying that you may have the strength to escape all these things that will take place, and to stand before the Son of Man.'

- The great danger of a trap is the suddenness with which it closes on its victims. Again and again the gospels urge us to 'Watch and pray!' so that we are not caught unawares. The early fathers of the church taught the ideal of living in a continuous state of prayerfulness. We pray to grow in our prayer life so that our whole life becomes a prayer. Only with God's help can this come about. Let us pray also to Mary the Mother of God to aid us in this and to intercede for us.

LOYOLA PRESS.
A JESUIT MINISTRY

Join a Worldwide Community of Prayer

Make a "Sacred Space" in your day with the worldwide prayer community at **www.SacredSpace.ie**. Inspired by the spirituality of St Ignatius of Loyola, the daily updates help you pray anywhere, anytime.

Sacred Space is brought to you by the Irish Jesuits.